The Midwest Associate:
The Life and Work of Perry Duke Maxwell

By Christopher Clouser
Foreword by Mike DeVries

 www.trafford.com

North America & international
toll-free: 1 888 232 4444 (USA & Canada)
fax: 812 355 4082

This work is dedicated to
Dora Harrison and Dora Horn,
and to my family,
Danielle, Jason and Emily.

Table of Contents

Part Two: The Work

Chapter 10: Tenets of Design

The Masterpieces of Maxwell

Appendices:

Acknowledgments

Bibliography

Index

Foreword

Having grown up working at Crystal Downs in northern Michigan, I have had an appreciation of Perry Maxwell's work for a long time. Perry's work as Alister MacKenzie's associate on that venerable course certainly had a great effect on his work and philosophy, as he spent three seasons there building the course now regarded as one of the best in the world. Maxwell's respect for a landscape's inherent qualities and use of those features in its design is one of the great aspects of the golf course at Crystal Downs. I became enamored with golf at an early age and with golf course architecture because of my exposure to Crystal Downs. I am certain that the beauty of the natural landforms of the site were an inspiration to Perry Maxwell just as they are to me to this day and I am positive that he made the course better due to his recognition of the intricacies of the land.

Maxwell was a hands-on architect who spent a great deal of time in the field, searching out the best features of a parcel and the most natural green and tee sites to fit his courses to the land. This is still the best way to produce a great golf course that is unique to itself and has its own quirks and intimacies unlike any other golf course.

Prairie Dunes is arguably Perry Maxwell's greatest course, and certainly the best nine holes he ever designed. It was one of only two required stops on my long honeymoon camping trip and my wife doesn't even play golf! I had read about Prairie Dunes and longed to see it in person, as its long natural prairie roughs, fierce greens, and constant wind are similar to the conditions of Crystal Downs and I wanted to compare these two "sister" courses. Then superintendent Doug Petersan was very hospitable, welcoming my interest in the course and setting me up to play with his green chairman, Quentin Lorenz. Quentin asked which tees I wanted to play and I said the back and hit a fairly good tee shot at the first, to which he responded, "We have a player here!" Of course, I had the usual ups and downs of a 14 handicapper, but it couldn't have been more fun and educational as he was very interested in showing me all aspects of the course, what they were doing, and allowing me to explore the putting surfaces and other intricacies of the course's features. It is certainly one of my finest golf memories that is enhanced by my fondness for Maxwell's work and the friendly atmosphere of the club.

Although my wife, Annie, doesn't play golf, she has a very fine talent in recognizing the architects of golf courses; just from the exposure my obsession gives her. She frequently tours courses with me when we travel and I want to stop and look at a golf course that some famous architect designed. I noticed her penchant for recognizing designers when I was looking at pictures of courses with someone and she said, "Isn't that a Maxwell course?" How memorable Perry's work is!

Maxwell's courses are challenging for the best players – witness the numerous major championships at Southern Hills – and fun for all levels of golfers. His wild green contours, the famous "Maxwell Rolls," add interest to all the courses he did and provide a challenge that any golfer can improve upon regardless of their physical strength and ability to hit the ball a long way.

Perry was sought after by the best clubs in the country – Pine Valley, Augusta National, and Merion, to name just a few – to remodel portions of their courses and it is a tribute to his ability to synthesize his work with the existing features, improving upon great courses and making them even stronger. Perry may not have designed as many courses, great or common, as some of his contemporaries, but he was held in the highest regard by them and their designs to be given the responsibility to alter a masterpiece. Such respect deserves notice by players who may have an affection for his work but not know it, especially when courses by the other "old masters" of golf architecture are noted in publications and marketing.

Chris Clouser's extensive study of Perry Maxwell's work will certainly bring to light this important designer's work, opening it up to more study and the preservation of his concepts and unique qualities. Credit for Maxwell's contributions to golf course architecture is long overdue and Clouser demonstrates how important it is for us to study and respect the classic designers and their works.

Mike DeVries

Introduction

Who was Perry Duke Maxwell? What was he like? Why write about him?
There are many answers to these questions. Maxwell was a loving father and
husband. He was kind and generous and spiritual. He pursued life and wisdom
as if they were lost treasures. He was a fixture in his community as well. The
Ardmore Presbyterian Church in Ardmore, Oklahoma has been a city landmark
since it was constructed in 1916. The original building was constructed with the
help of many and was spearheaded by Perry Duke Maxwell and is a monument to
his faith and devotion to his community and to God. Maxwell was well known at
the time of the construction of the church in his own community for service to the
town and for his role as a cashier and officer at the Ardmore National Bank. He
also had constructed and designed a four-hole golf course just north of town off
what is now US 77. But to many outside Ardmore, Perry Maxwell was a name
that may have only been known by a select few who happened to be in the oil
business. It was a strange sequence of events that led to him developing into one
of the select group of people associated with what has been termed the "Golden
Age of Golf Design."

From 1900 to 1940, the world saw one of the most amazing growths in one
area of business, art and culture in the history of the world. This phenomenon
has become known as the Golden Age of Golf Design and was a period when more
top quality golf courses were created before or since. The basic principle of the
designs of all of these courses revolved around a new concept termed strategic
design. The concept revolved around the player having multiple options while
playing the course and avoiding hazards that were created to impose a thought
process on the player. Thus the architect was both challenging the player
mentally and physically during the game. The result of which was a large number
of courses that were enjoyable to many levels of players and elevated the game in
stature from the basic levels of the Scottish links.

Some of this pantheon of architectural achievements became what many
have termed "classic courses," that were the best of their generation and became
proverbial "Mecca" for the masses of golfing brethren. This new taste of "strategic
design" has not staled in the mouth of players since the concept took hold. To
prove this out, just look at any ranking of the top golf courses in the country or
the world and you will see numerous examples from this golden era. Not only are
the courses household names, but also there were a number of giants in that
group that were involved with the designs of these courses. Alister Mackenzie,

Charles Blair Macdonald, A. W. Tillinghast and Donald Ross were almost household names. The George C. Thomases, William Flynns and Seth Raynors are truly as instrumental to the world of golf course architecture. Then there is Perry Maxwell.

Perry Maxwell is perhaps one of the least known designers of the Golden Age of Golf Course Design. He was a simple man, who preferred to go by P.D. He either designed or was involved with the original design on several of the top courses in the United States and has been involved in the renovation of other household names in the world of golf. Geographically his work has been isolated mainly to the Great Plains of America in Oklahoma, Texas and Kansas. This alone is probably a large reason for his anonymity, as none of his courses have been thrust into the spotlight of the major metropolitan areas of our country and except for Southern Hills and Colonial, very little of his work has hosted tournaments of any significant nature to most casual followers of the game. These factors alone would greatly eliminate him from the conversation of who would be the top architects of his time, but unjustly so. Tom Doak even negates to list Maxwell in the first chapter of his book, The Anatomy of a Golf Course. He mentions the likes of Colt, Fowler, Simpson and Abercromby from overseas. The domestic designers include Mackenzie, Alison, Macdonald, Raynor, Ross, Tillinghast and several others. But there is no mention of Maxwell on this list. Why? The simple answer may be that there are just too many to list. The more complex answer is that many people don't realize the contribution to the game that Maxwell made in his day as a designer.

Maxwell was somewhat similar to most other architects of his time in that golf was not where he started his career. Beyond that the similarities end. He was originally involved with the banking and oil industry in Oklahoma and was a man deeply devoted to his family and to God. Although he played the game, unlike Stanley Thompson or Harry Colt or Donald Ross he was not an exceptional golfer. Unlike George Thomas and Tom Simpson he did not heavily document his ideas on golf course design and strategy. Unlike almost every other designer from his time, he continued working during the Great Depression and after World War II. Maxwell was a renaissance man. He loved the arts, music and literature. He also was very practical, due to his earlier career as a banker and being a devout Presbyterian. But life wasn't easy for Maxwell.

He was born in a very rural part of Kentucky and by the time he graduated from high school, he had contracted tuberculosis. He left the state in pursuit of a cure for the disease. After returning to Kentucky and marrying Ray Woods he left to try and overcome his health problems in Carter County, Indian Territory, which would later become Oklahoma. Maxwell resided in Oklahoma the rest of his life. He and his wife would have four children by the year 1916. In 1919, Ray lost her life to appendicitis. It was then that Maxwell retired from the banking industry and went into the golf course design. This decision was aided by his wife, who for years had encouraged Perry to take on the craft once he completed the design of the first four holes of his home course in Ardmore, Dornick Hills.

It can be argued that Maxwell's designs were the definition of what the art and science of golf course architecture should truly be about. He designed his courses based on what nature gave him, plotted his holes with some strategy and let you play the game. Also he created a legacy through passing the trade on to his son Press, who would later design several courses in Texas and Colorado. He also brought golf to a group of people who had never really had a chance to experience the game. Maxwell took golf to "the desert." He was the first architect to make "greens" as opposed to the browns that people in Oklahoma and the other states in the region had played for years. He created a piece of Scotland in the sand dunes of Kansas. He brought something to people that they had never seen before and it spread like wildfire. This also proved to be an artistic release for Perry as he was a lover of the arts but lacked the ability to sculpt, write or paint.

Maxwell did get the notice of several others in the industry for his work. Alister Mackenzie requested his assistance. Augusta National came calling. Pine Valley, The National Golf Links and several others wanted the services of Maxwell. Over time he became famous for his amazing green complexes, which often contained large swales and dips termed "Maxwell Rolls." Maxwell was recognized in his time, but has been almost pushed off the face of the map in our current versions of this historical period, many others and I often wonder why. This during an era where major championship set ups, long drives, and green speeds rule the day. This for a man that some consider the greatest green builder in the history of golf course design is unjust treatment.

Most of this is due to a lack of understanding of his career. Many people that I talked with in researching this work were not aware of how many courses he had designed, that he actually did work before he became associated with Alister Mackenzie or that he did work outside of Oklahoma. One person who I consider knowledgeable in the area only thought that Maxwell was involved with approximately twelve to fifteen courses aside from some renovation work at five or six courses on the East Coast and Augusta National. People often dismiss him as a major player because they feel that his main influence was Mackenzie and that he was just trying to imitate his "teacher" in designing courses like Prairie Dunes. His career was basically shrouded in fog and was hidden by several "myths." Debunking those "myths" and providing the "truth" became a mission in this work.

The purpose of this book is not only to examine his life and career, but also to chronicle and analyze the virtues of Maxwell and his work. Maxwell is often difficult to place in the history of his chosen field because he is not easily categorized with others of the period. His style was a combination of the prominent schools of thought during that period. He was very silent about his work and beliefs. This obviously was due to his humble nature but also because he felt his work could speak for itself more times than not. But, what were the beliefs that Maxwell had about designing courses? Did he have favorite concepts that he employed repeatedly? How involved was he in the whole process of the course design and construction? What were the factors that inspired his particular style? These questions and many others are addressed in the chapters that follow.

It became obvious to me though after researching Maxwell's career and talking with numerous people about the man that there was something more that was attracting me towards him. It was the man himself. Do I think I could devote a book solely to his works in the arena of golf course design? Probably, but the beauty of what I found was the story that evolved out of the research and revealed the true character of a man that I have grown to admire. I am so thankful to his daughter and granddaughter to spend time talking with me and helping me to grasp what a truly remarkable individual Perry was. I can only hope that if we had lived at the same time, that we would have been friends. His devotion to family, love of life and faith to God are all things that we can all take away and use as an example in our own lives.

One of the people I contacted in researching for this book said that not only would a work like this be enjoyed, but it was a necessity. In the last few years there has been an amazing rebirth in the field of golf literature. Albeit not a large share of the market, it is an ever increasing one, and if we wish to inform and attract new people into the shared interests of the preservation of this great game, then we should not just give them the same information on the same four architects repeatedly or bore them with he annals of how American design rose from Scottish linksland golf, but give them stories about all the people who were part of the formation and the history of this, the greatest game.

Part One: The Life

Just Call Me P.D.

Prior to 1900 life was completely different from today: it was much more difficult. The life expectancy of the average American citizen was significantly less than today, disease was much more prevalent and death was seen as a normal part of daily existence. The country was still on the heels of the Civil War, which had torn the fabric of the union that was America. States still practiced slavery, even though it was constitutionally illegal. The divide between wealthy and poor was as dramatic as it is today. People were struggling to find jobs that were secure. The Industrial Revolution had not taken hold in the United States to the extent that it had in parts of Europe: agriculture was still the backbone of the nation. People made their money off the backs of others, from their own arduous manual labor or from a small trade or service. Rural Kentucky was perhaps an area that was even more extreme even tough it was not as reliant on agriculture as most other states.

In the 1870s, the main industries of Kentucky were coal-mining, tobacco-growing and stone-quarrying. In fact, Kentucky was one of the largest coal-mining centers in the United States after the Civil War: in 1879, the state extracted more than one million tons of coal from the ground. Most of this activity took place in the eastern portion of the state, but several small mining communities existed in Western Kentucky as well. Industry in the central part of the state consisted mostly of quarrying for the stones that were used to construct the fieldstone buildings that remain to this day. The western part of the state was much more conducive to the agricultural industry and the typical "family farm," which became associated with that area of the country. Western Kentucky was also the home of a third of the stone quarries in the state. At this time rural Western Kentucky was on the verge of the Industrial Revolution. Many of the communities that emerged to service the developing industries became company towns; such towns housed those who worked in the mines and quarries, and on the farms. A small number of residents provided invaluable medical and ancillary services.

Dr. James Maxwell owned and operated a small medical practice in the Paducah, Kentucky area. His father, Perry, was a local farmer who prided himself on the work he did with his hands. James' brother, Pressley was a willing hand on the family farm. James had decided to get out of farming after the death of his father, and he turned over the family land to Pressley. Pressley and James then decided to move to the Princeton area so James could expand his practice.

Princeton, Kentucky is a small community in Southwest Kentucky that serves as the county seat and also as a memorial to the life of one of the most important figures in the history of golf course design, Perry Duke Maxwell. Perry Maxwell was born on June 13, 1879 in Princeton. The house he was born in was built four years before the Civil War by a local named Rascoe, and was, eventually purchased by Pressley Maxwell and Dr. James Maxwell. While living in the house, James met and married Caroline (Carrie) Madison Harris of Paducah, Kentucky. Mr. and Mrs. Charles Ratliff, relatives of the Maxwells, soon purchased the house in June 1879. The Maxwells persuaded the Ratliffs to allow them to stay in the house until the birth of their child, Perry Duke Maxwell.[1]

The house stands to this day and looks almost exactly as it did back then. Two large trees protect it from the view of drivers passing by on the road that leads west from downtown Princeton. This house was to be the first house of four that the Maxwells inhabited in the first nine years of young Perry's life. They first moved to Paducah, and then returned to Princeton, after James purchased the old Childers Female Academy and renovated it for use as a house. They then moved to the old Gracey house in Princeton, where James died when Perry was just nine years old. The site of this house is now the location of the Princeton Elks Lodge.

Upon the death of James, Perry and his sister, Mary Belle, moved with their mother into the home of Perry's uncle, Pressley. By this time, Pressley had become a successful local businessman in Paducah. He later made an investment in a rice field in Texas, which would become a large oil field; the Maxwell family would use the resulting funds for generations. He also became a role model for Perry. Pressley was already wealthy from the sale of the land left to him and his brother and was able to provide well for the family. Perry and his mother lived with him for several years. Perry's daughter, Dora Harrison, recalled her paternal grandmother as a lovely little woman who wore white dresses, loved to play cards, specifically solitaire, and always had a smile on her face.

The birthplace of Perry Maxwell (courtesy of Dora Horn)

Indeed, Perry's mother was a genuinely happy woman who enjoyed life and never took a day for granted.

As a youngster, Perry Duke Maxwell entered the Merion, Kentucky school system and thrived. He became adept in all areas, including mathematics and

Early photos of Perry Maxwell and Ray Woods (courtesy of Dora Horn)

science; but he especially loved the arts, literature and music. During this period, Perry also started to attend church regularly at the local Presbyterian Church. He quickly took to the tutelage of the church and adopted the faith that would be instrumental to the rest of his life. Through his devotion to God, he would develop the formation of his life philosophy. It was also during this time that he developed a lasting friendship with the superintendent of the school system, Charles Evans. Evans would become one of Maxwell's closest friends over the years and would eventually write about Maxwell's life for the *Chronicles of Oklahoma* after his death. It was also during this time that Maxwell met the love of his life, Raymonde (Ray) Sophronia Woods.

Ray Wood's grandparents originally migrated from Virginia and, according to Charles Evans, soon became "a center of refined society in Western Kentucky."[2] Their son, Preston (Press) Holt Woods married Medora (Dora) Ellen Crumbaugh. Charles Evans recalls Dora Crumbaugh as "one of the clearest thinkers and most highly educated women he had known. Through more than forty years I visited her home which became, because of her intellect, beneficence and religious devotion a center of goodness and light in every village and city in which she lived."[3] Preston and Medora had several children, including Ray

After completing high school, Maxwell went to college at the University of Kentucky in Lexington. Perry was a very good student and excelled on the declamatory team. He won several speaking contests, including a regional event involving teams from Vanderbilt, Georgetown and Transylvania. He did a scene from "Quo Vadis" and won the crowd over. Perry loved the college life, but he contracted consumption, known today as tuberculosis and withdrew. At this time, consumption was rampant across the country and many panaceas were being tried. Some people opened health resorts to help those afflicted with the disease overcome the symptoms.

Noted philanthropist James Walker Tufts started one such resort in Pinehurst, North Carolina. Pinehurst would later go onto great fame as one of the first great golf resorts in the country when Donald Ross was hired to design a golf course. It was believed warm climates would often help to overcome the affects of tuberculosis, so Perry's family and Ray convinced Perry to pursue an education in DeLand, Florida at Stetson University. Ray and Perry's sister, Mary Belle, traveled with him and also attended the university. Ray and Perry intended to get married after graduating and move back to Kentucky; but although Perry excelled academically, his health did not improve. After one semester, both Perry and Ray withdrew from Stetson. Perry traveled over much of the next few years, including a trip to Oklahoma in 1897, before returning to Kentucky to live, while Ray returned home to Kentucky to attend teacher training in Louisville.

Perry traveled to many states and territories in the country to take in what existed at the time. Most of his travels were through the Deep South to try and find a possible place to live and rehabilitate from his disease, but also he had a desire to see the world. It was also during this trek that he developed his intenerate nature that would be so prevalent later in his life. But he did find one location that he thought would be ideal for he and Ray to eventually start a life together.

Perry did not give up his love of reading and learning during this time. This trend would continue throughout his life: he made annual trips to New York and Philadelphia to just take in the sites of the cultural centers of the country. He continued to learn from the masters of literature and from the Bible for the rest of his life. Though he never received a college degree, he was considered to be highly educated. Dean Julian C. Monnet of the University of Oklahoma was once quoted as saying; "I have just had a long visit with Perry Maxwell. Do you know that the more I am associated with him, the more thoroughly I am convinced that he is one of the most learned men I have met."[4] Perry would try to pass this thirst for knowledge onto his children and other relatives through the years.

Go West Young Man

In 1902, in Louisville, Ray Woods and Perry Maxwell were wed. They continued to live in the Marion, Kentucky area in a small village called Crayne. Here, they had their first child, Elizabeth Duke, in 1903. But Perry's health still suffered. The Maxwells decided to leave Kentucky; they needed a warm, dry environment to help Perry overcome his disease. There was no better place than the seemingly wild Indian Territory, which Perry had visited in his travels, in the area that would later become Southern Oklahoma. In 1903, they settled in a town called Ardmore.

It was the start of the new millennium and the Maxwells had journeyed to the new frontier. Oklahoma had not achieved statehood when they arrived and would not do so for another four years. Ardmore is in the southern part of what is now Oklahoma and was a vibrant area during the land rush. Ardmore quickly developed a pocket industry: cotton. Ardmore would become known as the greatest inland cotton market in the world. Contributing to this development was the fact that two new railroads came to Ardmore from the east, the Frisco and the Rock Island.

By this time Ardmore had a town government and a school system; it also had a number of banks. When the Maxwells first came to the area, Perry was enchanted with the possibilities of the new west and the opportunity to start over and pursue the "American Dream." He quickly found employment as a cashier at the local Ardmore National Bank, and his wealthy uncle, Pressley, purchased some stock in the bank in Perry's name. Perry quickly moved up the ladder at the bank. He soon became friends with Mr. Lee Cruce, who was the president of the Ardmore National Bank. Cruce would later become the second governor of the state of Oklahoma. The Ardmore National Bank was one of five national banks in the Carter County area. The growth of the cotton industry was able to support this with the investment and the growing population of the city of Ardmore.

Perry Maxwell kept up his Scotch Presbyterian faith. He was a devout follower of the precepts of John Knox, a noted Presbyterian preacher. Perry never drank alcohol, smoked tobacco, danced or swore; he also passed these values down to his children. They attended the First Presbyterian Church weekly, along with Sunday school, and they took the Sabbath to heart. Perry and Ray were instrumental in the development of their church and soon became actively involved. Throughout the years when Maxwell would frequently be out of town on business, he would make the time to attend church and maintain the many principles that he had exemplified through the years of faith.

Life in Ardmore had started well and was going along swimmingly. In 1907, Oklahoma would officially become a state. By this time the Maxwells had become a fixture in the community. Perry's uncle, Pressley, sold his Texas oil field, and made a small fortune. It was enough to finance the lives of three generations of Maxwells. Dora Harrison, Perry's youngest and only living daughter recalled, "You could tell uncle Press had money, he was the only person back in Paducah, Kentucky to have an indoor toilet at the time in his house." Pressley would eventually split his fortune between Perry and his sister, Mary Belle Strahley.

Photo of Ardmore National Bank circa 1903
(courtesy of Harold Pittman)

By this time, Ray's family had also moved to the Mill Creek in the Indian Territory. They would later move to Ardmore. Ray's family was headed by her father, who was a traveling salesman. She had five siblings, two of which, Par and Dean, would later help Maxwell in his golf course design business.

During the early years in Ardmore, Perry became quite accomplished at tennis, but Ray had started to become concerned at how strenuous this game was on Perry. That was when she found an article about a golf course in Southampton, New York (the National Golf Links of America) in Scribners Magazine. She showed it to Perry and he wondered if such a pursuit would interest Oklahomans. There was only one course in the state of Oklahoma at the time, located in Guthrie. Soon afterwards Perry visited the National Golf Links and made the acquaintance of Charles Blair Macdonald. Macdonald was the originator of the course and designer of the holes. As Maxwell would say later, "It was my wife who showed me the article. She also mentioned that there was a beautiful piece of ground for sale nearby. Also she thought tennis was getting too strenuous for me."[5] Press Maxwell recalled about his father, "My father was a very good tennis player in his younger years, but my mother used to needle him about giving up the game because he was getting old. He finally quit tennis... and took up golf, enjoying it so much he built several holes on the family farm."[6]

The golf bug had bitten Maxwell. In 1909 he began to play the game that would alter his life and to study golf course architecture. This was also the year in which Perry and Ray's second child, Mary Belle, was born. Three years later Perry and Ray had their third daughter, Dora. The three girls were extremely close and grew up to be the best of friends. While the Maxwell's were busy growing their family the town of Ardmore would remain a sleepy cotton haven until 1913. The tiny world of the inland cotton capital changed dramatically with two events. The first provided the opportunity for people to get to Ardmore; the second gave them a reason to go; and both events happened on August 4th.

17

On that date, the first spike was driven for the Ringling Railroad that would go west of the city and help to open up the areas west of Ardmore in the former Indian Territory; but the larger event of the two was the discovery of the famous Healdton Oilfield. Oil quickly supplanted cotton as the key industry in Ardmore. Newfound wealth was evident all over the city; new churches, schools and public facilities lined the streets. Oil also helped to line the pockets of many investors and many banks, including Perry Maxwell and the Ardmore National Bank. After the discovery of the oil fields, Ardmore had more millionaires per capita than any other city in the country. Perry would later make the acquaintance of many influential people and leaders of this powerful industry. One of these contacts was William Hume of Tulsa, who became one of Perry's best friends. William Hume was a Scotsman who migrated to America to work for Dundee Petroleum and was based in Tulsa.

In 1913 some amazing changes took place in Perry Maxwell's life. The first great golf boom in the United States began. It was triggered by the dramatic victory of Francis Ouimet in the United States Open that year at the Country Club in Brookline, Massachusetts. To capture the title, Ouimet defeated two of the best players in the world, Ted Ray and Harry Vardon. This event increased Maxwell's interest. In 1914 he attended the United States Amateur tournament, which Ouimet also won. Maxwell and Ouimet would meet and they immediately became friends. Ouimet helped Perry pick out his first set of golf clubs for $9.

The Homestead

In 1914 Maxwell purchased a "beautiful piece of ground" that his wife had pointed out years earlier. It was 320 acres of rolling terrain with two large ridges on either side of the property. The property also featured a meandering creek running through it and a natural lake. This description of the land was taken from an abstract about the property provided by a Maxwell family member:

> The property was previously deeded to Carter County for use as a "county poor farm." The county decided it was not needed and unsuitable for such purposes and on March 19, 1914, the court of Carter County, Oklahoma, after hearing the resolution of said Board of the County Commissioners, and taking testimony of witnesses and being fully advised in the premises, finds it to be best interest of Carter County, Oklahoma, that said farm be sold. Land to be sold in a public auction. Said bids were opened and we (Carter County Commissioners) find that the bid of P. D. Maxwell was the highest and best bid, same being for $7,025.00, same being more than 90% of the appraised value. [7]

The "poor farm" was a place for the local government to house the destitute and try to make them productive for society as a whole. When Maxwell purchased the property, he shut down the "poor" farm and set up his own dairy farm. Morton Woods, Perry's brother-in-law, was brought in to oversee the operations of the dairy farm. Morton converted it into a Golden Guernsey dairy farm. The dairy farm existed for several years and sold Golden Guernsey milk until 1957, when it was shut down and the Golden Guernsey brand discontinued. When Morton died in 1977, the land was sold for a housing development adjacent to the golf course. Over the years the land has not only been the home to Perry and his family but also many other relatives, some of whom still live in what is now referred to as the Dornick Hills Addition. The whole area was setup with a Scottish theme, paying reverence to the homeland of the Maxwell family. There are many outcroppings of stone, including a stone wall that runs along a street named Stonewall Road. The farmland itself was very large and consisted of a large stone barn and two large silos. The silos have since been destroyed but the stone barn remains as a symbol of the times on Primrose Hill.

The first Maxwell home was built on the southern rise overlooking the property on the opposite corner from the dairy farm. Even when it was built it was somewhat small for five and soon to be six as the Maxwells were expecting another child. James Press joined the family in 1916. It was like most modest farmhouses on the plain at the time: a wooden frame with a fence around it. But the house was just the start of the development of the property. Along with the dairy farm, Maxwell was able to take the large acreage and create what would later become the area known now as Primrose Hill, an important part of the area north of Ardmore. Over the years Primrose Hill would include clay tennis courts, a dairy farm, and Dornick Hills Country Club, the social center of the city of Ardmore.

Photo of Maxwell House in Ardmore (courtesy of Dora Horn)

Life in Ardmore

After seeing Francis Ouimet triumph over the mighty legends Ted Ray and Harry Vardon, many Americans realized the potential of the game of golf. It soon became a popular American sport. Maxwell was so infatuated that, with the assistance and spurring of his wife, he developed the large piece of land their home was on and Dornick Hills was born. Referencing the number of small rocks in the area and Perry's Scottish ancestry, Maxwell had used the Gaelic term for little rocks, dornick, to create the name of the course and the club that would eventually be formed.

At this time Perry had only studied one course, the National Golf Links in Southampton, New York. The designer of the course, Charles Blair Macdonald, was seen as the father of American golf architecture. After touring the course in early 1914 and talking extensively with Charles Blair Macdonald, Maxwell decided to take Macdonald's concept, which revolved around the "ideal course," and the use of conceptual copies of famous holes, to create his own course on the land he owned in Ardmore. He first created a fashionable four-hole course, simply because there were no other courses in the area.

The routing still exists almost as Maxwell laid it out, with the exception of one hole. A description of the layout was offered by a local man named James Watson, a friend of Maxwell's, in a brief discussion of the course written in 1924:

> The original course consisted of only four holes. The first tee was just north of the Clubhouse; just behind the first tee was a pro shop possibly ten by twenty feet building. The first Pro was Hamp Veal who later became the pro at Bartlesville, Oklahoma. He lived in the home near the Springer Road west of the clubhouse, which is now gone. The course layout was this; you drove north from the tee, which is now the West nine. The second hole was the same as now, you drove back south toward the clubhouse and went west to the now third hole green. From there you went across a small creek to a tee and played on the north side of the creek and east back to a green just north of the second tee. This was the original layout of the four-hole course. [8]

The three original holes that remain would become the opening three of what is today the second nine holes on the course.

Maxwell had only seen a small number of courses and was new to designing them. At the time he designed the first four holes at Dornick Hills, the main influence on his design was easily the National Golf Links in Southampton. This was evident in the very first hole he ever laid out. Its design was a combination of the famous Leven and Sahara hole concepts popularized by Macdonald. Not only was the completion of these first four holes an achievement it really was a step forward in golf in the Southwest United States. Dornick Hills would eventually become the first course to have grass greens in the state of Oklahoma. Maxwell would use a Bermuda strain of grass that was resistant to the heat of the summers in the state and was able to stay green throughout the winter as well. But that would come a few years later. The original four holes were mainly designed to serve as a way to be entertained by the game and have a short leisurely round with friends and family. Perry had little foresight as to what the four holes would mean to him, his family and the community as a whole.

After completing the original four holes of his own course in Ardmore, Perry went around the southern United States and toured many courses. The purpose for the trip was to do research about the possibility of implementing the grass greens at Dornick Hills. One of the more influential parts of the trip were the constant opportunities to see the golf course architecture of the pre-eminent designer in the United States at the time, Donald Ross. Ross' style of architecture and the technique to use the many elevated portions of the site were an obvious trait that Maxwell would use extensively in his designs later in his career. Perry also read the only book available at the time about golf course architecture. It is believed the book was the Horace Hutchinson work, Golf Greens and Green-Keeping. Hutchinson was a leader of the Heathlands movement in golf course design south of London and was a widely read writer for Country Life Magazine. Perry also found time to spend with his family, work and devote time to his other concerns in Ardmore.

Maxwell was a much better at designing golf courses than at playing them. Charlie Coe, a famous amateur golfer from Oklahoma, was once asked about Maxwell

Photo of the Maxwell girls. From left to right: Dora, MaryBelle, and Elizabeth (courtesy of Dora Horn)

on the course, "I used to play a little golf with him, both he and his wife, when I was just a kid. We'd go out and play nine holes after church. I wouldn't say he was much of a golfer, but he was a gentleman golfer, played with his family, a great family man. I always thought the world of him. He wasn't much of a golfer, but he knew how to lay out a golf course."[9] It is believed that Perry could shoot in the mid-80s, but even his own son would question that years later.

Between 1914 and 1919 Maxwell developed a complete set of nine holes at Dornick Hills using the original course as a start, with the exception of the last hole from the original four. Perry and Dr. James Watson, a close friend and fellow Ardmorite, organized the funding of the original course. Several prominent citizens donated $100 each to help with the building of the course and the country club. Once the funding was received Perry began with the construction of new holes. The course was completed in 1918. Perry's wife and children also helped with the development of the holes. Perry's youngest daughter, Dora, has often told the story of her and her two sisters helping her father at the course one day by clearing rocks from the playing areas. "Father went home for Thanksgiving dinner without us for some reason, Mother asked him, 'Where are the girls?' Father said, 'Oh, I must have left them. I forgot all about them.' So he drove back out and brought us back home."[10] This began the organization of the Dornick Hills Country Club that vitalized the area north of Ardmore and led to the first expansion of the course to nine holes.

Away From the Course

While the completion of the original nine holes took place at Dornick Hills, Maxwell became a fixture in the community. He was known as a loving father and a dedicated businessman. As the oil boom continued to bring wealth to Ardmore it brought more acquaintances for Maxwell. His dedication to work was amazing with all the other distractions including golf course design and family. Though living outside the city, Perry seemed to make it into town quite often. To get to town Maxwell took a streetcar to work in the morning. Literally, he would drive the car from home to the beginning of the line and let the engineer take it from there. The line stopped at a station about a half-mile from the house, but the tracks ran to the Maxwell house. Maxwell would often take the car, with the engineer's permission of course, from the station to the house and would bring it back down in the morning. Perry was the first person on the train, so no one ever knew except for Perry, his family and the engineer. Perry's dedication went far beyond the office though; his children were also a priority in his life.

Perry and Ray were insistent on their children acquiring a good education and appreciating the arts. They often took trips to the northeastern part of the country. Perry always saw Philadelphia and New York as the cultural centers of the country. They would also vacation at Barnegat Bay in New Jersey. The Maxwell family loved to ride in the car, as Perry would drive them across country.

Maxwell would stop at odd times though, often to check out a golf course he spotted from the road. Perry would continue to make yearly trips to New York until very late in his life. In Jim Finegan's article, "The House of Maxwell," Dora Harrison recounted some stories about her father's trips:

> "Sometimes he would drive on those long trips, especially when he was also taking my sisters and me back to college. Other times, he would go by train. He always reserved an upper berth, which he felt was more comfortable than a lower berth once you got into it, but some people thought he chose it because it cost less. When he would leave home, we would all be sad as we stood in the doorway saying goodbye, but at that moment we weren't crying too much because he would always have forgotten something and we knew he'd soon realize it and come back.
>
> Music and art and literature were all very important to him. He gave each of us a book every Christmas, maybe a novel by Dickens or a collection of poems, sometimes a book about ancient Greece or Rome, always something worthwhile. He tried to take in as many concerts as he could while he was away. I remember that in Philadelphia he would go to the Academy of Music on the spur of the moment without a ticket, and it would be sold out, and he'd say 'I've come all the way from Oklahoma and you've got to let me in,' and sure enough they would, even if it was only to stand in the back.
>
> The Metropolitan Museum in New York was a great favorite of his. My mother's sisters lived in Ardmore, too, and Father would come back from New York with a little statue of Winged Victory, for instance, that he bought them. And he would tell them the story behind it, which he knew they would appreciate. He was for the most part self-educated, but he could quote great authors and he could add columns of figures in his head."[11]

On September 27, 1915 a great tragedy occurred in Ardmore. Tank cars of natural gasoline exploded in the railroad yards at 1:30 in the afternoon. In an instant downtown Ardmore was destroyed. 42 people were killed and hundreds were injured. The Ardmorites quickly rebuilt their town. This town recovered and became the center of the oil business in Oklahoma. At the center of the rebuilding process was the Ardmore National Bank led by Perry Maxwell. He was a full vice-president at the bank by this time and helped the city to overcome the adversity.

In 1916, there was another addition to the Maxwell family. Press Maxwell was born. He would be the last child of Ray Woods and Perry. Press not only was the baby of the family but also the only son in a family with three sisters, who were surrogate mothers. It was also in 1916 that the Ardmore National Bank began negotiations with the First National Bank of Ardmore to consolidate the two institutions. G. W. Stuart was the President at the Ardmore National Bank. Perry was the largest stockholder and an influential person in the deal. Maxwell was beginning to wrap up his career as a banker and saw this as the first step. The consolidation was finalized in 1917. The notification was released in the local

Ardmorite newspaper and the Ardmore National Bank closed its downtown location in late 1917.

In 1917 that Perry successfully spearheaded a fundraiser to build the Von Keller Hospital by bringing in $30,000. The hospital opened on the corner of 12th Northwest and Commerce in downtown Ardmore and still stands today. Maxwell also helped with the building of the Presbyterian Church in town and even donated the funds, almost $10,000, for the purchase of the church bells that still chime every Sunday morning.

Just as Perry was ready to begin his semi-retirement with his wife and family, tragedy struck again. In early 1919, the love of his life, Ray, died quickly from a ruptured appendix. The loss was devastating. Maxwell had lost the person he had devoted his life to. He had no clue where to turn. He would turn to his friends, specifically Charles Evans and William Hume. Hume had just been married in New York City when he received a telegram about the death of Ray. Instead of going on his honeymoon, he and his new bride, Josephine, headed to Ardmore to be with Perry. Perry knew that Ray would want to be buried where they had lived much of their lives together, Primrose Hill. Perry received special permission from the local authorities to setup a private cemetery on top of a bluff overlooking the land that the Dornick Hills Golf Club occupied. The cemetery featured a stone wall that surrounded the southern edge of the plot and the northern portion of the burial grounds was encircled by a structure composed of white Grecian columns. This is where Perry would be buried as well when he passed away. The Maxwell-Woods cemetery remains today and is a testament to the life of Perry Maxwell and his family.

With the consolidation of the banks and Maxwell not having any demands on his time, he decided to take up the career that his wife had been advocating for five years. He would become a golf course designer. To start his career, Maxwell decided that the best way to learn more would require a trip to Scotland. He had decided on a whirlwind tour of famous courses, including St. Andrews. Before going, it is believed he had communication with Charles Blair Macdonald and received some guidance on what courses to visit while overseas. Many of the locations that Perry would visit were located in close proximity to his ancestral home, Anstruther, Scotland. Perry also thought it would be wise to try to make connections with his heritage and attempt to meet his Scottish relatives while returning to his native country.

Early photo of the Dornick Hills clubhouse and many of the founders on the southern rise looking over the property. Maxwell and his wife are in the last car to the right and Press and Dora are standing in front the vehicle just to the left. (courtesy of Dora Horn)

A New Career

The trip to Scotland, in Maxwell's day, was not a quick flight across the Atlantic. It was a weeklong voyage across the ocean. It is believed that the boat actually landed in Liverpool, England and Maxwell then traveled by train to the Kingdom of Fife in Scotland. Maxwell had specific objectives he wanted to get out of his only trip to Scotland. His time in Scotland was precious. He had left four children at home in America with relatives and he needed to get back to Ardmore as quickly as possible. The objectives of the trip were to visit some of the championship courses in Scotland and to visit some of his family. He would come out of Scotland with much more.

The first priority for Maxwell was to track down his family. The Maxwell family roots came from a small community, south of Edinburgh, called Anstruther. Anstruther is a community halfway between Crail and Elie and a stone's throw away from St. Andrews and sits on the Firth of Forth in the East Neuk of Fife. The Maxwell family roots come from two clans in Anstruther, the Dishingtons and the Adamsons, and were related on Perry's paternal side. The Dishingtons were proprietors of a prominent furniture shop in Anstruther. On his maternal side Perry was a direct descendant of Captain Thomas Harris, a settler in the Virginia Colony at Henrico County, Virginia in 1611. Harris was a member of the House of Burgesses in 1623, 1639 and 1646.

Maxwell quickly found his brethren and reminisced with them. He took a photograph of the house, known as Fernbank, and brought that home. His daughter, Dora, would follow in his footsteps and go to Scotland in 1938. She used the original picture to find the house in Anstruther. She knocked at the door and told the resident of the home that she was a relative from America. The response of the woman was, "Have you had your tea yet?" Dora again said that she was from America and thought they were relatives. The woman again replied, "And I asked, have you had your tea yet?" Dora replied, "No," and they went in had a wonderful conversation and of course drank their tea.

Perry quickly began studying the great courses of Scotland. None made a greater impact on him than the Old Course at St. Andrews. He often raved about how well the holes in Scotland were "incorporated" into the surrounding terrain. This trait was one feature Perry implemented into his designs. The other major feature he would take from his study of St. Andrews were the famous rolling greens. The large greens at St. Andrews used these rolls as strategic elements in their design. Maxwell would later in his career begin to use these with great success. They would become known as "Maxwell Rolls," a play on words of the names of two popular automobiles. Another key aspect of the green designs that Maxwell took note of were the fact that many would slope from the front to back. After his study of the Old Course, Maxwell considered St. Andrews the greatest golf course on the planet and worthy of emulation in his own designs.

The other major event of the trip, and one that was not planned, was meeting Alister Mackenzie. Mackenzie at the time was the consulting architect for the Royal & Ancient Golf Club in preparation for the 1921 Open Championship to be played at the Old Course. Mackenzie was beginning to see the possibility of a career in the United States. The two discussed the possibility of a partnership, if Mackenzie came to the United States. Maxwell agreed. He saw great advantages to being associated with such a well-known designer as Mackenzie. Maxwell and Mackenzie also had many things in common. Both of their fathers were medical practitioners. For each, their first experience in the industry of golf course design was a project in their hometown.

Photo of Fernbank in Anstruther (courtesy of Dora Horn)

They both enjoyed playing the game, though neither was a great player. Also, both had made livings with a different trade before turning to golf course architecture.

Before the trip home from Scotland, it is believed that Maxwell toured other courses such as the New and Eden courses at St. Andrews, Crail, Elie, Gullane, Muirfield, Troon, Prestwick and Hoylake, in Liverpool. The short trip across the Atlantic was very eventful and productive as Maxwell decided he was ready to take on a career of golf course design. He eventually returned to Ardmore in September of 1919.

Return to America

When Maxwell returned to Ardmore, he was in the midst of a scandal. While in Scotland, an associate from the Ardmore National Bank had forged Maxwell's signature on several large notes drawn upon the Ardmore Bank. Due to his office and amount of stock held in the bank, Maxwell had to help repay the lost funds at a two for one share. He eventually paid the funds with a large loan from his sister and her nest egg from the wealth that uncle Pressley had left her. Maxwell would repay the loan to his sister over the next few years. The man who perpetrated the crime was a gentleman with a solid reputation in the community, which added to the shock of the whole thing. He was found guilty and sentenced to nine months in jail. After this incident Maxwell significantly reduced his involvement with the bank and began his career in golf course design. He would remain associated with the First National Bank until 1929 on a part-time basis.

Perry added nine more holes to the course at Dornick Hills over the next four years. These nine new holes begin the round at Dornick Hills today. Before designing the original nine holes, Maxwell had only studied the works of Charles Blair Macdonald and a few courses in the South by Donald Ross. This would account for his deference to the "National Style" of design. By the time he worked on the second nine, Perry had toured some of the great courses of Scotland and many of the top courses in the United States. There are fewer conceptual copies on the second nine holes based on the formula that Charles Blair Macdonald had used at the National. This was a strong indication that Maxwell's style had changed and was becoming his own.

Perry's philosophy took a quick change to incorporate what he had learned on his trip to Scotland and also to apply the lessons learned from his friend in New York. He saw many things in the terrain at Dornick Hills that could be applied to other sites and he developed his own set of template holes on the new nine holes that he would use over his career. The most obvious was the elevated tee shot on the first hole that provided a great view of the fairway and much of the rest of the course on the south side of the creek.

The first course Maxwell ever built was also one of his best. The varying approaches to the greens with the natural use of the terrain make the course truly memorable in every fashion. The club does a wonderful job of memorializing Perry Maxwell and is proud of its heritage. Though the course has changed through the years and lost some of what the original design consisted of, the intentions of the club are to service the members and to honor the man who built the course and was a local hero.

Adding to the ambience of the course is the Maxwell-Woods cemetery that is located down a path that leads from the 16th green. The path is the only way back to the resting place of Ray Woods, Perry Maxwell and other family members. The walk seems to lead you back into nothingness, and about the time you think you should turn around you see a fork in the path. If you take the right hand fork you will see the Grecian columns of the monument that Perry Maxwell constructed in honor of his wife in 1919. Also around the perimeter of the plot is a stone wall with a stair step entrance that Perry constructed. Originally the cemetery provided views of all of the original land owned by Maxwell and was visible from other elevated locations on the site.

Maxwell was proud of the lack of expense involved in the design and upkeep of the course. When asked in an interview for American Golfer, Maxwell had the following response, "You will never see it until you play each of its eighteen holes, for the simple reason that it does not obtrude and is not an eyesore. Not a square foot of earth that could be left in its natural state has been removed. No pimples or hummocks of alteration falsify its beauty. There are but six artificial bunkers, the rest are natural, and all the driving tees are within a few steps of the putting greens. To date no man has played Ardmore in par, yet my daughter, still in her teens has broken 100 on it. Professionals and topnotch amateurs, who have played it, pronounce the greens and fairways perfect. The total cost of construction and upkeep over a period of eleven years is less than $35,000. By that I mean about $3,000 per annum. Nature has been kind because we have not denied her. We cooperate with the seasons and dividends never fail."[12] Dornick Hills would always be known as the course that Maxwell built for himself, his wife and his family. The fact that his first course is still one of his best designs to many modern experts, speaks to the vision and imagination that Maxwell had built into his home course.

The course has been modified over the years to deal with distance and other issues of the modern game, but the original routing is almost as Maxwell put it on the face of the valley of Primrose Hill. The first dramatic changes were actually implemented by Maxwell himself in 1936. He moved the green on the tenth and the tees on the eleventh and twelfth holes. The movement of the tenth green was the most significant as this indicated a true change in Maxwell's design philosophy. He moved the green to the opposite side of the creek and created a forced carry.

There was a minor green remodeling in 1965 and another large renovation in 1985 by Dick Nugent and Joe Black, two noted architects in the 1980s, to the opening nine holes. The greens did have some of the contours softened as the modern day grasses would not allow for the green contours and allow people to putt on them. An article in the Daily Oklahoman from April 27, 1986 outlined much of the renovation work on the front nine in two paragraphs:

> Original bunkers were put back in place on four holes. The No. 1 green was moved in order to avoid a blind second shot and the tee box on No. 2 was moved so that the carts would drive north of a pond instead of south, where they had dangerously headed into the line of tee shots of No. 9
>
> Greens were enlarged and given undulations on almost every hole on the front nine. The tee box on No. 6 was moved south to its original location, cutting some 30 yards off the distance. The result is a 500-yard, par 5 that dares golfers to go for the green on their second shot.[13]

Other major alterations by Black and Nugent would involve the elimination of the large waste bunker on the sixth and the carry bunker on the eighth hole.

The course also went through a controversial renovation in 1992 that affected many of the greens and bunkers on the back nine by Jeffrey Brauer, a former president of the American Society of Golf Course Architects. The work by

Brauer affected almost every hole. The tenth green was rebuilt to the left of where Maxwell had moved the green. The most dramatic change was the elimination of the waste bunker between holes seven and seventeen. The bunker was replaced by a large pond. The contrast between this and the original hole cannot go unnoticed.

After seeing the course, the blueprint for Maxwell's idea of strategic golf and using the land to shape the hole is apparent. But does this course just cater to the play of the members or is it a challenge to the best the game has to offer? Dornick Hills has seen its share of notable tournaments, even having a PGA tour stop briefly in the 1950s. But the biggest success recently has been the collegiate tournament the course hosts every May, The Maxwell Invitational. The annual tournament brings to Ardmore the best college teams in the country to compete in a unique format in the most important invitational tournament in the country. Many programs including the University of Oklahoma, Oklahoma State and Tulsa have won the tournament. It has also seen players like David Duval and Charles Howell III, both excellent professional golfers, walk off with medalist honors. All this to maintain the legacy of Perry Maxwell, while also getting local golfers exposure to some of the more high profile golf programs in the country.

The Maxwell-Woods Cemetary located on top of the hill over the seventh hole at Dornick Hills

With the continuing test of Dornick Hills being equal to the challenge of many of the best in the game, the small layout of just over 6,400 yards seems to always hold its head up high. The course represented what Maxwell's early design philosophy was about. The course to this day still looks like he had laid out 18 holes on his farm. The contours of the land are subtle and gentle but do provide some elevation changes that could not have been created by man in the early part of the century. The routing uses many of the natural features. If Maxwell were to go back ten years later, after his techniques had evolved, he may have laid the course out differently; but the largest part of the course would have remained. This along with the green contouring that existed on the course made for an incredible test to the golfer. Dornick Hills is a true jewel from the Golden Age of Golf Design that should be studied and treasured for its impact on the career of Perry Maxwell and on golf in Oklahoma.

The First Contracts

Dornick Hills was Maxwell's testing ground for his theories on golf course design and as a test site to see if grass greens could grow in Oklahoma. The course met with huge success in the state, especially with two men from Oklahoma City. Press Maxwell once told a story about two men from Oklahoma City that played at Dornick Hills and were impressed. They offered a project to Perry on the spot. Those two men were Keefe Carter and Bob Conliff. They were interested in starting a club in Oklahoma City, along with other investors, but needed to hire an architect for the course. In August 1920, a group of businessmen came together and founded the Twin Hills Country Club in Oklahoma City and officially hired Perry Maxwell to design the course.

The site contained all of the noted trademarks of Maxwell's design philosophy; rolling terrain, elevated tee and green locations, exposure to the wind and natural water hazards. Twin Hills would be the first course that Perry would get paid to build. It is believed that the acreage purchased for the course was actually bought from Perry Maxwell. An acquaintance of Perry's uncle persuaded him to invest in an oil company and it quickly brought in some large profits for Maxwell. Allegedly, he used these funds to finish paying off the debt to the Ardmore National Bank and his sister, and then purchased 160 acres that would later become one of his greatest designs.

Construction of the course went by quickly. The largest bulk of the work was done by the end of 1921. The major obstacle was that the clubhouse needed to be moved and that forced the movement of the ninth green. The new clubhouse was completed in 1923. Once the clubhouse was moved the course was completed. The course is one of the premier golf courses in the state and many have said that Twin Hills was the best in the state during this early period of golf in the state of Oklahoma. Soon after completion, the course was sold to Dorset Carter, Keefe's father.

There has since been only one major alteration to the course, the leveling of the eighth fairway took place during a late 1960s renovation. Since then, only minor modifications had been done to the layout. It is believed that shortly after the PGA Championship in 1935 at the course, Maxwell came back and made some slight adjustments to the course as well. But the course still has much of what Maxwell originally designed.

The course still has the feel of an open course with a lack of trees that directly impact the line of play. Ironically, the course was laid out by Maxwell on a densely forested piece of land. Over the years, care has been taken to keep the trees in line with the design intent. The layout of the course is within a small rectangle, exemplifying the mastery of routing that Maxwell demonstrated early in his career. The front nine of the course takes up the western part of the lot. The property was blessed with an abundant amount of rolling ground, which was one of the components that Maxwell saw as a necessary ingredient to a good course. The holes on the course constantly switch direction so that wind will impact shots differently throughout the round. The course also makes use of the natural water and large elevation changes. The course features a core routing much like most of Maxwell's work; with many tees and greens close to the clubhouse. The routing could almost be divided between the back and front nines by a diagonal line being drawn from the northeast corner to the southwest corner of the plot.

The fourth hole at Twin Hills (courtesy of Larry Newman)

In the first set of nine holes, Perry provided variety in the type of holes and the demands on the player. This particular strength is what has endeared Maxwell to many members of clubs that have one of his designs. The varied shot demands with the use of the terrain as a defense for the green make it so that the player never tires of the holes. Maxwell also brought the player back to the "axis" of the course three times in the first nine holes and provides that again in the round two more times. The course at Twin Hills radiates out from the "axis" or clubhouse much like the spokes of a bicycle wheel radiating out from the center. Maxwell did this because he had a high, central elevation point and wanted to use this as many times as possible for green sites and for tee locations. The front nine is dominated by the small creeks and the drastic elevation changes found throughout. It also provides an excellent study in how Maxwell used the terrain to accomplish a key factor to successful golf design, drainage. Elevated tees and push-up greens can create dramatic effects for the golfer to enjoy but without the drainage that is needed to take place, especially in the red clay of Oklahoma, a course would soon die out. This is also a main reason why Maxwell seemed to be particular about sites in Oklahoma, as he understood that drainage would be the key to his minimalist concept of design.

The course at Twin Hills met the approval of Alister Mackenzie. He toured the course and was quoted in a 1926 Oklahoma News article about the course. "Better than the three American courses I have been hearing about all of my life; The Links, The Lido and Garden City." Mackenzie did find the fifteenth somewhat of a boring hole but that was the only weak hole he found on the course and he raved about the fourth, seventh and eleventh, all par three holes. When one looks at the course at Twin Hills they often wonder how difficult the greens may have been in Maxwell's day. The current green designs were created from the work of Mark Hayes in 2000 when he came in to perform a restoration of the original design. Much of the work was on the greens, which were severely altered in the only other work done on the course. The greens at that time were altered to become much more rolling in nature. The restoration has been wrongly criticized by some as not being true to Maxwell's original design intent. Maxwell's green designs did not really begin to have the more famous severe contours until later in the 1920s and with the development of better drainage systems through the use of clay tile by Maxwell and his crew and not relying solely on surface drainage for the putting surfaces.

In 1935, the PGA of America came to Twin Hills. The team of Carter and Conliff had convinced the organization to host its annual match play championship at their site. It would be the first major championship on the professional golf scene in Oklahoma. The main story of the tournament was Walter Hagen. Del Lemon provides a wonderful perspective into what Walter Hagen was like in his book, The Story of Golf in Oklahoma.

> *Hagen's presence invited respect, as much among his fellow pros as with the fans. In Hagen's early years, when golf professional were considered by most club members as little more than overpaid caddie masters, he had ignored the "Members Only" signs at private clubhouses and traipsed in anyway, as if he belonged. His gregarious personality charmed them, his golfing skills dazzled them. He drank their whiskey and topped their stories with his own.[14]*

During the 1935 PGA, the qualifying consisted of a 36-hole qualifying event based on stroke play and then went into match play to determine the eventual champion. Hagen took the medalist honors of the 36-hole qualifying event, while other players like Sam Snead, Ben Hogan and Byron Nelson were eliminated. For the qualifying, hordes of spectators included several notable Oklahoma sports heroes. Perry Maxwell even came to town for the event. The match play portion of

34

the tournament was determined by drawing names out of a hat. Hagen was matched up against a tough, young player named Johnny Revolta. Revolta was a good player that was respected by the entire field, and defeating him would put Hagen well on his way to claiming a sixth PGA Championship. The match was hotly contested, with the key turning point being a missed putt by Hagen on the par three 14th. But even with that Hagen had a chance to square the match on the 18th hole and missed his putt for par.

Revolta escaped a match with Gene Sarazen, the first player to win all of the Grand Slam tournaments, after his defeat by Al Zimmerman. Several of the favorites fell early in the match play portion as well. The finals, though, featured a match between Revolta and the famed "Silver Scot," Tommy Armour. Armour had won the PGA, US Open and British Open previously and was the odds makers' favorite to win in the finals. The match was not close with a final score of 5 & 4. Revolta had won the first major championship ever contested in Oklahoma. It would be the last until after World War II.

Twin Hills has all the components that go into the making of a legendary golf course, but it has remained under the radar of the national golf scene. The championship history is littered with accomplishments of the legends of the game, including a professional major championship that saw the end of perhaps the greatest player in his generation. The origins of the course are an interesting story and the course has played a key role in the history of other clubs in the general vicinity. It is a difficult test and still is a "member friendly" design. Twin Hills, though not the first work by Maxwell, is perhaps as significant to the career of Maxwell. It was the first for-hire job and is a blueprint for other Maxwell courses. All of the template holes that Maxwell would use over his career can be traced to a similar hole on the Twin Hills or Dornick Hills courses. This is what makes Twin Hills a lasting tribute to his career and a course that anyone studying Maxwell must see to really understand his design philosophy. Once the work at Twin Hills was finished, Maxwell began his assault on the state of Oklahoma in a career that would influence what golf courses would look like in the state for almost thirty years after his death.

Maxwell's fame spread quickly around Oklahoma due to his work at Dornick Hills with grass putting surfaces and the challenge of Twin Hills. Beyond the fact that Dornick Hills had grass greens, many immediately recognized the fact that Maxwell designed excellent golf courses. Because of this ability, Maxwell's services were in high demand. But to become an architect and designer of a high level he knew he would need help. During his study of the National Golf Links and conversations with Charles Blair Macdonald, it must have made an impression on Maxwell how important Macdonald's partner, Seth Raynor, was to the operation. Maxwell contacted his late wife's brother, Dean Woods, and asked him to join in the designing and constructing of golf courses. Dean was employed as a civil engineer for a copper mining company outside of Tucson. Dean agreed and moved his family to Oklahoma City from the copper mines of Arizona.

One of the reputations that Maxwell has around the country was as a golf course designer that specialized in redesigning sand green courses into grass green circuits for his acquaintances from his days as a banker in Ardmore. This did comprise a portion of his early designs, but it was not the main part of his portfolio. Contrary to Maxwell's reputation this list included at least five sand green golf courses. Maxwell thought the success of the grass greens at Dornick Hills was due to the fact that Ardmore was so far south. He was often hesitant to even test grass greens north of Oklahoma City until after better strands of Bermuda grass had been developed. Also, only two of the courses he worked on were actually redesigns of sand green courses early in his career, Muskogee and Ponca City.

Vintage photos of the 18th hole at Duncan CC (courtesy of Stephens County Historical Museum)

The other major myth is that he designed several courses for his friends in the oil industry. This is seemingly due to golf exploding as a popular sport in Oklahoma shortly after Maxwell's decision to start his second career. This popularity had more to do with many more people having the discretionary income to play the game and many more investors had the funds to develop courses. Maxwell did design courses for some people that were associated with the oil industry but this was not the primary source of his contracts. In most cases he won the job through underbidding the competition or because of experience the developer had with one of his previous designs.

Maxwell, prior to the Depression, only took jobs in Oklahoma with just a few exceptions. The main reason for this was that he wanted to stay close to home while his daughters attended school until they were ready to attend the Abbot Academy. Also, the abundance of work in the area was enough to keep him busy. Maxwell was involved with roughly twenty courses in Oklahoma during the 1920s starting with the Twin Hills Country Club. During the work at Twin Hills though Perry took on several contracts. Many of these very early contracts were for sand green designs.

Sand Green Courses

Contrary to conventional wisdom many of Maxwell's courses during the early part of his career were designed with sand putting surfaces. It is due to this misconception, that many feel that Maxwell's designs have not been fully recognized over the years. Sand greens were a normal form of golf course design during this period. Maxwell was concerned about how the Bermuda grass strain would fare in parts of Oklahoma north of Ardmore. Over the years the sand green courses were often used by Maxwell as guinea pigs to see if grass could be sustained in the particular area before Maxwell would design a grass green course nearby. Of the sand green courses that Maxwell designed, only a few have been documented to date. A large portion of the work done initially by Maxwell and Dean Woods remains to be identified on many of these courses. The best preserved of the bunch is the Duncan Golf & Country Club.

The Duncan Golf & Country Club got started when local entrepreneur Fred Schafer, Sr. sold some land to the group that originated the club. The club originated in 1919. In 1921, the club accepted Maxwell's offer to build a course. The land was a wheat field with rolling hills and it was located in a natural valley, which helped to accentuate the nature of the course. The valley deceptively hid the amount of elevation change existing on the property.

During the Depression and World War II the club experienced some financial difficulties and went bankrupt. The local Elks Lodge purchased the club. The Elks Lodge decided that they would tear down the old clubhouse and build a new one near the original sixth green. This necessitated the renumbering of the holes and due to the proximity of the green to the projected location of the clubhouse, the green on the ninth hole was moved. Aside from this, the original nine holes stayed in tact until recently. Over the years, as with a large part of courses in the United States, trees have started to grow into the line of play on the course. The trees have made the course significantly tighter than originally designed by Maxwell.

The course did go through a minor renovation in 1987 that saw the rebuilding of two of Maxwell's greens. The first and fourth were rebuilt due to drainage issues. The fairways were somewhat sloping with slight doglegs. The greens are open in the front and are built-up green sites with tight greenside bunkering. The bunkering on the course was very basic at the time, with the small circular bunkers that Maxwell has become stereotyped with from his career.

The other major sand green design that remains in tact is in Shawnee, Oklahoma. The course now known as the Elks Country Club, dates back to 1923 and was originally called the Shawnee Country Club before being purchased by Elks Lodge #657. The original design included all of the existing holes. The front nine of the course has the best terrain and provides the more scenic walk for the golfer. The holes take advantage of water, numerous specimen trees and ideal push up green sites. The greens on the course are small with several sloping from back to front. The course was littered with many bunkers when it opened. The terrain of the back nine is much less to talk about, especially in comparison with the front nine.

Another sand green design was the Kennedy Golf Course in Tulsa just over the fence from the Tulsa Country Club. The Kennedy course fell under during World War II. The land today is part of a city park and actually is only blocks away from where Perry would live in Tulsa on Denver Avenue. Perry Maxwell was one of the people that turned golf into a sport that people wanted to play; due to his incorporation of grass greens. It is due to this that many forget, or ignore, the designs of Maxwell that used sand greens. The best example of the sand green layouts that Maxwell completed was the Hardscrabble Country Club.

Hardscrabble Country Club

Hardscrabble is often referred to as farmland that is almost impossible to grow anything on due to the rocky nature. So just imagine how bad the land must have been on the farm actually named Hardscrabble located outside of Fort Smith, Arkansas. E. F. Creekmore, a local resident, headed up a group of investors who purchased the farm for the purpose of building a golf course. Perry Maxwell was hired to do the original design work on the course for a fee of $1,500. The original layout by Maxwell at Hardscrabble was a sand green design. Hardscrabble was also the most unique routing Perry would design. The original routing of the club was an out and back layout. In the late 1960s the course was changed significantly as five new holes were added to make the routing into two groups of nine and to make room for a practice facility.

Two holes were a true loss due to the work done on the course. They were two holes that would be unique to any course in the country. The third hole required a semi-blind tee shot up the hill to a crest in the fairway. From this spot, the player had a view from above the fourth fairway and also had a wonderful view of the green for a drop shot style approach. The fourth then featured an elevated tee shot that played through a corridor with steep hills on both sides all the way back to the green located at the end of the natural spillway. The amphitheater setting of the fairway provided some interesting lies as the player hit to the green that sloped towards the water. Two other holes on the course were template style holes. One was a Maxwell template and another was a version of Charles Macdonald's famous cape hole. The 14th features a downhill approach with a green guarded on the left by water. The shot from high above is very intimidating and many people bail out to the right. The plateau landing zone is very wide and provides a multitude of angles into the narrow green. Maxwell designed the hole to reward the longer player off the tee. By this point in the round the player has noticed the ruggedness of the terrain. The difficulty Maxwell had in routing through the many ups and downs on the site becomes evident. The best example of this is the par four sixteenth. It features a drive that must clear a deep chasm then clear the crest of a hill. The shot down to the green is almost a fifty-foot drop shot with water surrounding the green. Short of the green is a swale that will only allow bump and run approaches to get on the green. This hole was also a drivable par four if conditions were fast and firm. The hole is a version of the famous Cape hole designed by CB Macdonald at the National Golf Links. The concept of the Cape hole revolved around the green being surrounded by water of at least two sides and most often three, much like a cape of land jutting into a bay of water. Maxwell's version on this hole protruded into the water on two sides.

The Hardscrabble Country Club has a long and impressive amateur championship history. The most famous event the club has held is the now defunct Willard Memorial Amateur. Hardscrabble has twice hosted the Trans-Mississippi Amateur. The ladies have also been well represented by the club as the Women's Southern Amateur, Women's Western Amateur and Western Junior Girls' Amateur have been hosted there as well. Perhaps the most famous winner at Hardscrabble though was from the lone USGA Championship held at the club. Alice Dye of Indianapolis, Indiana won the U.S. Women's Senior Amateur, which was contested at Hardscrabble in 1979. Alice later went on to greater fame as the wife and several time co-designer with Pete Dye, one of the greatest architects of the modern era of design.

The early years of Perry Maxwell's design career can be catalogued and used as a preview of what was to come later on. Many of the holes that are famous at his later courses were first laid out on similar terrain at courses like Hillcrest, Muskogee and Melrose. Perry worked his crew into a fine oiled machine during this early era of his career. He had also taken the concepts learned from Charles Blair Macdonald and used them throughout the state of Oklahoma. He had taken the National style of design and tweaked it to not only include emulations of famous holes form Great Britain, but to also include holes of his own design that seemed to be more adaptable to the terrain in Oklahoma. Maxwell designed over twenty courses in Oklahoma alone and three in other states from a period of 1920 through 1928. A study of these is necessary to understand Maxwell's evolution as a golf course designer.

Indian Hills Country Club

After Twin Hills, Maxwell went to Catoosa, just north of Tulsa, to design Indian Hills Country Club. The course was an 18-hole layout. Like the rest of the

Tulsa area, the terrain was hilly and rocky. The course has several of the usual Maxwell design traits from early in his career. The course emphasized small greens and accurate approaches that were made difficult with the tight greenside bunkering. As with many courses, the trees on the course grew and seemed to take over the site. In 1993, though, the course switched back to what Maxwell originally laid out. A tornado swept through the course and destroyed many of the trees on the front nine holes. Very little has changed about the layout, but there have been numerous changes to the ownership of the club. The club was originally owned locally under the name of Indian Hills. In the mid-1950s the club was purchased by the Aberdeen Company and the name was changed to Rolling Hills. After 25 years, the club was sold to an individual in the area. The club renamed the Spunky Creek Country Club. After the renaming, a housing development was built around the course and greatly increased the value of the property. The course was fixed up and sold once again to an investor group from Colorado. Then in August of 2001, the local Cherokee Nation purchased the club and renamed it Cherokee Hills. The Cherokee Nation has long term plans to develop the course into a tourist location. The fact that the course still remains and didn't fall by the wayside during the Depression, World War II or due to all the ownership issues is a minor miracle.

The course though has recently been through a major change. The course was renovated in hopes of expanding the gaming facilities for the resort. To do this part of the original course is going to be eliminated. The owners purchased additional land to make room for a new set of holes. The construction and design was undertaken by Tripp Davis. Davis commented on the possibility of the design in the early stages, "The Cherokee Nation bought it and is attaching it to a hotel and casino. They are taking part of the land the front nine was on, but I think even Maxwell would admit that this was a weak nine. It was really flat and Maxwell had to make some compromises. However, the back nine is on a wonderful piece of ground and the new land we have for expansion is as good or better. We will be taking the existing holes and renovating them and we are building eight completely new holes while pretty much rebuilding four others." Fortunately, for the club Perry Maxwell originally laid out the location of 27 holes for the final plan of the facility. These additional nine holes are the framework of what the new holes will look like. The area where the opening nine holes were located will be replaced by a much more appealing piece of property with more natural features for Davis to use in his work.

Muskogee Country Club

The Muskogee Country Club was founded in 1903 under the name of the Muskogee Town and Country Club. It was incorporated a few weeks later with 53 original members, including Tams Bixby, the club's first president. Originally located outside of Fort Gibson, in two buildings. In 1907 the Club decided to expand and purchased 100 acres. That same year Alex Findlay designed a nine-hole golf course. In 1911, the game had caught on so well, they bought an adjoining forty acres and developed another nine holes.

In 1924, Perry Maxwell was brought in to redesign the entire course into the current 18-hole layout. The other major goal was implementing grass greens to replace the sand greens on the course. It was also at Muskogee that Maxwell set a standard for all architects to meet. He, Dean Woods and the club pro at the time all slept in cots on the grounds at night while the work took place. As with other Maxwell designs, the course uses the rolling terrain to its full potential. The routing that Maxwell conceived has been altered since his work. The original layout has been altered mostly in the stretch of holes three through five.

The tenth hole is the first on the course that makes use of the natural lake on the grounds at Muskogee with the approach over the green.

The Muskogee Country Club features a list of notable championships that have tested it. The LPGA tour visited in 1962. The Muskogee Civitan Open was organized by a group of local businessmen to try and attract a future U. S. Women's Open. The 1962 tournament was notable as the last victory on the LPGA tour by Patty Berg. She has the record for the most women's major championships of 15, second only to Jack Nicklaus for the most in all of golf. The following year, Mickey Wright dominated the tournament. Mickey Wright also won the 1964 Muskogee tournament as she defended her title. Susie Maxwell, no relation to Perry Maxwell, would go on to win the tournament in 1965.

The course has since hosted other events, with the most noteworthy being the 1970 U. S. Women's Championship won by Donna Caponi. This was the 25th championship and to commemorate the special occasion many of the past champions attended. Of all the prior champions only three did not enter the tournament. Donna Caponi though would be too tough for them even though she made things difficult for herself. Caponi had a two-stroke lead coming to the last hole and double bogeyed it.

The strength of Maxwell's layout is the beginning sequence of holes and the use of the natural hazards on the site. The opening hole is a slight downhill dogleg. The player is faced with a difficult shot into the angled green that uses a

41

delayed dogleg feature around a nest of trees. The wide fairway slopes from right to left and makes the drive to the correct side important. The nest of trees, combined with the slope of the land make it easy to "con" the player into thinking a shot to the left side would be the appropriate line. Maxwell's philosophy on the use of trees is evident on this hole. He would often use specimen trees or a nice nesting to provide interest to a hole and provide some strategic impact.

The solid first is followed by the most difficult hole on the course. The long second is a slight dogleg left that goes downhill. The fairway rolls away from the player and creates a hanging lie. The green that is perched on a rise about 75 yards past the lowest point in the fairway. The green is protected by a swale that also appears to make the hole shorter and acts as a deceptive tool.

The third hole as Maxwell originally designed it was a 550-yard par five that was a great risk-reward hole. The player could play to the edge of the fairway and take the chance of going over two deep swales to the green. The player that didn't take the risk could play to an island between the two depressions and have an iron into the green. The hole was eventually split into two holes to become a short par four and a par three, to make better use of the two ravines on the course. Holes four and five were then combined to make the new fifth hole of 532 yards. Since then, Tripp Davis has performed a renovation that included work on all of the first six holes, except for the fifth.

The back nine also features some excellent holes. Three in particular stand out as the lake is the focus of the back side and Maxwell's ingenuity at using hazards in a variety of ways is demonstrated. The tenth hole is the most famous hole, and perhaps the best on the course. The fairway slopes away from the player and rolls towards the lake. Just past the fairway bunker at the corner of the dogleg, the fairway becomes extremely wide. The difficulty is that the lie is downhill and the approach must clear the water. From the tee, many players are fooled into thinking that Maxwell used the same strategy on this hole as on the first. With the angle of the green, the best approach would come from the left side of the dogleg just beyond the fairway bunker. Perry provided the player a chance to use the terrain to his advantage from the tee. But he also gave a wide berth in the fairway, as it is almost forty yards in width, if the player who could not hit a draw from the tee.

The eleventh uses the lake in a different manner. It has a beautiful tee shot over the water to a rolling fairway that flows from right to left. The longer player will want to cut the slight dogleg in the hole and avoid the fairway bunkers. This is at the cost of carrying more of the lake and tempting disaster. The green is clearly divided into two sections. The right side is very difficult to master due to a hump in the middle of it while the left is very flat. The problem with the left side is that it is a peninsula between two bunkers. Any pin location here will be difficult, at best, to touch. It is only ten paces from front to back. The fairway at one time stretched all the way to the edge of the water. It has been cut back due to tree growth on the left side.

The last hole to really flirt with the water is the 16th. The fairway slopes from left to right on this hole. The green is perched just to the left of the water. The green also slopes towards the lake. The green features three separate areas with a slight false front. Two large rolls on the right side split that side and a spine running from the back creates the third section of the green. The entire hole feeds the player to the water and anything to the right side of the putting surface will end up wet. Hole locations on the left side of the green force the tee shot to the right side of the fairway and must flirt with the leading edge of the water. The pin location dictates the strategy on this hole.

Maxwell's strength at routing a course was most evident with his layout of Muskogee. His use of the natural hazards around the course was inspirational. A natural depression that ran through the course was the primary factor affecting the routing of several holes and the second nine holes were routed around the natural lakes of the course. Maxwell also implemented some new template holes on the course including the masterful tenth hole. The course has received some notoriety but has often been one of the most overlooked courses in Maxwell's portfolio.

During 1924, Maxwell also completed the design of the Pennsylvania Golf Club in Llanerch, Pennsylvania. The course was built for the Pennsylvania Railroad and was the first design by Perry outside of Oklahoma. From aerial photos it appears that Maxwell again used a small plot of land effectively to lay out a difficult test. The course was only in use by the club for eight years as they relocated in 1932 to Malvern and renamed the club to the Chester Valley Country Club. Once the club relocated it is uncertain what happened with the course. Aerial photos prior to World War II show the remains of the course, but it was in a state of disrepair. Today the area is grown over and contains houses and a small forest.

Early in 1926 Perry received notification that Alister Mackenzie would be interested in beginning a partnership with Perry Maxwell and using him as his "Midwest Associate." The Good Doctor had already reached agreements with Wendell Miller and Robert Hunter to be his other associates. The first time they would meet since their exchange at St. Andrews seven years earlier, would be at the Biltmore Hotel in Oklahoma City. Mackenzie was on his way across the country en route to Australia for some work he had accepted at the Royal Melbourne Golf Club. Maxwell was accompanied by his close friend Charles Evans. During the meeting, they discussed what would be their first collaborative effort at the Melrose Country Club in Philadelphia. It was arranged for Maxwell to hire Mackenzie as a consulting architect on the project. Maxwell also took Mackenzie on a tour of his design at Twin Hills. They also toured the recently started work at the Nichols Hills Country Club on the north side of Oklahoma City. Maxwell added Mackenzie's name to the contract, but Mackenzie had little involvement with the actual design. It is also believed that they traveled south to visit Maxwell's home course at Dornick Hills. A few months later, Mackenzie was traveling through the United States fresh from his trip to Australia and returning for one of his annual visits back to England. On his way through, he would meet Maxwell in Philadelphia to make his initial visit to their first cooperative design at the Melrose Country Club. It is believed that Mackenzie came back one other time to visit the site during construction and one more time just before completion.

Melrose Country Club

The Curtis Country Club opened in 1912 complete with swimming pools, tennis courts, baseball and other activities. The club also eventually built a rudimentary golf course. In 1926, the Curtis Company sold the club to a new group of owners led by Bob Smiley and Wayne and Malcolm Harkness. Their first goal was to build a world-class golf course. They hired Perry Maxwell for his second design in the Philadelphia area. As part of his partnership, Maxwell set up a deal that named Mackenzie as a paid consultant on the project at Melrose.

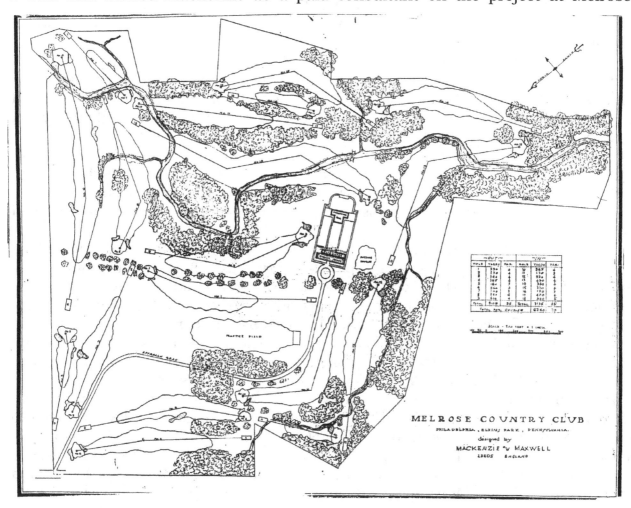

The routing of the Melrose Country Club (courtesy of Melrose Country Club)

Maxwell would be the lead on the construction and design of the course. The consummation of that partnership took place with a large amount of whistle blowing and fanfare. While there, Mackenzie made suggestions for the layout and made pre-arranged visits to the nearby Merion Golf Club and Pine Valley Golf Club. After the course was opened it was said to "resemble more the famous Pine Valley than any other Philadelphia course."[15]

The routing was laid out over a small piece of property. The site has been cut down even more over the years due to highway expansion. The original layout measured roughly 6,240 yards. The original course would not survive for very long. A WPA project was started to build the Tookany Parkway and also alter the path of the creek, which required re-routing of the course. The Tookany Parkway was expanded again in 1968 and housing editions began to encroach on the course, so more work was needed as holes disappeared. Melrose is often overlooked with all the great courses in Philadelphia. The course today bears almost no resemblance to the original design in 1926.

Melrose is significant mainly because it was the first work that Maxwell collaborated in any fashion with Mackenzie and after the completion of the project in 1928; Mackenzie wrote a letter to Maxwell that stated the following.

> *My dear Maxwell:*
> *When I originally asked you to come into partnership with me, I did so because I thought your work more closely harmonized with nature than any other American Golf Course Architect. The design and construction of the Melrose Golf Course has confirmed my previous impression.*
> *I feel that I cannot leave America without expressing my admiration for the excellence of your work and the extremely low cost compared with the results obtained. As I stated to you verbally, the work is so good that you may not get the credit you deserve.*
> *Few if any golfers will realize that Melrose has been constructed by the hand of man and not by nature. This is the greatest tribute that can be paid to the work of a Golf Course Architect.*
>
> *Yours very sincerely,*
> *Alister Mackenzie*

This was high praise from one considered by many to be the greatest architect in golf. Many excellent holes were laid out on the original course. But the heart of the course was routed through the natural elevation changes provided by the Tookany Creek. The first five holes of the course were fairly flat in nature and somewhat ordinary, but starting with the sixth hole the course took a drastic change in direction and feel. The longest hole on the front nine was downhill all the way from the tee to the green. The drive was tested by the creek that ran along the right side of the hole. A different fork of the same creek was then used to challenge the second shot as a diagonal hazard. Those that attempted the carry

45

were given an easy chip. The eighth was a short hole of 140 yards that had the green delicately placed at the junction of two forks of the Tookany and was perhaps the most tranquil hole on the course. The next hole was a test from the tee as the Tookany was used as a carry hazard for the player. The other test was to hit it straight down the middle as the fairway was pinched by trees in a bottleneck fashion. The approach to the green was to another skyline green setting for the eighth hole.

Perhaps the most interesting was the ninth hole on the front side. It still remains as the second hole but has been lengthened by sixty yards to a short par five. The hole has been described by some as a "roller-coaster". The hole crosses over two deep ravines during its journey to the green. The rise that occurs between the two chasms is the ideal landing zone for the golfer. Originally the view from the rise would provide an excellent vantage point into the green that was protected by two beautiful bunkers. One bunker was directly between the player and the green and was built into the rise fronting the putting surface, with the other bunker playing along the right side of the green. The right front of the green was open and allowed the player to either try an aerial approach or a running draw.

The best hole on the course and one of the best in the city was the thirteenth. At 430 yards, the length was frightening for many, but once the player was on the tee they became more anxious than nervous. The player was provided another elevated tee shot that looked over the fairway that ended in a flat area that was surrounded by the Tookany Creek on three sides. This is perhaps where the comparison to Pine Valley originated from as the Maxwell design at Melrose created similar demands off of the tee on some holes. The wide fairway accepted many shots but only the ones to the left side were given a clear view up the hill to the elevated green site almost thirty feet above the lower fairway. The green was also among the best on the course.

The last two holes on the course, a difficult combination, were eliminated with the Parkway work in 1938. The seventeenth was a 420 yard hole that was bottlenecked near the green by a grove of trees. The fairway sloped slightly from right to left. The green was placed directly on the other side of the creek. The shot from the left provided a slightly better angle into the green. The eighteenth was a long double dogleg par five of 540 yards. This hole again exhibited some of the target style tendencies seen previously on the thirteenth hole. The fairway featured a dogleg to the left that would allow the longer player a chance to play towards the green on their second if they liked. The shorter player could play straight out and then take their chances on the second as the fairway was divided awkwardly by the creek. The player that wanted to lay up could place their second in the location they wanted for their short pitch to the elevated green.

The work in Elkins Park was key to Maxwell's career for many reasons. It allowed him to get a start in the golf mecca of Philadelphia. This would prove beneficial many years down the road for later work in his career. The design also began the partnership with Alistair Mackenzie. Although the work by Mackenzie at Melrose was limited to some bunker placement, contrary to many other claims. The other major impact was the opening of an office in Elkins Park that Maxwell would make annual trips to and conduct work. The work that was conducted by Maxwell in Philadelphia between the completion at Melrose and the renovation work of the 1930s has gone mostly unrecognized, but it would only make sense there was something bringing him back to the city if he opened an office there. To do so would be a wasteful expense and something out of character for Perry. With Melrose having undergone so many changes to the course it is important to document what was actually constructed by Maxwell so that it does not get lost in the annals of history.

The course at Melrose was the beginning of the partnership between these two giants of the design industry. The partnership would also include courses at the University of Michigan and the Ohio State University, with the greatest effort of the collaboration being the grand design of the Crystal Downs Country Club. While the work at Melrose was being completed, Maxwell also ventured back to his home state and began working on more projects in Oklahoma.

Hillcrest Country Club

Frank Phillips, one of the co-founders of the Phillips Petroleum, decided that he wanted a new facility as a setting for entertaining his poential business conacts. At the time, Phillips was planning a national expansion of his company. He was the driving force behind the development of the Hillcrest Country Club and helped organize and finance it. Phillips, however, was not as

The beauty of the eleventh at Hillcrest is beyond measure. It features a Maxwell ideal elevated tee with the mountain behind.

enthusiastic about having a golf course. He actually hated the sport and couldn't stand to play it. The Hillcrest Country Club members insisted on developing a golf course. It is believed the inspiration from this was due to the encouragement of Willie Brown and Ed Dudley, two notable golf professionals in the area. From what can be gathered from available information, it appears some of the Hillcrest members were in attendance for a tournament at Indian Hills and it was through the insistence of Brown and Dudley that Hillcrest should build a course similar to the other Maxwell design. The club decided, against the wishes of Phillips, to build a course. The Bartlesville Engineers Club was trying to determine between two sites, which would be more ideal. They had also recommended A. W. Tillinghast or Walter Travis to handle the design of the course. Maxwell had heard that Hillcrest was going to try and build a course. Maxwell consulted the club on which site was best to choose and they selected the current location. He was quoted when discussing the site, "The new grounds are ideal for a golf course. I would not have been interested had it been on a prairie on which you expected a course, but the topography of the Hillcrest course site is fine. It will make one of the best eighteen-hole golf courses in the state."[16] They brought in, noted architect, Tom Bendelow to survey the site in November 1925. Maxwell then was given the commission of the job by underbidding Tillinghast and Travis. Maxwell began designing the course in the following January. The original design of the Hillcrest Country Club was to include sand greens. Maxwell suggested this, "You are just north of the 36 degrees or in that region where you are too far south for bluegrass and too far north for a good stand of Bermuda. The Bermuda greens at Tulsa, Muskogee and Oklahoma City were killed out last winter by the heavy sleet. Those at Ardmore came through all right. I am of the opinion that you would make a mistake here in trying anything except sand."[17] The issue revolved around the fact that the year before the subsoil was harmed due to a very hard frost and the ground could not support the growth of Bermuda grass. The greens though were seeded and grass grew. The course officially opened in the spring of 1927. The final cost of the project was approximately $25,000.

Over the first part of Maxwell's career he had been developing several of his own template holes, to add to the repertoire provided by his mentor Macdonald. At each course he seemingly found another to add and tried to use on later designs. With the design of Hillcrest, he was able to implement almost each of these template holes somewhere on the course. Dornick Hills and Twin Hills, earlier in the decade were places that Maxwell tested out his general theories on design. By the time of the design at Hillcrest he had mastered the application of those theories into a group of templates that were among his favorite individual hole designs. Using these techniques also created some significant items about the course.

The eleventh hole is the best on the course while also being the most photogenic and natural hole on the course. The hole is farthest from the clubhouse and also the most peaceful. It runs sixty feet downhill from tee to green in a stair step manner with the land also flowing slightly left to right. Short of the green is another swale that goes down another ten feet. The green is two tiered with several rolls that dominate the play on the green. The view from the tee shows an excellent view of a mountain in the distance and provides a scenic view of the hole. When this hole was laid out, one must wonder if Maxwell intended for this to be the opening hole on the course as it uses many of the same characteristics as his other opening holes. Strategically, the secret to the hole is trying to get the ball onto one of the plateaus in the fairway and to avoid the downslopes. The approach is best played if from the right hand side as that leads into the open portion of the green. This beautiful hole is one of the best ever created by Maxwell. Though he would have loved to include this hole in his repertoire of prototypes, the natural landforms needed to do this were just not in existence at many courses that he would later design.

Hillcrest was also significant for one other major factor. It was the last course that Maxwell did before the real contractual partnership began with Mackenzie and he started to receive high-profile jobs around the country. Hillcrest was perhaps the last of his low-key designs until after World War II. After this his style truly began to evolve. Some of that was due to the influence of Mackenzie, but most of it was due to his own maturation as a designer and learning in the first few years of his career.

Maxwell had received much acclaim locally, which drew the attention of an old acquaintance named Nichols. This led to one of his finest designs, the Oklahoma City Golf & Country Club, originally called Nichols Hills. It was only fitting that the final design of the pre-depression era by Maxwell would be the course at Nichols Hills, which owes much of its inspiration directly to the National Golf Links and is a shining example of the influence that CB Macdonald and his prize course had on the philosophy of Maxwell.

Nichols Hills

In 1926, Dr. G. A. Nichols hired Perry Maxwell to design and construct two golf courses for him in Oklahoma City. Nichols was an acquaintance from Maxwell's days in the banking industry in Oklahoma. The course construction was started in early 1926. It is known that Maxwell brought Alister Mackenzie to the site in 1926. The course was contracted under the Mackenzie and Maxwell partnership umbrella. The 36-hole complex ended up being an 18-hole course when Nichols sold off part of the land. The plans called for Maxwell to develop a course on land east of the current clubhouse. It is believed the sale of the land eliminated the possible routing by Maxwell of the East course and led to an odd characteristic to the current routing. This created one of the few courses ever designed by Perry that does not have two returning loops of nine holes. Three years after the completion of the course Nichols became interested in the area where the Oklahoma City Golf & Country Club was located. He offered to exchange his golf course for the land where the club was located, which contained a course designed by Alex Findlay. That course was quickly destroyed and used for residential and commercial purposes.

The original design at Nichols Hills consisted of approximately fifty bunkers, a creek, and two ponds on a plot roughly 150 acres in size. An access road that ran through the property caused some issues with the layout of the course at the time of design. This road was later converted into a city street. The design has subtle elevation changes, a few forced carries, few fairway bunkers, subtle sloping greens and numerous greenside bunkers. As with every Maxwell design, the wind was a major factor. The greens often slope away from the golfer when the prevailing wind is in the players face. The greens also are generally small with some false fronts. Many of the green locations were inspired by Maxwell's study of the National Golf Links. No course by Maxwell, aside from Dornick Hills, shows as much of this reverence for MacDonald's design as the Nichols Hills layout. Most of the exemplary holes have a direct connection to the templates that inspired Maxwell for much of this early portion of his career.

The front nine features many excellent derivations of the classic concepts preached by Macdonald in his "Ideal Course" philosophy. The back nine goes in a different direction with using some of Maxwell's personal templates that he had used over the first ten years of his career. The first part of the second nine was designed across the access road that split the property. Since the original design, this has been expanded to full city street. Also, the numbering of the holes has changed since the Maxwell's original layout. The club felt it made for better sequencing of the holes.

Due to his contacts in the area and the notoriety that Maxwell received for this design, it was a huge step in getting much more important designs down the road in Oklahoma and in the Great Plains. It would open the door later for his most noteworthy design at Prairie Dunes as the owners of that course would first notice Maxwell's work at the Oklahoma City course and thought that style would work best on their course. This would be a testament to the skill that Maxwell had in designing a golf course. His courses may have similar traits in green or bunker design, but he made the courses to fit into the landscape.

By the end of the decade Perry was well known in the state and he was a good friend with many of the top individuals in Oklahoma. The list included Lee Cruce, Wiley Post and Will Rogers. Lee Cruce was the second Governor of Oklahoma and was the man who oversaw Maxwell's growth in the banking industry in Ardmore. Will Rogers is perhaps the most famous person ever to come from Oklahoma. He was a world-renowned entertainer. He is so well known that people still try to use his image to market products on television. Wiley was an Oklahoma original. Wiley was the only person that ever got Maxwell into a plane. That happened only once as Perry agreed to fly over one of his designs so he could see what it looked like from above. Flying was perhaps the only fear Maxwell had, but it was a major phobia. Unfortunately, two of Perry's friends, Post and Rogers, died in 1936. Perry developed relationships with other captains of industry and famous individuals all his life. People such as Waite and Frank Philips and other heads of oil companies in Oklahoma would be just some of the acquaintances for Perry. The list would also include Eugene Grace, J.P. Morgan, Grantland Rice, Bobby Jones and Clifford Roberts.

Maxwell's second career had taken off quite well and his personal life was also going very well. Even though he still felt the loss of his beloved wife, he was getting on with his life. His daughters were all in college during the decade at

50

Wellesley. The only setback appeared to come early in the decade when Perry suffered a radiation burn while getting treatment for eczema in Philadelphia.

In 1929, the Great Depression took hold of the country. Maxwell saw the personal fortunes of many friends disappear overnight. Fortunately, Maxwell had long ago divested himself of all the stock in the banks he owned and was able to sit back on the fortune he had due to his investments and to the funds that his uncle had left him. Maxwell was worried, however, that his second career was over. But he would work directly with Alister Mackenzie in their much-acclaimed partnership over the next few years. And this would lead to Maxwell landing several plum assignments down the road.

The Doctor and His Associate

After the completion of the Melrose job, Maxwell and Mackenzie had limited communication, if any at all, until 1928 when a group wanting a course in Northern Michigan contacted Robert Hunter, Mackenzie's other lead associate at the time. Walkley Ewing headed up the group of investors who wanted to build a more suitable golf course than the nine-hole course they currently were using. After reading Hunter's book, The Links, Ewing knew that he wanted a course similar to the wonderful designs he had seen in the pages of Hunter's literary masterpiece. Hunter recommended Alister Mackenzie to design the course for Ewing. Mackenzie decided he would check out the site and contacted Maxwell. Maxwell and Mackenzie met in Grand Rapids, Michigan and were escorted to Frankfort by Ewing. Though initially somewhat perturbed by the whole thing, because it broke up his trip back home, Mackenzie quickly became enthused about the possibilities after seeing the landscape full of sand dunes and trees. Maxwell and Mackenzie then began to work on one of the best designs during the "Golden Age," Crystal Downs. Mackenzie was at the forefront in laying out the first nine holes, but Maxwell came back over the next three summers to oversee the construction and addition of the second nine and subsequent changes to the course. He lived in a house that existed near the property. Perry constructed the front nine and then added the second using notes from Mackenzie but making alterations as he saw fit.

The whole Frankfort, Michigan area is set upon glacial sand dunes that provide some dramatic elevation changes. It is also set between Crystal Lake and Lake Michigan. The club opened on July 4, 1929. The course itself is located north of Frankfort, off of a rural highway. Once you pass through the gates you see the fifth fairway and green. Then you go back into the trees on a narrow curvy road and suddenly you appear out of nowhere next to the third hole. The parking lot is a piece of level ground between the first and third tees that speaks of the simplicity of the club. To the left of the road on a towering dune is the clubhouse. From the windows in the pro shop you can see the dramatic elevation changes that Mackenzie and Maxwell had to work with. The large dune that the pro shop and tees for the first and tenth are set upon is accompanied by other dunes and a valley that runs the width of the front nine. This was used perfectly by Mackenzie on holes five through eight. These elevation changes make these holes special. If left as a nine-hole course, this would have rivaled the original nine holes at Prairie Dunes as the best nine-hole course in the United States. Another stretch of holes, twelve through sixteen, were set upon a ridge that runs parallel to the Lake Michigan shoreline. The remaining holes make use of the dunes and an amazing drop off that creates a dramatic effect on the seventeenth. The attention to detail on the course was directly attributable to the amount of time Maxwell spent in Northern Michigan.

Crystal Downs was not just another contract to Perry Maxwell. The course encompassed almost eighteen months worth of his energy over a three-year span. He lived on the site and was focused almost singularly on the goal of completing the course. First glance and conventional wisdom would just say that the course

The puzzling tee-shot on the 5th hole at Crystal Downs (courtesy of Jeff Reel)

is a testament to the design philosophy of Alister Mackenzie. But some feel the course more closely resembles the early work done by Maxwell in Oklahoma. Study of those early courses by Maxwell would also lead many others down that same thought process as it appears after careful analysis that many of the holes at Crystal Downs were developed as successful template holes in Oklahoma.

During the initial stages of the routing of the course, there was some difficulty in determining the proper way to lay out the opening nines holes. It supposedly resulted in a quirky circumstance that was resolved after some quick thinking by Maxwell. The story was relayed in the wonderful biography of Alister Mackenzie by Doak, Scott and Haddock in this fashion.

> *Mackenzie and Maxwell stayed on for several days to establish a routing plan for the course and to begin the design of the greens. At one point, finding themselves stuck on a final solution to the beautifully undulating but rather tight front nine, Mackenzie sent Maxwell into town for provisions. When Maxwell returned an hour or two later, he found the doctor sitting on the hill where the pro shop is now located, bottle at his side. "I have the front nine finished," declared Mackenzie. "Come and see what you think." After studying the plan, Maxwell's reply was that it was wonderful, but there were only eight holes. Mackenzie promptly added a short hole along the ridge on which they sat: today's celebrated and deadly par-3 ninth.[18]*

Crystal Downs is undoubtedly the type of course that Mackenzie hoped would come from the partnership with Maxwell. This course perhaps more than any other, held up the principles of architecture that Mackenzie had laid out on paper many years before. It would also prove to be the course that exemplified how well the styles of Mackenzie and Maxwell blended together. Over the years, it has been just assumed that Mackenzie was the key player in the design of the course, but after analyzing the layout of the course and the amount of time that Maxwell invested in the construction, one cannot deny the fact that Perry was a much bigger player in the design and layout of the holes than has been the common wisdom for many years.

An interesting note about the work at Crystal Downs included Maxwell being partially paid with a piece of land that was next to the course along with the fee of $5,000 split between Maxwell and Mackenzie. From talking with family members, it appears that Maxwell on several occasions received a piece of real estate as part of his compensation. Many of those were quickly sold after he received them. This was to keep cash coming in to help pay the way for his children going to school at Wellesley and Dartmouth.

Mackenzie was able to leave Maxwell in charge of the projects and go on to other work and not have to worry if the person he left behind would understand what his design intent was for each hole, or if they would water down the design with their own beliefs. If anything, Maxwell possibly took Mackenzie's work to a level that few other people could have due to his similar views and ability to understand what Mackenzie intended with his design. Though this partnership was not unique, it was definitely not ordinary for two such esteemed architects to work so closely together. The combination of their similar beliefs and the way they worked in the field meshing was what made this partnership such a success. This was proved with their next partnership just a few hours south of Frankfort.

University of Michigan

While in Michigan to look at the site for Crystal Downs, Mackenzie also received the contract to do the University of Michigan course in 1928. With him leaving the country shortly and Perry already being in the state to work at Crystal Downs contract. Maxwell was left in charge of getting the plans started on the course. Maxwell submitted the original layout of the course after his first visit to the site in 1929. The preliminary layout by Maxwell identified several of the green sites and many of the holes in the final routing. Mackenzie visited the course after the preliminary plans were created and made modifications to holes two through five, changed the green designs on holes six and fourteen and made recommendations for some bunkering changes. The changes by Mackenzie increased the length of the design from 6,250 to 6,600 yards and created a par 71 design.

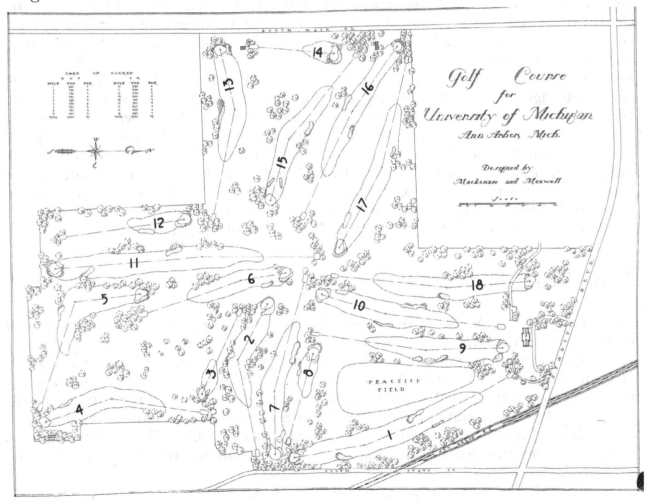

The original routing submitted by Maxwell for the University of Michigan course in 1929

With Maxwell's love of learning and reading, he relished the idea of being able to work on a course at one of the premier centers of education in the country. During this job, Perry would make the acquaintance of a young Marshall Eldred in 1930. Eldred was a native of Princeton, Kentucky and paved the way for Maxwell to come to his boyhood home a year later and design a golf course.

The most famous bit of information about the University of Michigan golf course is the fabled rumor that the course was in disrepair for many years because of the parking of cars for all the home games of the University of Michigan football team. The course that actually parks the cars for the games is the neighboring Ann Arbor Golf & Outing Club, a nine-hole course that often does this for the Wolverines. What should be the most famous fact about the course is that it is the home of a classic design by Alister Mackenzie and Perry Maxwell.

Perhaps the main item that Maxwell would draw from his exposure to Mackenzie was the development of bunkers with an artistic flair. Prior to his work with Mackenzie, Maxwell's bunkers would be somewhat regular in shape or were large waste bunkers like those found at Dornick Hills. After his exposure with the Good Doctor, his bunker work was much more freeform as demonstrated at later courses. The work at Michigan also was very economical. Maxwell and Mackenzie completed the construction of the Michigan course for under $100,000 and provided one of the best collegiate courses in the country and came in under the original budget of $200,000. Maxwell was quoted in 1945 when talking about the course, "Although we did spend a lot of money on it. Money was no object at Michigan. They wanted something distinctive and different. So we spent $35,000 decorating the fairways with pine trees 25 and 35 feet tall. It's very pretty now."[19] This was in response to a statement by Fielding Yost of Michigan that the course was the best course in the country, which Maxwell quickly refuted. If not for the wonderful work at Crystal Downs, this would undoubtedly be the course that would exemplify the melding of the two styles of Maxwell and Mackenzie.

Ohio State University

In 1925, L. W. St. John originally started the pursuit of opening a golf course for the university, as it was his next step in getting top-flight facilities at the prominent midwestern school. He had already achieved the success of striking a deal for a large football stadium and thought a golf course surpassing those at Yale and at rival University of Michigan would be a great achievement. Once the site was purchased, the search for an architect ensued. Mackenzie and Maxwell were invited to Columbus in early October of 1929. The Board approved their ideas on the design and Mackenzie was commissioned to undertake the project.

After this though, the project still carried forward slowly. It took Mackenzie over two years to get detailed plans to St. John. In January 1931, St. John finally received the plans and the work could finally begin. Wendell Miller would be the lead builder on the assignment as he was a Columbus native and could easily oversee the construction. He had been on other Mackenzie projects before this, including St. Charles and Augusta National. Mackenzie was slow to get detailed hole drawings out to the Ohio State people and progress was slow. Unfortunately, Alister died before he was able to get the detail plans completed and forwarded to St. John.

St. John though was intent on fulfilling his dream of having a "Mackenzie" course. He eventually acquired the hand drawings that Mackenzie had completed. With Miller on board already and the funding from the WPA in place, St. John thought the work could finally begin on his dream. However, Miller was struck down with a heart attack while assisting Maxwell in Tulsa on a project.

OSU immediately began searching for an architect to perform the job. Two names were forwarded to them by Robert Hunter, Perry Maxwell and Robert Trent Jones. Bobby Jones, of Augusta National fame, was asked his opinion of the two men and he responded that he had never seen the work, nor heard of Perry Maxwell, but that Trent Jones would be a fine candidate. The University ended up selecting Maxwell. He along with a professor from OSU, George McClure would be handling the project. This was a highly unusual situation as in most cases the architect would be the one in charge of the project. Maxwell was also involved with other projects at this time and would spend time going back and forth, but he would spend much more time on site than many of his contemporaries. McClure however did not see it this way and constantly complained to the higher ups at Ohio State. Eventually, Maxwell would oversee the construction of a majority of the holes of the complex, before dropping from the project and it was completed by McClure and, a gentleman by the name of, John McCoy.

A constant source of frustration during the construction of the course was that Maxwell had failed to provide McClure with detailed plans for the project. It appears that those plans were eventually provided before Maxwell left the project. Eventually the plans provided by Mackenzie and Maxwell would be used by McClure to construct the course. Before leaving though Maxwell constructed a large portion of the course.

The Ohio State Golf Course may not be the best collegiate course in nation but it has an amazing legacy and history that was touched by two of the greatest architects in history. One can only imagine what the course would have looked like if Mackenzie and Maxwell had seen the project through to its completion together. One of the niches that Maxwell seemed to cover in his career was to take contracts for universities to build golf courses. The mid-1930s were also instrumental for Maxwell as the period opened the door to the area of work that Perry would become most famous for in the years to follow his career. Maxwell became a master of renovation work during the Depression due to a limitation on funds at many clubs, his penchant for low budget work and due to other circumstances that would arise later in the decade.

Construction photo from Ohio State and photo of newly finished twelfth hole
(courtesy of Ohio State University)

The Dust Bowl and Elkins Park

The "Roaring Twenties" was a decade of decadence and economic growth. Businesses had made large gains and profits due to the industrial revolution. Labor wages had not kept up to the same standard. The wide berth between the rich and poor had grown exponentially. This, combined with the large increase in personal debt finally broke the back of the economy. October 29, 1929 was the day the New York Stock Exchange crashed. People began to jump out of buildings, banks went under, 15 million people became unemployed, countries fell and it set the stage for 15 years of conflict.

Due to his lack of reaction, Herbert Hoover was defeated in the next presidential election by Franklin Delano Roosevelt. Hoover had assured Americans that the "passing incident in our national lives," would be over in sixty days. Roosevelt was quick to jump on the attack in trying to defeat the Depression. He declared a four-day bank holiday and in the first one hundred days of his administration passed a series of legislative orders quickly termed the New Deal. The emphasis of the New Deal was to put people back to work and rebuild not only their lives, but their spirits as well. One of these programs was the Works Progress Administration, also known as the WPA.

Of all of Roosevelt's New Deal programs, the WPA was the most famous. Over the life of the program it employed over 8.5 million people for an average monthly salary of $41.57. The employees of the WPA built such items as bridges, roads, public buildings, parks, airports and golf courses. The administration was under the direction of Harry Hopkins. Under Hopkins' direction the WPA would spend more than $11 million in relief funds before it was shut down in 1943. Due to the nature of the program it was much more extensive than just giving out the funds. Hopkins was quoted about his thoughts on this, "Give a man a dole and you save his body and destroy his spirit. Give him a job and you save both body and spirit."[20] The WPA did not employ every person seeking employment but it took a large burden off of the state support systems that still had to deal with over five million unemployed people around the country.

Golf course architecture seemed like a trivial point in comparison to the circumstances of the period. Unfortunately, many great architects saw their careers go up in smoke. A. W. Tillinghast, Alister Mackenzie and Stanley Thompson all lost fortunes or were bankrupt. Donald Ross effectively was without work except for his continued professional job at Pinehurst and the courses directly surrounding the famed resort. One of the few that actually increased his workload was Perry Maxwell. The twelve years between the stock market crash and the start of World War II were the most prolific of his career. It was also during this time that Maxwell retired officially from the banking industry.

Maxwell could live comfortably for a few years from his sale of stock in the local banks and from his real estate and oil investments, but repaying the debt due to his sister and his daughters attending college would put a drain on his savings. Perry began to pursue jobs around the country and would start to work two to three courses at a time for almost the entire depression. This was all made possible by his experience in the early years of his design business that helped him to fine tune his design strategy and philosophy and developed a competent construction crew.

It was during this time that Maxwell started to branch out from his stomping grounds of Oklahoma and started to take jobs from outside of the state. Much of this expansion was due to his partnership with Alister Mackenzie and the notoriety gained with that association. Other key components to his rising popularity as a designer were his skill as a green builder and his reputation for low cost construction. The work that Maxwell did during this period can be split in half between renovations and original designs. His renovation work included stops at Pine Valley, the National Golf Links, and other courses in the Northeastern United States.

During this period, Maxwell was also getting the involvement of other people to help manage his crews and provide labor for him. Included in this was Wendell Miller. Wendell and Perry were associated from dealings with Alister Mackenzie. With his downturn in activity, Wendell was more than willing to provide an able hand and body for Maxwell. Wendell was the East Coast Associate for Mackenzie in the past and was the construction lead on many Alister Mackenzie projects in the eastern part of the country, including the magnificent Augusta National design.

Maxwell also had mastered his trademark "Maxwell Rolls" by this time. It was during this time frame that Maxwell's designing career started to take a turn towards a new style influenced by Mackenzie and his visit to Scotland in 1919 and away from the design philosophy of Macdonald.

But all of this would not have been possible if not for the Works Progress Administration. This program was instrumental in the construction of several of Perry Maxwell's courses during this period. The next design that Maxwell did apart from his partnership with Mackenzie was actually made through a contact at the University of Michigan. Perry went back to the town he was born in and created a nine-hole course

Princeton Country Club

It seems that American history is filled with stories of people who end up coming back to their hometown and contributing to the community after they have made it famous in the outside world. The life of Perry Maxwell is not any different. Local resident Marshall P. Eldred was attending the University of Michigan at the time that Maxwell and Alister Mackenzie were building a golf course. Maxwell and Eldred became acquainted and Eldred discovered that Maxwell was originally from Princeton, Kentucky. Eldred informed Maxwell that there was interest in Princeton of opening a golf course. Maxwell volunteered his services and told Eldred to contact him when they were ready to start the process.

Soon afterward, Eldred and a group of local residents, including Grayson Harralson, formed the Princeton Country Club. They quickly contacted Maxwell and he came to Princeton and laid out the original nine holes of the course at a rate of $80 a week. The course construction began in 1931. The club survived through the Depression and World War II through the generosity and wealth of Grayson Harralson, a local captain of industry.

The original nine holes were laid out with five bunkers and provided a variety of holes in length. Maxwell also routed the holes based off of an axis in the center of the plot, similar to most of his other routings. Due to the large trees at the time of the design, the wind was not much of a factor. The course was designed with several mounds surrounding the greens. These along with the original grass depressions made the short game a premium. The grass bunkers were viewed as a way to lower the maintenance costs of the project and also make maintenance easier for the facility. The greens on the course are not as problematic

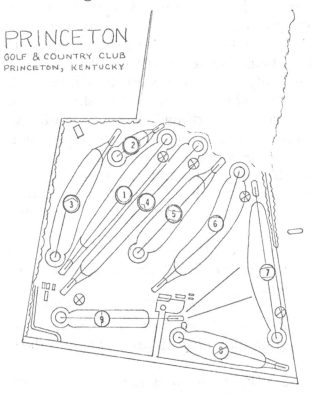

Layout of Princeton Country Club in 1931
(courtesy of Princeton Country Club)

61

as some of the other Maxwell courses. This is in all likelihood due to the fact the course was constructed without the direct supervision of Maxwell, but by Dean Woods. Maxwell was working on the course at Crystal Downs and the University of Michigan during the construction of the Princeton course and only laid out the routing of the course. Everything about the construction of the nine-hole course was handled by Woods. Maxwell would go from Princeton to another small town in Southern Kansas just north of the Oklahoma border in Coffeyville that would also point towards the innovative nature of Perry.

Hillcrest Golf Course

Though the course was designed in the early 30s the Hillcrest Golf Course is a fairly new Maxwell design. Well, perhaps that should be explained a little better. The course has always been a Maxwell course, but until recently it was popularly believed that the course was designed by E. Smiley Bell, who designed the Coffeyville Country Club. In 1992 that all changed. The course hired Sandra Graves as the superintendent of the course. Ironically, "Sam" and her husband, Steve, had heard a rumor from two golfers at the Hillcrest course, Wilma Buckner and Eleanor Kee, that the course was actually a Perry Maxwell design. When the Graves began experimenting with restoring the original 4th fairway, they took the opportunity to follow up on the rumor with lifetime Coffeyville resident and golfer, Harry Strasburger, Jr. Strasburger quickly enlightened the couple to the discovery they had made and they quickly brought him out to the course to see if any changes they had made were consistent with the original design and if the work on the 4th was correct. Soon after, the Graves found even more proof that Maxwell had completed the design. They found articles that included details surrounding the design, fund raising and construction. One even had a detailed description of the layout as presented below.[21]

1 – Tee off north of clubhouse northeastwardly, left dogleg fairway, 361 yards, par 5. Slight downgrade, then upgrade with plenty of trouble on the left.

2 – Straight south for 395 yards, with trouble and ditches on the right and out of bounds only 15 yards beyond the green. Par 4.

3 – Ditch and trees along straight fairway, 171 yards north. The par is 3.

4 – Longest hole of the course, 587 yards, par 5. Has a slight left dogleg with lots of rough. Some shots have to go between clumps of trees.

5 – A straight hole, running west by south so as to avoid the bright sun at any time of day. Par for the 372 yards is 4.

6 – A big ditch in front of the green is a handicap to the tee off. Runs northeast 174 yards, par 3, and is very much like the No. 1.

7 – The prettiest hole on the layout. Runs straight north 365 yards across several ditches, which make it also the most exasperating hole on the course unless your first shot is perfect.

8 – Straight southwest again, 421 yards for a par 4 plenty hard.

9 – Runs northeast to the foot of the clubhouse hill, 423 yards, par 4, straight fairway. Steps provide an easy ascent up the hill to the clubhouse.

Strasburger was instrumental in bringing Maxwell to Coffeyville and hit balls for him to help with the layout of holes. Another notable fact about the course is that Maxwell may have created the first amphitheater used for viewing golf matches. Instead of routing holes over the hill, Maxwell thought it would be an ideal setting for onlookers and left it untouched. The Coffeyville Journal even noted this feature in its original review of the course: "From the high point in the northern part of the course, every green and tee can be seen. It probably is the only course in the country from which a gallery may watch an entire match with a pair of field glasses, without having to take a step."[22]

The Coffeyville government saw an opportunity for a city wide park restoration with the restoration and expansion of the Hillcrest Golf Course is at the center of this movement. The first phase of this project was the addition of nine holes to the current course. This was completed in 1999 by Jerry Slack, who is also the development planning of the restoration project. The recently finished Phase II restored Maxwell's original nine holes. Though it will be considered the back nine, the holes are as Maxwell originally designed them. Slack worked on refurbishing the original nine holes and added a second nine. Slack recognizing his responsibility to the Maxwell legacy, was quoted about the time devoted to the project, "That's why I spent two years routing, instead of two months."

Another major factor in the spread of Maxwell's talent out of Oklahoma was the drought that had started in the western Oklahoma region now referred to as part of the Dust Bowl. The drought began in 1930 in the eastern part of the country but spread slowly west over the plains and by 1934 the Great Plains were literally a desert. The Dust Bowl was an area of land that measured 500 miles by 300 miles in size. This equated to 100 million acres of land that was truly decimated. The drought was just part of the problem.

For years transplanted Southern farmers had been stripping the soil of what it needed to stay fertile through farming practices. Wheat crops had exhausted the topsoil and overgrazing of cattle and sheep had stripped the plains of the grass cover needed to prevent the erosion that would take place in the sand storms of 1935. The greatest storm hit on what is termed Black Sunday on April 14, 1935.

The following passage was taken from a PBS documentary titled Surviving the Dust Bowl.

April 14, 1935 dawned clear across the plains. After weeks of dust storms, one near the end of March destroying five million acres of wheat, people grateful to see the sun went outside to do chores, go to church, or to picnic and sun themselves under the blue skies. In mid-afternoon, the temperature dropped and birds began chattering nervously. Suddenly a huge black cloud appeared on the horizon, approaching fast. The storm on Black Sunday was the last major dust storm of the year, and the damage it caused was not calculated for months. Coming on the heels of a stormy season, the April 14 storm hit as many others had, only harder. [23]

In the aftermath, 2.5 million people moved out of the plains and headed to other parts of the country. The experiences of such journeys are famously portrayed in John Steinbeck's The Grapes of Wrath. Ernie Pyle described the remaining land, "If you would like to have your heart broken, just come out here. This is the dust-storm country. It is the saddest land I have ever seen."[24] Robert Geiger even added his own comments, which were almost like a daily mantra to the remaining residents of the area, "Three little words achingly familiar on a Western farmer's tongue, rule life in the dust bowl of the continent – if it rains."[25]

With the western portion of the state dealing with the awful conditions of the drought and the eastern portion of the state feeling the effects of the Depression, it forced Maxwell to begin to look in other areas of the country for work. His greatest fame during this period would be for a series of renovations in the Philadelphia area to some of the treasures of golf.

Elkins Park

The Maxwell family loved vacations. They even went so far to make annual trips to either Philadelphia or New York City. Due to Perry's fascination with the cultural sites in the Northeast, Perry would take his family to opera houses, theaters and many other tourist stops on their trips. He also always brought home gifts from the trips. Over the years after the death of Ray, the trips to Philadelphia and New York evolved into business trips, as Perry would try to drum up business at golf courses. He went so far as to have a family physician in the area due to his frequent visits. He would make annual visits to receive care for a radiation burn he had received years earlier during treatment for eczema. It would prove to be great foresight by Maxwell in his later years to have the doctor in Philadelphia. Even during the years of the Great Depression, Maxwell traveled extensively and achieved his greatest success during this period. The favorite destination though was Barneget Bay in New Jersey. It has often been said that

Perry dreamed of building a course on the sandy stretch of land, but it never came to pass.

The work that Maxwell did in Philadelphia just seemed to build upon itself. He would do work at one course one year and by the time he returned the next summer the good word had spread about his work and other clubs would be interested in his services. Maxwell had already established a reputation with the fine work he had done at the Melrose Country Club just outside of Philadelphia, so he was a familiar name when he began searching for work. Along with his reputation, Maxwell established an office in Elkins Park, a Philadelphia suburb. Perry used this office throughout the 1930s as he took on projects throughout the decade in Philadelphia. The first of these was at the Philadelphia Country Club

The Philadelphia Country Club was in need of Perry's services to help remodel the greens on the original William Flynn design. The greens had settled in a fashion that made them unplayable in some instances. Maxwell was hired in 1933 to come in and remodel nearly all the existing greens. He used his trademark rolls extensively on the course. The humps and convex contours, though sometimes dramatic, positively affected play as they added elements of strategy to the greens. Aside from the greens, the only other alteration that Maxwell did was to redesign the original sixth hole. The hole originally was a dogleg right to an elevated green site. Maxwell eliminated the dogleg and created a hole that went straight from tee to green with the terrain sloping from left to right. The green was not relocated but Maxwell added several contours to the surface.

Eventually, the Maxwell greens would have problems as evidenced by letters from the club that indicated the greens did not drain well during large rainstorms

MACKENZIE & MAXWELL
GOLF COURSE ARCHITECTS
ELKINS PARK, PHILADELPHIA

A. MACKENZIE, LEEDS, ENGLAND
P. D. MAXWELL, ELKINS PARK, PA.

Letterhead for the Mackenzie and Maxwell partnership out of Elkins Park (courtesy of Dora Horn)

in 1938. The Philadelphia Country Club course was not the only one with these problems, but it was even more of a problem as they were preparing to host the U. S. Open the next year. The greens were constructed using the clay-based soil found at the club and drainage became too difficult due to the intense rainfalls. It should be noted that other greens where drainage tile was implemented were not draining appropriately either due to the clay. The same letters that identify the issues also talk of alterations that the USGA recommended to the club before they hosted the tournament. Several of the greens still retain the Maxwell contouring.

Perhaps the best example of Maxwell's work still in existence is the fourth green with a hollow in the middle of the putting surface.

Another Philadelphia club touched by Maxwell was the Flourtown Country Club. The Flourtown Country Club at the time that Maxwell did his work was an 18 hole facility called the Old Sunnybrook Golf Club. It was an old-money golf club in Flourtown, Pennsylvania. Maxwell only did some minor green renovations that were eliminated in the 1950s. The Sunnybrook Golf Club decided to sell its land to the township and moved a few miles up the road to their current location in Plymouth Meeting. The most famous work that Maxwell would do up to this point in his career would actually come in a Philadelphia suburb across the New Jersey state line in Clementon that he visited with his friend Mackenzie some years earlier. He would get to work at one of the pre-eminent golf clubs in the country, Pine Valley.

Pine Valley Golf Club

The Pine Valley Golf Club, with the possible exception of Augusta National, is the most prominent club in the United States, largely due to its amazing course, but also due to its amazing membership. The course over the years has stayed amazingly true to the vision that George Crump had set forth from the start of construction in 1912. There had only been the addition of some tee boxes and the second green to the ninth hole in 1928. Maxwell was called in to do what at that time was the top renovation work in his career.

In 1934, Maxwell began working on rebuilding the eighth and ninth main greens. The eighth green was originally a small green that was just being eaten away due to wear and tear over time. Maxwell was brought in to rebuild it from the ground up, but to make it as close to the original as possible. The green basically was increased in size with the same dimensions. The one big difference was that the original had a small L-shaped landing area short of the green that some would land on and chip into the green from there. This was eliminated as the green was raised. The eighth green is one of the smallest and most fearsome targets in all of golf. The green was reconstructed with two tiers and slopes dramatically from back to front with sand all around it. Due to the amount of usage associated with the number of rounds on the small green, a second green was added several years later.

The ninth hole was the second hole that Maxwell would work on. The ninth green was a skyline green with nothing on the horizon, as the trees on the opposite side of the eighteenth fairway had not grown to their current height. Over time, with players hitting longer shots, a problem arose with the lack of a backdrop behind the ninth green, as many shots going long would run down into the eighteenth fairway. This created a safety risk. Maxwell was asked to move the green forward and provide some sort of protection to the players below on the 18th fairway. Maxwell moved the green forward about twenty yards and behind the green he added a bunker to catch any shots going long. Maxwell used the same green dimensions but added one of his notable rolls in the left side of the green. Also, over time some trees have grown in behind the green eliminating the skyline look of the green. Unlike the eighth hole where the majority of play is on one green, the two greens on the ninth hole split play.

The other change that Maxwell made at Pine Valley was on the fifth hole. For years, players were vexed by the steep drop off to the right of the green. Maxwell was charged with eliminating this problem. His solution was to place a series of bunkers along the edge of the slope with steep vertical walls. This eliminated the lost ball problem and created an opportunity for the players to make a heroic recovery on a difficult par three of over 230 yards. Pine Valley was so grateful for the fine work that Maxwell did that they granted him a lifetime honorary membership. Though his most famous work in the area was at Pine Valley his best was perhaps at the Gulph Mills Golf Club in King of Prussia.

Gulph Mills Country Club

Gulph Mills was originally a Donald Ross design from 1916. The membership brought in Maxwell to take care of a few holes that seemed to be forced in by Ross to make the routing work. Maxwell's first trip of three to Gulph Mills was in 1934. The work at Gulph Mills was to be spread out over a five-year span. Maxwell would ultimately work on five holes at the course.

The work on the course began with the eighth and tenth holes. The eighth is a short par four that doglegs around a pond. The pond comes into play as it reaches out to the corner of the dogleg. This would be the signature hole of the work that Maxwell did at the club. The green complex was rebuilt at the base of a hill. To some the hole is hauntingly similar to the seventh at Augusta National. The bunker scheme was reversed from right to left from what Maxwell would design some three years later. But Maxwell had not yet stepped foot on the grounds at Augusta. The hole also featured some wild bunkering unlike most Maxwell had designed to that point in his career. The large bunker in front of the green contained a small turf island and erratic shaping.

The renovations on the tenth involved moving the green fifty yards forward and creating another all or nothing approach over a narrow pond to a green with "Maxwell Rolls." Maxwell also added bunkering around the green to make the hole much more dramatic for the approach. The dramatic tee shot from the elevated tee to a fairway that rolled down to the pond that fronted the green made for a beautiful hole. The green sloped from back to front in the form of two tiers.

Over the next two trips to the course Maxwell would alter three other holes. The second visit by Maxwell came in 1937 and saw him revise the eleventh and fourteenth holes. The eleventh was originally a par three that was lengthened to a par four by Maxwell. This was facilitated with the now seemingly long walk from the new tenth green to the current eleventh tee boxes. Maxwell moved the tees back and created and admirable par four that fits in perfectly with the rest of the course.

The fourteenth hole was originally a short par four that had an odd tee shot associated with it. Maxwell was asked by the members to convert it to a par three, partially because of the odd tee shot and partially due to the fact that it would keep par the same for the entire course. The last trip to Gulph Mills by Maxwell came in 1938 and saw him only touch one hole, the seventh. Originally the Ross green site was located further up and away from the quarry. Maxwell moved the green back to the edge of the quarry and created a long dogleg long par four. The hole has an all or nothing approach that must carry a quarry short and left of the green. Maxwell encouraged that this hole be played from the forward tees of 420 yards, but the club uses the back markers of 460 yards and calls it a par five.

Even though clubs like Gulph Mills have excellently documented the work done to their course. That is often the exception to the rule. The renovation work of Maxwell is perhaps even more difficult to identify than his original work. This is due to much of this work being changed over the years or not even being documented. This lack of documentation would also be a hindrance in identifying the entire Maxwell portfolio, as it was against the better nature of Perry to write about his work. With the existence of the office in Elkins Park it is likely that Perry would have a consistent source of revenue. Otherwise his conservative nature would not have allowed him to maintain such an extravagance.

Two great projects would soon provide Maxwell the chance to make more

Perhaps the best renovation work completed by Maxwell was at Gulph Mills. Note the artistic bunkering that surrounds the 8th hole. (courtesy of Ian Andrew)

headlines outside of the Philadelphia market and make him a force in a new city, Dallas. The Colonial Country Club started out as a dare from a member of the Rivercrest Country Club to a man named John Marvin Leonard. Leonard was a local "workaholic" that helped build a family empire with his brother Obie. The empire included retail, ranching, real estate, banking, oil and gas. The two brothers decided to build a course in Fort Worth that would bring the first bent grass greens to the state of Texas. This was unfounded territory in the Lone Star state. People at Rivercrest and the Glen Garden Golf Club scoffed at this idea. People thought the grass would never survive the heat of the Texas summers.

Leonard found a spot near the Texas Christian University campus in Fort Worth. In late 1934, he purchased 156 acres and at once began working on building his dream. He started by selecting two noted architects in the region. John Bredemus was involved with courses in the Houston and Galveston areas and Perry Maxwell was noted for several courses in Oklahoma. It is believed that Leonard had played Maxwell's course at Dornick Hills, which first brought the designer to his attention. Leonard then requested that each architect submit five layouts and plans for the course. He then started picking and choosing the best portions of each and used them to create the top course in the state. The course was constructed by Claude Whalen, the club's first manager, pro and greens super. Joe Cano was also involved with the construction. He would work at the course for more than forty years, many as the course superintendent. Dean Woods was also involved with the construction of the course. It is also believed that Maxwell was present for a large portion of the construction and Leonard considered his input during the construction of the course.

The bent grass greens were a combination of seaside bent grass, sand and cow manure. Leonard kept the greens heavily watered and kept close observation on them. Leonard was not done though. He wanted everyone to see his masterpiece and the jewel of golf in the southwest. He would immediately begin petitioning the USGA to hold their national championship on his course. The courtship would last a few years until the USGA relented and rewarded Leonard with his heart's desire.

Maxwell's next noteworthy work would soon follow at a course that would be one of the chief inspirations for his career. While looking at a 1909 Scribners article on a golf course in Long Island, New York, Perry Maxwell would never have guessed that he would be working on that same golf course some 25 years later. The National Golf Links is one of the oldest and greatest golf courses in the history of the country. It was the dream and favorite work of Charles Blair Macdonald. Macdonald ran the course with an iron hand and after he completed the design, no work was done on the course until he said it could be done. He was so extreme that he wouldn't even allow rakes on the course for the bunkers.

By the mid-1930s Macdonald had gotten well along in age and was beginning to acquiesce some of the responsibility with the upkeep of the National. But he still had to provide the approval of the work. It is apparent that Perry Maxwell was brought in to do some work on the National. But documentation as

69

to the actual work is non-existent. Due to the reverence that Maxwell had for the design of the National, it is doubtful that he would leave his impression on the course. So the amount of work he did is assumed to be minimal and was possibly only the reworking of one or two greens. It is likely that Macdonald was present for all the work and that Maxwell had little if any input into the final product. The beauty of whatever work Maxwell did is that it blends in so well with the original work. Obviously, whatever work Maxwell completed at the National impressed Macdonald as he was then sent to the Links Golf Club, also a Macdonald design, for some renovation work there.

Maxwell received national notoriety when he was interviewed for the magazine, American Golfer, early in 1935. This brief interview projected him onto the national stage and made him known to a legion of readers of the publication. His ability to state what his ideas were on course design resonated with the cost-conscious developers of the time and instantly gave him an audience that would hire him over the next five years. The entire interview is provided below.

American Golfer, January 1935

Photo-Biographies – No. 33

Out of Oklahoma Comes a Golf Course Builder Who Strives to Leave the Good Earth Unscarred

By Bob Davis

Can it be, at last, that a Moses has appeared out of the wilderness, into green pastures, over rolling hills and onward to inviting landscape where the beauty of fields and brooks and alluring undulations born of kindly nature merge in loveliness? Is it to be that we are to have tees and greens and fairways, yea even rough, that rain and sunshine and the cleansing winds have brought to perfection through the seasons?

Is the Great Architect of the terrain, the Landscape Gardener of all outdoors to be approved, after all these centuries by a mere mortal who would leave undisturbed the splendors time hath wrought?

Hail to the newcomer who craves not to remake the world. Salute to simplicity. Hosannas...!

Oh pshaw; I can't go on this way indefinitely, like a duffer addressing the ball. Don't seem right. Anyhow, getting down to brass tacks, I've just had what I consider a swell chat with Perry D. Maxwell, who hails from Ardmore, Oklahoma, out where the west separates from the east and goes its own way, regardless.

Unless I am mistaken in my measure of this man, it is my desire to communicate to the cock-eyed world that "P.D." by which alphabetical abbreviation he is affectionately known to his numerous and rapidly increasing disciples, has started something in the construction of golf links that will sweep the maimed and mutilated continent that for years has writhed under the constant assaults of blasting powder, ploughs, stump pullers, hydraulic miners, deforesters, sod-sockers and canal diggers.

Now comes the Oklahoma obstetrician who lays gentle hands upon mother earth only to bring forth beauty which fills the eye of all beholders. Wherever he is called to perform his service there springs to life a playground for those who follow the ancient game; a course that blends with the natural lay of the land, retaining its comeliness.

Twenty years ago, in Ardmore, Oklahoma, "P.D.," a duffer by declaration, and a banker by profession, organized a golf club of one hundred and sixty members, none of whom had ever before dubbed or sliced a ball. He then set about the task of laying out a course that would meet all modern requirements without courting bankruptcy.

"The minimum of expense was the first consideration," he said. "That and the importance of creating a course that would be a legitimate tax upon the skill of the players. It is my theory that nature must precede the architect, in the laying out of links. It is futile to attempt the transformation of wholly inadequate acres into an adequate course. Invariably the result is the inauguration of an earthquake. The site of a golf course should *be* there, not *brought* there. A featureless site cannot possibly be economically redeemed. Many an acre of magnificent land has been utterly destroyed by the steam shovel, throwing up its billows on earth, biting out traps and bunkers, transposing landmarks that are contemporaries of Genesis.

"We can't blame the engineers, surveyors, landscape experts and axmen for carrying out the designs in the blueprints, most of which come into existence at the instigation of amateurs obsessed with a passion for remodeling the masterpieces of nature. A golf course that invades a hundred or more acres, and is actually visible in its garish intrusion from several points of observation, is an abhorrent spectacle. The less of man's handiwork the better a course."

I express the hope that some day it would be my pleasure to see Ardmore.

"You will never *see* it until you play each of its eighteen holes," replied the builder, "for the very simple reason that it does not obtrude and is not an eyesore. Not a square foot of earth that could be left in its natural state has been removed. No pimples or hummocks of alterations falsify its beauty. There are but six artificial bunkers, the rest are natural, and all the driving tees are within a few steps of the putting greens. To date no man has played Ardmore in par, yet my daughter, still in her 'teens, has broken 100 on it.

"Professionals and topnotch amateurs, who have played it, pronounce the greens and fairways perfect. The total cost of construction and upkeep over a period of eleven years is less than $35,000. By that I mean about $3,000 per annum. Nature has been kind, because we have not defied her. We co-operate with the seasons, and dividends never fail."

Audibly I cursed various bunkers and traps that in the past have had to do with my silvering hair.

"Far too many exist in our land," said Maxwell. "Oakmont, Pittsburgh, where the National Open will be played this year, has two hundred. Other courses famed everywhere average one hundred and fifty. From twenty to twenty-five, plus the natural obstacles are ample for any course. Millions of dollars annually are wasted in devastating the earth; in obstructing the flow of the rainfall; in creating impossible conditions.

"Don't blame all of this on the architects; the guilt lies primarily with the influential misguided club members who take sadistic joy in torturing the good earth. As a result the majority of American golf clubs are in the red, gore of the steam shovel, blood drawn by the mound-builders. We have learned nothing from Scotland or England where the ancient and honorable game can be enjoyed on marvelous links at one tenth the admission fees, dues, green fee, etc., that prevail in the land of the free."

"What caused you to take up the economical construction of courses?" I asked.

"It was my wife's suggestion that Ardmore be built. She did not live to see the course completed. I have since made golf architecture my life work, having built several along the lines of Ardmore, never, at any time attempting a piece of property devoid of natural features.

"Frequent visits to Scotland and among our home courses have convinced me that the time is ripe for a stupendous revision looking toward a saner and simpler plan for turning the good earth into playgrounds for those who follow through."

More power to you "P.D."

The Architect of Choice

With the consummation of the partnership with Alister Mackenzie, Maxwell began to take steps towards becoming a legitimate force in golf course architecture outside of the state of Oklahoma. He got his foot in the door of the tough Philadelphia market and designed several courses in the Midwest. After the completion of the great design at Crystal Downs and one of the pre-eminent college courses in the country at the University of Michigan he began to focus on smaller contracts that provided quick return simply because of the lack of original course design work. This renovation work would lead to Maxwell becoming a fixture in the Philadelphia area for almost a decade. He received work at excellent courses like Gulph Mills and the Philadelphia Country Club but the next large achievement was the renovation work he was hired for at Pine Valley. To have the work at Pine Valley on his resume meant instant recognition, as this was one of the prominent clubs in the country. All of this work was coordinated out of the Elkins Park office that Maxwell had the foresight to open some years earlier as part of the Mackenzie partnership.

Soon after this his renovation skills were requested in the Long Island area to do some work for Charles Blair Macdonald and actually to do work on the one course that started his long journey to becoming an architect, the National Golf Links of America. This was followed by recommendation by Macdonald to the Maidstone club and sojourning across the Long Island area to do work on almost any course that he could find after the havoc done by a large hurricane in 1938. During this period of time Maxwell would also take on a handful of contracts that would be the designs that he would be recognized for over fifty years after his death.

These "Classic" designs are exemplary of his style and philosophy from over his career and how he was able to adapt to the necessary situation. The flexibility that Maxwell displayed with the development of the Colonial Country Club course was a credit to him as he was involved with the original design and due to Dean Woods being retained to help with the construction was able to provide input during this phase and was a natural selection for the renovation work that Marvin Leonard wanted done for the 1941 US Open. The work by Maxwell at Colonial went far beyond what many people associate with him. Though he deserves the recognition for the development of the "Horrible Horseshoe," a group of three holes that he recreated for the course, he was much more of an influence on the course as the course added almost another 300 yards to the design from the original routing that opened in 1934. The fact that the course was also an experiment to see if bent grass greens could grow in hot climates allowed him to use the idea on his next major design.

Perry looking over his work
(courtesy of Dora Horn)

Shortly after the American Golfer interview Maxwell received the contract for a new project in Tulsa. The course at Southern Hills was perhaps the one job that Maxwell wanted more than any other. He pushed to have a course at the same location developed years before it actually came about. He was hired due to the recommendation of the person who donated the land simply because he had the idea a few years previously to create a new course in Tulsa of championship caliber. This was to be the first bent grass course in Oklahoma. Maxwell was involved with other grass green courses, but all of those used the slower Bermuda grass. The faster bent grass was believed to not thrive in warmer climates until the development of Colonial in Fort Worth, Texas. Southern Hills was a bold step as it was originally designed to be a championship test and was not well received by the membership of the club. Fortunately, now the course has reached the place in golf lore that Maxwell envisioned as one of the premiere layouts in the country.

Southern Hills

Every artist has a selection of work that is the standard by which all his or her other work is judged. Southern Hills has been referred to as Perry's "Crown Jewel" by more than one analyst. Southern Hills was developed in the midst of the Great Depression. The Depression had taken hold of Oklahoma by the time 1935 rolled around. The price of crude oil was down to ten cents a barrel, which was much worse than the stock market crash to the Oklahoma economy. 3,000 wells were shut down by order of the Governor. This caused the lay off of thousands of workers. This led to the migration of thousands of Oklahomans to California. One local newspaper even called it the "End of the World" when a giant dust storm came through Oklahoma. That was also the summer that Will Rogers and Wiley Post both died in a plane crash in Alaska. All of this led to perhaps the worst period in the life of many an Oklahoman and also to one of the more prominent clubs in the city of Tulsa.

A popular Tulsa country club was being turned into a public facility due to financial problems. This created an instant need as the downtown Tulsa club members would be without a golf club to play on. Also a prominent Tulsa family lost their daughter to a tragic death that was blamed on a lack of recreational opportunities for the youth of Tulsa to occupy their free time. These two items prompted two men, Bill Warren and Cecil Canary, to pursue getting a new country club established in Tulsa. Their plan was to convince Tulsa's most prominent citizen, Waite Phillips, to finance the building of a new facility.

Waite Phillips was one of the two founding owners, the other being his brother Frank, of Phillips Petroleum Co. At the time, his estimated wealth was in excess of $50 million. Even during the Depression his fortune was being pressed by other demands. He was referred to around town as the Fifth National Bank and Trust Co. Below is recounted the story of the meeting between Warren, Canary and Phillips and the resulting actions that made the course possible as told in the Southern Hills Country Club history.

There was not one timorous cell in Bill Warren's body, but it was with great apprehension that he and Cecil Canary entered Waite Phillips office to, more or less, persuade him to finance the new country club they envisioned. Both men did their best to explain the need and advantages of constructing a family oriented facility that would include a swimming pool, stable, horseback trails, a polo field, skeet range, tennis courts, a clubhouse, and of course, a golf course. Actually golf was not as popular in these days as horseback riding, trap or swimming and certainly not enjoyed by as many people as those playing tennis at the fashionable Tulsa Tennis Club. Swimming pools were relatively rare in Tulsa and the magnificent pool they planned should attract members. The city should also welcome a gourmet restaurant that would please the most discerning connoisseur.

When they had completed their sales presentation, Waite immediately labeled the proposal as being "ridiculous." He explained that there were more important financial demands to be resolved. Then he added, "I will, however, donate the land for the club if you can demonstrate that there is a sufficient number of people interested in such a project. I'll give you two weeks to garner pledges from at least one hundred fifty Tulsans, for $1,000 each, but I will personally not give a nickel to finance the project."

The two men walked down the street without saying a word. In a way, they had gained a partial victory but neither had any idea how that much money could be obtained in two weeks...A party was held at George Bole's home where the first effort to sell membership pledges was held. Most of those invited came because they were curious, not because they intended to make an investment. Fifty of the guests pledged $1,000. The job of finding *some 100 other Tulsans who could write a check for $1,000 fell to Bill Warren. It turned out to be two jobs, not one. He managed to gain the pledges but getting the payments was more difficult.* [26]

Seventeen days later a total of 140 people had pledged $140,000. Waite Phillips later would pay for two pledges and would provide a gift of money to landscape the clubhouse. He also was the person that strongly urged the group of investors to hire Perry Maxwell to design the golf course. Phillips and Maxwell were acquaintances from Maxwell's days as a banker in Ardmore. Ironically, the same land that Phillips donated was the same parcel that Maxwell had inquired about developing into a golf course and residential community two years previously. Maxwell had approached Phillips, asking him to create a championship course that Phillips could make millions from by selling home sites around it. Phillips himself wasn't a golfer, so Maxwell tried to tug on his civic pride by saying in his prospectus, "Tulsa is ten years behind what it should be in the way of a championship course."[27]

Once Maxwell was selected he was given an odd contract. Due to the financial concerns regarding the start of the project, it was decided Maxwell would have a budget of $100,000. He would be paid the first $7,500 he saved from that and half of every $10,000 not spent after that. The going rate at the time for architects was $3,000 per job. The final costs came in at approximately $113,000, $52,000 of which was on the irrigation system. Maxwell did, however, receive $7,500 for his services. The entire complex was completed for roughly $150,000. The golf course was seen as a distraction during the time of the construction, due to the amount of dust in the air. It was a hindrance during the members Sunday lunches on top of the hill where the clubhouse was to be located.

Maxwell had anticipated an issue in regards to water availability for the course. An expert from Chicago created the irrigation system that is still used today. The system was made up of seven wells, a storage lake and miles of drainage pipe. The system has only added a second storage lake since inception. All of this was to create the first bent grass course in the state. The construction met with few issues other than delays that were caused when Maxwell was out of town working on his other projects. This was due in large part to Maxwell and part of the crew living on the site and sleeping in tents overnight. The course used WPA labor to do most of the work. Press Maxwell once remarked that they would at times have 500 men working at a time. One of the few roadblocks during the entire project was the death of Wendell Miller.

Miller was a good friend to Maxwell and was a great loss. Miller was also a supervisor on the project. Perry had known Wendell due to their mutual friendship with Alister Mackenzie. Due to the death of Mackenzie in 1934, Wendell had very little work available to him and was hired by Maxwell to work on his Tulsa project.

The course also had to be resowed in January of 1936, as cottonseed hulls were used in the soil mixture and did not allow the grass to take hold in the clay filled Tulsa dirt. The club also had to take out loans during the down time to pay for operations with the Atlas Life Insurance Company and the First National Bank. The course opened and much to Maxwell's dismay only 29 people, including one woman, came to the opening festivities.

The course would soon gain notoriety for its difficulty and attracted national attention. It was initially called "Phillips' Folly," but it was a roaring success with the community and helped to promote a groundswell of local pride. Southern Hills has hosted a number of tournaments of significance. The first event was a charity pro event run by a group called the Tulsa Golfers for the War Wounded. Perry even visited during the tournament and was proud of how the course stood up to the challenge of some of country's top players. Sam Snead won the tournament. His winning total was 277, three under, while the great Byron Nelson, who had just come off of his famous eleven tournament winning streak, could only muster eight over par. The USGA also took notice. After the urging of Ben Hogan to have a tournament at Southern Hills, the 1946 US Women's Amateur was contested at the club and won by Babe Didrickson Zaharias. The course also hosted the 1953 Boys' Junior Championship, which was won by Rex Baxter, Jr. The success of these two events was what convinced the USGA to schedule the 1958 US Open at Southern Hills.

The course matured and had only some minor alterations by Robert Trent Jones in preparation for the 1958 U.S. Open. Jones, who was hardly ever hesitant in renovating the work of another architect, only put in five fairway bunkers. He would be quoted as saying, "You've got one of the greatest golf courses in the world. You'd be a fool to let anyone make any further changes." Technically speaking the course at Southern Hills is the closest product to the ideals of what Maxwell had in mind for golf course design. He moved little land, was cost effective in his work and created a strategically sound course using the attributes of the land to mold the golf holes. It was a huge step forward as he created the preeminent golfing test in the southwest that is still seen today as one of the great courses in the United States. But the biggest step was the development of a complete course with bent grass. Bent was believed to not be nearly as heat resistant as Bermuda but with the irrigation system installed by Maxwell, the course was the first in the state to feature bent grass throughout the entire layout, up to this point bent grass had only been used on greens, as many courses had transitioned to a seaside bent mixture earlier in the decade.

The course was much more difficult than the players at the 1958 Open expected. Gene Sarazen called the course ridiculous. Hogan, Snead and several other players had a difficult time. Hogan actually withdrew due to injury from trying to hit a shot out of the wiry rough that he later equated to steel wool. Native Oklahoman Tommy Bolt, would be the victor of the tournament with a score of three over par with a young 22-year-old Gary Player four shots back. The main story of the week aside from the difficulty of the course, were the ninety plus degree temperatures that bestowed the nickname of the "Blast Furnace Open" on the event. Fortunately, this tournament did not sour the USGA to the course.

The US Open returned to the course in 1977 and provided one of the most memorable Opens in modern times. Hubert Green, an Alabama native, was mastering the course and dealing with the typical Tulsa hot weather. He had a one shot lead over Andy Bean and Lou Graham. Unknown to Green, there was a death threat made against him. The Tulsa police had informed the USGA that a warning was given to the local FBI office about a plan to kill Green. The USGA immediately added security to the course as Green reached the tenth hole. By this time Bean had faded and it was a two-man race between Green and Graham. Green was informed of the threat as he left the fourteenth green and was told they could suspend play if he wished. He decided to continue and went on and won the tournament by one shot over Graham and posted the lowest winning total in a major tournament at Southern Hills, 278.

The course would also host two more PGA Championships, in 1982 and 1994. Both of the tournaments were dominated by players on incredible hot streaks going into the tournaments. Ray Floyd won the 1982 tournament and highlighted his run with a streak of nine straight threes on holes six through fourteen in his first round. Floyd's first round tied a major record for a low score in a round of 63. Though Lanny Wadkins tried his best to catch up, he was a distant second to Floyd by three strokes.

The 1994 PGA Championship was the Nick Price show. Price was on an incredible streak that saw him win over ten tournaments in an 18-month span,

Looking back down the last fairway at Southern Hills

something unheard of in the highly competitive mid 90's tour. He won the tournament easily and showed that hot players could handle the Oklahoma heat just fine. The PGA in 1994 though was not supposed to take place in Tulsa. Originally the championship was to take place at the Oak Tree Golf Club in nearby Edmond. But the worst possible situation erupted at the club. The parent corporation of the club fell victim to government rule changes for banks. The club assets were seized and expenditures were frozen. That was when Southern Hills stepped in. The impact that Tulsa and Southern Hills made on the new generation of players and organizers was felt almost immediately. It was after this tournament that the course decided that it needed to remodel the course to remain competitive for the current day professional.

The club decided to undergo a restoration of the original design that Maxwell had laid out in 1935, this included repairing some vandalism done to the greens in 1999. Keith Foster did the restoration work. Also, the club added a third set of nine holes by Ben Crenshaw and Bill Coore which provides a similar feel to the course that Maxwell originally designed. It is believed by many that Maxwell originally designed 27 holes for Southern Hills and that only 18 were built and the other nine hole routing has since been lost.

In 2001, the USGA finally came back to Southern Hills with the US Open Championship. The course had gone through a restoration and was back to what Maxwell had originally designed the course to play like with some additional yardage. Leading up to the tournament there were two overwhelming stories. The first was a young man, Tiger Woods, who had won the last four major championships. The other major story was the course. Again Southern Hills was being seen as unfair to the players. It had several holes with slick greens, including the eighteenth, which was the source of much of the bemoaning of the players. Eventually Tiger would fall to the wayside and leave three men standing at the end. Retief Goosen had led most of the tournament, but Mark Brooks and Stewart Cink made late charges. Brooks had already completed his round and was waiting in the locker room one shot back of Goosen. Cink needed a birdie to force a playoff and had a fifteen-foot putt. Then one of the most odd exchanges in US Open history took place. Cink missed his putt and decided to putt out, obviously dejected because he missed the tying putt and Goosen being less than ten feet from the cup, he knew he was defeated. He immediately missed his tap in par. Thus putting him one shot behind Brooks also. Goosen then attempted his birdie putt and missed. Then he missed the three-foot come backer to the amazement of the entire crowd. He made the bogey, but was faced with a Monday morning playoff with Mark Brooks. If Cink had made his tap in, he would have been in the playoff as well. He later said, that he didn't even realize he missed the playoff until after filling out his scorecard. The next day Goosen immediately took charge and showed the skill that he used for 71 holes of the tournament and won easily.

Southern Hills has sweeping fairways that directly affect the shot to the greens. The greens are well bunkered and require accurate approach shots, but they do in most cases allow for someone to run the ball onto the green. The bunkers provide a player an opportunity to make an exciting recovery, but also are penalizing to the player. The course becomes even more frightening when the Oklahoma wind kicks up. The greens are of a rolling nature associated with the traditions of the game. There is even a subtle use of trees by Maxwell that would be frowned upon by many other architects of his time. The rough is said to be so vigorous that spectators are warned to not take off their shoes, as the rough may cut their feet. One feature that Maxwell used more extensively at Southern Hills, as opposed to his other courses, was the fairway bunker. Many of his other courses, especially those prior to his association with Mackenzie have very few fairway bunkers. But Maxwell intended for this to be a more difficult test than his other courses from the start.

The Southern Hills Country Club is not one of those courses that pops into the mind of the casual golf fan. But as anyone that has played the course can attest it is a true test to the average golfer and provides for enjoyable golf, while still being rigid enough to withstand the play of the upper crust of the golf world. It is also the course that any other in the state of Oklahoma is ultimately compared against. Though Maxwell would have only cared somewhat about what the professionals would think of his course, he would be delighted to see that his design had stood the test of time and that it was still something that could vex even the golfing elite from time to time and still provide a good solid course for the members who play it day after day. The course was such an influence over the architecture in Oklahoma for almost fifty years after its creation. Every course created after that was compared to Southern Hills. Southern Hills was the last landmark course that Maxwell would design in Oklahoma. Part of that is due to the fact that Maxwell knew he had a special project on his hands when he was given the contract for the course. His sense of civic pride for the Tulsa area was what drove him to want to design such a masterwork and put the state on the "golf" map as it were. The other part is that after this, Maxwell concentrated on smaller scale projects in the state to help bring back in line the costs of golf as he saw it. He designed several public courses in the last few years of his career in the Tulsa and Oklahoma City areas. Perry would also relocate to Tulsa after the completion of the Southern Hills course. But much like the rest of his career Southern Hills was not the only work in the area.

Tillinghast and Oakhurst

Perry also had a significant project going on across town at the Oaks Country Club, formerly Oakhurst. Maxwell has been credited in some sources with as many as fifty renovation projects in his career. The ability to determine the actual number is limited due to his willingness to leave a club with documentation of his work in any manner. He was an itinerate at heart and loved to move quickly from job to job on his renovation projects. He would often leave details of what he wanted the club to do and then move on and then come back later to see if the plans were followed. Maxwell was seen as the top renovator of golf courses in America at the time of the Great Depression. Ironically, none of the prime examples of this were in Oklahoma, his base of operations. This was mainly due to his love of traveling, and with the aid of the automobile this was made much easier. Perhaps the three most famous renovations in Oklahoma would be the work at Lincoln Park in Oklahoma City in 1926, a green renovation of Mohawk Park in Tulsa and his work at the Oaks Country Club in Tulsa in 1935. Early in his career Maxwell saw the opportunity to go in and touch up golf courses and work on areas of the courses that clients saw as weaknesses. The Oaks Country Club was a major player in the golf scene in Oklahoma as it was one of the longest standing courses in the state. Before the creation of Southern Hills, Oaks and the Tulsa Country Club were the dominant clubs in town. They were both designed by A. W. Tillinghast during the same visit to Tulsa in 1920. After the completion of the Oaks, Maxwell opened an office in Tulsa and would eventually move to town.

Tillinghast was employed by the PGA of America in the mid-1930s and took a tour of several courses around the country. In January of 1936, he toured several courses in Oklahoma. Many of these were Perry Maxwell designs. The courses included stops at Twin Hills, the Oklahoma City Golf & Country Club, Ponca City, Indian Hills, Southern Hills and Hillcrest. He also was able to review the changes proposed by Maxwell to the Oaks before the work was started. Below are some excerpts from the letters that Tillinghast wrote to the President of the PGA of America.

"This morning, at the request of the P.G.A. member Francis Scheider, I visited the course of the Oklahoma City Golf and Country Club. With Scheider I went over every hole on this truly fine course. As a matter of fact there was so little to criticise, as he asked me to do freely, that I was only able to help him in one instance...The seaside bent greens of this course are very good, after five years, and so is the Bermuda fairway. I made many notes concerning their methods of turf production and maintenance, which will add much valuable knowledge tot hat which we already have."[28]

"...it was suggested that I call on the Carters at Twin Hills Golf Club. I did that this afternoon...and generally outlined the motives of the P.G.A. work. Seeing that they had no immediate problems confronting them I limited my observations to general recommendations and they appeared to be please with my call."[29]

"...I went to his course, the Indian Hills Country Club at Catoosa...Seaside Bent greens were established here in 1930 and today there is a truly excellent turf. By frequent spikings the greens are kept open at all time, which explains their excellence without any doubt. Tile drains have also been an important factor.

82

The layout is commendable and fortunately there are practically no unnecessary pits through the fairway."[30]

"Several new holes are proposed to give a little more length and my advice was sought regarding them...Tonight a dinner was given to Tulsa P.G.A. members, their greenkeepers and their clubs' committee chairman, by the Tulsa Country Club. There were twenty five present, including Perry Maxwell, prominent course architect of this section."[31]

Maxwell completed the large renovation of the Oaks course in 1936. He worked on seven holes with most of the work involving green renovations. The nature of the course is very subtle to the observer. The rolls that Maxwell added to the greens then become very apparent. Also, it appears that Maxwell may have also slightly rerouted a few holes by moving tees to their current locations when roads were added to the grounds for access from 71st Street. The beautiful and short sixth hole is the most photogenic hole on the course and features the first hint of Maxwell on the grounds. Later holes that show Maxwell's influence are the eleventh and twelfth holes. The thirteenth hole is the only green on the course with major contouring in the green complex and uses a typical Maxwell shelf.

The work in Tulsa, specifically at Southern Hills, was also a chance for Maxwell to again go back to his simpler and less flamboyant style of design. Though it seems that he admired the artistic side of Alister Mackenzie's designs and the influence they had on him, it is probable that he felt that style was only truly useful in a much more dramatic setting. His early success with that style in Oklahoma prompted his return to it when he completed what many would consider his finest course. This would also be the standard bearer of what many people associated with a Maxwell design for years. But less than a year after the completion of the crown jewel of his career, Maxwell was given the perfect setting to design a golf course in a place many would least expect it, Kansas.

Next up came what many, including Perry, thought was his finest work. He was hired by the Carey family of Hutchinson, Kansas to design two golf courses for them in their hometown. Eventually, he only designed one course, with only nine holes actually being constructed. The scenic beauty of the land that encompassed what would become Prairie Dunes made Maxwell hearken back to the trip he had made to Scotland almost twenty years previously. The construction of the course involved large sand dunes, with amazingly contoured greens. Press Maxwell completed the eventual 18-hole course almost twenty years later. One of the greatest mysteries in golf is what would the course by Perry had looked like if he were able to complete it. Some argue that the land would have afforded him the opportunity to build something that would rival Pine Valley and Cypress Point as the best course in the country.

Prairie Dunes

Prairie Dunes was the most artistic of Perry Maxwell's work. Prairie Dunes would be considered the epitome of what Maxwell wanted his designs to look and feel like. His family members have also stated how Perry felt it was his "masterpiece" and favorite design. Prairie Dunes is set in the sand hills of Kansas, surrounded by tall fescue, plum brush and yucca plants with a small town in the distance. Prairie Dunes harkens back to Scottish traditions in golf course design and feel. It was all the dream of Emerson Carey and his sons.

Emerson Carey was the founding father of the Carey Salt Company in Hutchinson, Kansas. Carey had made his fortune off of the discovery of a large sodium chloride deposit in Hutchinson. Carey was responsible for originally bringing golf to Hutchinson, which would include three courses. His sons, Emerson, Jr. and William, were the instrumental people in bringing about Prairie Dunes. The three Careys toured England and Scotland on a golfing holiday and were smitten with the linksland style of golf so prevalent in Scotland. They quickly became convinced that the sand hills outside of Hutchinson would be the perfect place to introduce an American version of the same style of golf. With the hiring of Maxwell and the completion of the course, that is what was accomplished. As Tom Watson would describe the course years later, "Prairie Dunes is a little bit of Scotland in the Land of Oz. Sunflowers instead of heather; oceans of grain instead of the sea. But, like Scotland, be prepared the wind always blows."[32]

Maxwell made his trek to Hutchinson in 1937 and was amazed at how the topography reminded him of some areas of Scotland that he had not seen since his trip in 1919. His son, Press, traveled with him on the trip and recalled Perry as being excited by the land and that it would make a wonderful site for a Scottish-type course. The selection of the site was relayed by Press in the first history of the course, <u>Prairie Dunes: the First Fifty Years 1937-1987</u>.

> "I'm not certain, but I think my father took a month to walk the site and not two weeks, as some say. You see, he had so much ground to work with that he wanted to see it all, and form all directions. He didn't design courses from maps. He went out in the field because he wanted to be right in the place where the game was to be played. He was not an engineer, nor was he college trained. His method of working was to make sketches of everything. They were rough sketches and he made them right in the field where he stood. He'd sketch in the location of the tee, the fairway and the green."
>
> The location that was eventually chosen was one of stark magnificence, combining the burnt-brown yet ever-challenging beauty of the sandhills with an occasional green oasis of ancient cottonwood groves. At the end of Maxwell's explorations, he reported: "There are 118 holes here...and all have

84

to do is eliminate 100." The Careys purchased 480 acres of ground at Maxwell's direction asking him to lay out an 18-hole course and to construct nine holes immediately.

As Press recalls, Maxwell's superintendent of constructions (Dean Woods) "was an old fellow who was opposed to the use of tractors," and so the first nine holes were built without the use of modern equipment. Teams of mules hauled dirt to create swales and mounds that nature had overlooked.[33]

The Careys bought the site of the course, 480 acres, for $10,000. The club originally consisted of approximately 150 members. During World War II the club was kept afloat due to the membership from the nearby U. S. Naval Base. Several of the officers were members.

Actually, the plan was for Maxwell to build a 36-hole complex. But due to financial consideration only nine holes were completed for the opening of the club. A second nine holes remained as drawings on pieces of paper in Maxwell's house. After the initial rounds were played on the course, Maxwell was quoted, "I told you the boys would agree with me when I said that there isn't another nine-hole course like this one in the whole United States."[34] Undulating greens, sloping and rolling fairways, and nasty bunkers around the green were skillfully planted in the midst of one of the most dramatic settings in the United States. Prairie Dunes quickly gained a reputation as the finest nine-hole course in the country, and possibly the world. In a 1939 ranking by The National Golf Review, the nine-hole Prairie Dunes course was ranked at number 100 in the world. The course stayed as a nine-hole course until 1957 when Press came back to finish the design his father left incomplete.

The construction of the original nine holes and some of the other key elements of the course are revealed in interviews in the first course history. The construction of the famous greens at Prairie Dunes was explained by Claude Morris, a supervisor of one of the crews, "They told me the new greens were harder than the old ones. That's because we had horses in those days and not tractors...we'd come in with scoops and fresnos to level off the greens, and then they dumped the dirt around. But we took the topsoil and stacked it separate, because the next layer was sand and stuff. When we got it shaped as we wanted it, we'd bring the top soil back in and level it with horses. We'd then finish it by hand. A green built that way can stand up for fifty years or more. You can't find that on modern courses, because the tractors pack it down too tight. Horses' hoof marks sort of aerated it."[35]

Prairie Dunes has been the host to many notable tournaments since the additional nine holes by Press Maxwell. The Trans-Mississippi Men's Amateur has been hosted here three times, with noted television announcer Gary Koch winning in 1973 and Ron Richard winning in 1987, but the most famous of these championships was contested the first year after the completion of Press' work. In 1958, Jack Nicklaus battled the course to win one of his many amateur championships before his stellar career on the professional tour. Though he won, he did not break par in any round on the course.

The original fourth green (courtesy of Peter Herreid)

The most decorated champion at Prairie Dunes, however, is Julie Inkster. In 1980 she won the first of her three straight U. S. Women's Amateur. To top this, she came back 22 years later at the first ever U.S. Women's Open at Prairie Dunes to win that championship as well. Going into the final day she trailed the talented Annika Sorrenstam by two strokes. She made this up by the seventh hole and was the sole leader after she completed the front nine. She eventually would win the championship by two strokes over Sorrenstam at four under par. The course has also hosted two other U. S. Women's Amateur Championship in 1964 and 1991. It has also hosted some USGA Men's Championship. The 1986 Curtis Cup, 1988 Men's Mid-Amateur and the 1995 Senior's Amateur Championships have also been hosted at the isolated course in Hutchinson, Kansas.

The maintenance of the course was a major area of concern for many, with the awarding of the 2002 U.S. Women's Open. The greens at Prairie Dunes are regularly maintained at a stimpmeter speed between 8.5 and 9.5. For the Open, the decision was reached not to increase the speeds beyond that due to the problems they would have with the undulations in the greens being too severe to play. The rye fairways and rough would be maintained through a preventative treatment plan until after the tournament. Another major concern was the use of the native areas for the tournament. A plan was developed to mow down selective areas for galleries and walkthrough areas for those attending the tournament.

The course at Prairie Dunes has also been a standard that many have held up since its construction as a way to maintain a golf course. The trademark has been the fast and firm conditions through the green while maintaining areas of native grass and brush for over sixty years. The course is spread over a 200-acre area, of which, 100 acres is undisturbed prairie. Within the course, 75 acres of natural habitat still exist. This area is maintained through a prescribed burn plan. Resource conservation is a large part of the maintenance as well. Through the use of an on-line weather station connected to the club's irrigation system they can minimize use of water. The course only uses spot pesticide treatments and built a chemical storage facility in 1997 to reduce the chances of pollution. Through this plan the course has also received national acclaim from environmental organizations like Audobon International. In turn, the course has served as a research site for nearby Tabor College and as a host of the 1997 Birdwatching Ryder Cup.

The course, since the completion by Press has been constantly applauded for efforts to maintain the design and feel of the unique nature of the course. Though an inland site, the feeling of the course is summed up best by Joe Dey, former head of the USGA and PGA Tour. "The entire course is such an excellent example of the links concept. That is, that Prairie Dunes could be transported 'as is' from the beautiful prairie to the coasts of the Irish Sea or the North Sea, where the roots of the game will always be, and it would be right at home...a good logo to symbolize this course would be of a lone golfer standing deep in the rough looking for his ball."[36] Ben Crenshaw, who along with Bill Coore did some work at Prairie Dunes, also provided some wonderful comments on the course, "Anybody who has ever visited Prairie Dunes will be treated to real golf; the kind that tests you in the most enjoyable manner, with your brains and your body. The holes tumble and toss and turn very quietly and naturally with the most properly placed bunkers telling you where and where not to go. Yes, this is golf of the first order."[37] It is hard to top such flattering comments about a course. Prairie Dunes was an opportunity for Maxwell to take the perfect setting and design a course as close to those of Scotland that he could on the Great Plains.

Iowa State University

Even with all of this activity, Maxwell found time to work occasionally on one project that would cover over half of a decade from start to finish and would be a consistent source of income throughout the period. The course was commissioned by the Iowa State University in Ames, Iowa. At the time Maxwell was hired Ames, Iowa only had one nine hole course at the Ames Country Club. The largest part of the popularity of the course was with the college students at ISU. The major problems revolving around the Ames Country Club was the fact that it was not right on campus and required a vehicle to get to and that it was somewhat exclusive. That was when a movement was started to get a college owned golf course on the Ames campus. The cause of a golf course for Iowa State University was championed by college president Raymond Hughes. The other major supporter was athletic director and football coach, George F. Veenker.

A location, north of the campus, was selected. An alternative source of funds was necessary if the course was to become a reality. Hughes began checking into the possibility of getting federal funding to build the course. As luck would have it, the Depression actually helped the growth of sports in the country

Original routing of the Iowa State Golf Course (courtesy of Jason Chrystal)

and at Iowa State. One of the programs from the New Deal of president Franklin Delano Roosevelt was the Works Progress Administration. Harry Hopkins was a native Iowan and was willing to provide the funds and labor for the project. The WPA had already had an impact on the university, as it was the source of the funding of the Arboretum west of the campus. After the selection of the North Woods as the location of the course was finalized. The college hired Perry Maxwell to come in and design the golf course. After the final costs were calculated the college would end up paying approximately $30,000 according to the early estimates, due to the significant funding from the WPA. Work on the course began in August of 1934. The largest part of the early work involved the following, cutting and removing trees, moving hills, filling holes, making ditches and piling dirt for fairways and greens. According to the supervisor of the project, R. R. Rothacker, "60 men, 10 trucks, 2 Cletrac 35 tractors, and 2 Cletrac 55 bulldozers"[38] were involved in the early phases of the construction. Rothacker and J. David Armstrong were two of the landscape architecture professors at the university and they were overseeing the largest portion of the construction. The college nurseries contributed numerous trees and the grass that was seeded on the course, colonial bent. Armstrong was convinced of the course's merit and of the rest of the recreational area developed around the course, which included bridle trails. Opening of the course was delayed until the arrival of irrigation pipes and the moving of manpower to other projects. The final year of construction included a caddy house, shelters and a "rustic bridge" to cross the Squaw Creek that ran through the course. Drainage soon became an issue and a tile was placed for the fourth and eighth fairways. A final reseeding was needed due to the drainage issues and the course opened in the summer of 1939, over one year after the official dedicated on May 12, 1938. After the opening, the course proved exceptionally difficult including the sixteenth hole, a par five of roughly 500 yards, called Big Boy.

In 1938, in conjunction with the official opening of the course, Veenker organized the first Iowa Master's Golf Tournament, which is now hosted annually at the Iowa State Golf Course. Veenker invited 100 of Iowa's best golfers, as he wanted a representative from each club in the state to compete. The first champion of the tournament received a "traveling trophy" and an autographed picture of Bobby Jones. Soon after the opening of the course it was determined to hold the 1949 NCAA Golf Championships at Veenker. The team competition was won by North Texas State, but the top story involved a teenager from Wake Forest. Arnold Palmer was the favorite to take home the individual honors of the tournament but Palmer was defeated by Tommy Veech, of Notre Dame early, and the stunning defeat was also the end of the coverage by the student paper.

In 1972, the City of Ames underwent a street expansion project that directly affected the Veenker course. 13th Street was to go directly through the course and this would eliminate three holes from the original design. In the end three holes, the practice facility and the clubhouse were all moved. But the fears of the landscape architect handling the job, John Harrod, were that the new pieces of land would not fit in with the current course. The site lacked the topography and mature trees that were present throughout the course before. But grading and the planting of some new shrubbery helped to alleviate this issue. A second redesign occurred in 1982. With this work four more holes were eliminated or altered significantly. Today, just over half of Perry Maxwell's course remains.

The Iowa State Golf Course is one of the courses in Maxwell's portfolio that bears a unique distinction, being an eighteen hole circuit instead of the customary two loops of nine. This was dictated by the shape of the land selected for the course and the fact that a railroad line ran through the site. Unfortunately, much of the original design was eliminated. The first and eighteenth were very reminiscent to the first and eighteenth at The Old Course at St. Andrews. The two holes shared a wide fairway with out of bounds directly to the right of the first hole. The only thing missing was the Swilcan Burn but the first was named after the primary feature of the hole, a punch bowl green. The eighteenth was a replica of the famous Home hole at the Old Course. The tee on the hole was elevated well above the fairway next to the railroad line and the green featured a gigantic depression short of the green much like the infamous Valley of Sin.

The "Big Boy" was the feature hole in the original design, for no other reason than that it was the longest on the course. Strategically, the hole also was of extraordinary merit. It was a masterful use of the terrain to create a hole that required the player to use the terrain to shape the shot. The elevated tee shot went out to an open fairway with the preferred shot going along the edge of the tree line to produce the right angle into the green. The railway at the time of the original design was against the border of the course and all along the right side of the driving zone for the hole. The approach to the green was downhill and could use the slope of the hill to get onto the green. Those that were foolish enough to try and carry to the green, would more often than not bounce over the green and into the Squaw Creek that ran directly behind the intended target. Iowa State was a blip on the screen when compared to the goliaths that Maxwell worked on in this, his greatest era. But the course was extremely difficult and was a rival of many of the courses on the second tier of his career including Muskogee, Melrose and Hillcrest. This alone makes it worthy of mention and inclusion in any detailed list of his masterpieces.

Other Contracts

Maxwell started working on the Arkansas City Country Club in 1937. Arkansas City was a throwback for Maxwell to his early years of designing in Oklahoma. Maxwell came in and designed nine holes using the hilly terrain in a similar fashion to his other courses in Oklahoma. Maxwell actually had plans drawn up of an 18-hole course. Due to the proximity to Prairie Dunes, it is possible Maxwell planned on coming back to the courses, but this chance was eliminated primarily due to World War II. The routing of the nine original holes is exactly as Maxwell had designed it. The original greens were sloping and rolling like many other Maxwell greens in the Depression era but have been somewhat toned down due to them being rebuilt since the original construction, with the exception of the eighteenth hole.

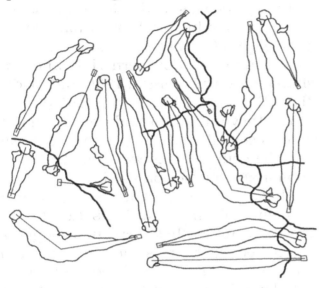

Pencil drawing of the Arkansas City Country Club
(courtesy of Arkansas City Country Club)

The current front nine of the course was built by Dick Metz in 1965. The original course also featured two winding creeks that have since been closed off to create two ponds on the course. Maxwell's 18-hole diagram used these features on twelve holes. The holes that don't make use of the creeks are set upon the highest points of the course and provide some wonderful views of the surrounding area as the course is set on top of a large bluff just east of Arkansas City.

The Topeka Country Club is one of the oldest and most prestigious clubs in the state of Kansas. It is actually the longest standing club in the state at its current location. The club opened in 1906 with a nine-hole course that had sand greens. In the late 1937, Perry Maxwell came on board to create a new course with 18 holes and grass greens. At the time Maxwell had just completed working on Prairie Dunes over in Hutchinson.

Perry's mode of operations would involve the contracting of one high profile job in an area and then go around to other clubs and offer his services as well. In many cases they would want some work done to their course, but would have to get bids on the job. Maxwell would always underbid his competition and would in most cases have overages, but his final cost was always below what the next lowest bid would have been. The course would save money, pay Maxwell and the members would be delighted his work. This was probably how the Topeka contract was obtained.

The redesign of the 18 holes was composed of sloping fairways with small undulating greens and some tight greenside bunkering. The course contains no forced carries, but allows players to shoot aggressively or defensively due to the nature of the hazards on the course. As with almost all courses built during the Depression, trees have grown and started to crowd the fairways of the course. At Topeka, this has only amplified the design. The sloping fairways have become even more of a strategic key as the trees often force the player to make a daring shot or play to a safe area.

91

The work in Kansas that Maxwell did involves several of the top courses within the state. It also saw the completion of Perry's favorite design, even above his own course in Ardmore. The state also contains more of Maxwell's work than any other state except for Oklahoma and Texas and shows just how dominant of an architect he was in the region. Even though he was so dominant in the region for many years he would still go unrecognized for his work on a national level. That would quickly change with his next high profile contract.

During the construction of the fine courses at Southern Hills and Prairie Dunes, Maxwell visited the Masters Invitational tournament in 1936 and made the acquaintance of Bobby Jones and Clifford Roberts. After finding out that Perry was a one-time partner of Alister Mackenzie they hired him to do some renovation work on their wonderful course. Perry accepted and over a two-year period proceeded to change at least ten holes on the course. This would make Perry the first architect to have touched the two dominant courses on the East Coast of the United States. Augusta National, though only open for a few short years was quickly becoming the American country club of choice with its ties to Bobby Jones. This along with Pine Valley were the courses that everyone thought were the cream of the crop and to have touched each in some way was a real accomplishment. Due to this work Perry also was given the opportunity to work on another stellar project in Winston-Salem, North Carolina for the Reynolds family known as the Old Town Club. Having been influenced by his friend's ode to St. Andrews at Augusta, he attempted a similar idea with the work at Old Town. The results were a course that is perhaps the most undervalued design in the South today. After the completion of the Old Town course Perry fulfilled a handful of contracts in the North Carolina area but had to say goodbye to his son as he went off to fight in World War II in the European Theater.

Perry also seemed to focus more on his children and their future during this period as well. Before Ray passed away, they had decided that their children would have the best education they could provide. The daughters were the first to benefit from this as they went away to the Abbot Academy, a preparatory school, and went to Wellesley College for their higher education. Only Dora did not complete her degree, due to health reasons. All three of them would meet their husbands while there. Even though Dora did not finish her schooling, she became an excellent photographer and studied with the famous George Platt Lynes. MaryBelle was an accomplished artist and would help out her father by sketching greens for him, as his artistic abilities were limited. Press would also benefit from an Ivy-league education, as he would go to Dartmouth. Press then would go into the Air Force and upon his return would become the top assistant for his father, though he was never made partner, and would continue the family business until he retired in the 1970s.

The Golden Age Ends

Perry Maxwell had just come off the completion of his two greatest works at Southern Hills and Prairie Dunes. He was still an unknown to many not in the golf architecture industry. That changed with his acceptance of a contract with the Augusta National Golf Club in 1937. Augusta National, though only a few years old at the time, was already one of the top clubs in the country due to its association with Bobby Jones and with the Masters Invitational. Before Maxwell's first visit in 1936, he had never seen the course except for photos in newspapers. Even though he had worked at many other clubs, Augusta would be one of the top honors that Maxwell could ever attain. Ironically, after Robert Tyre Jones had said he had never seen the work or heard of Perry Maxwell in regards to the Ohio State University job, he was hired by the Augusta National Golf Club to rework some of the holes that Mackenzie had designed. Roberts had announced they were hunting for an architect and Maxwell was immediately recommended. Perry's connection with Mackenzie was seen by Roberts as an easy way to have him implement the changes that Roberts deemed necessary without anyone second guessing his bringing another architect to alter the course so soon after it opened.

A newspaper article that commemorated the opening of the Veenker Memorial golf course in Ames, Iowa made reference to Maxwell altering ten holes at Augusta over two years. The work would have taken place in 1937 and 1938. The work by Maxwell revolved around three basic ideas; rebuilding controversial greens that were unplayable in previous Masters Invitationals, making some holes more difficult and challenging for the level of player in the tournament and eliminating any issues on the course in regards to drainage. All of this was under the guidance of Clifford Roberts and most of the suggestions were provided by two-time champion Horton Smith and Bobby Jones.

The alterations by Maxwell and Dean Woods began with the first hole on the course. Maxwell filled in the bunker on the left side of the green. The bunker was reinstated in the 1950s in one of the later renovations on the course. The elimination of the bunker actually helped to accentuate the plateau style green that Mackenzie used on the hole in the original design but it did reduce the strategic nature of the hole as Mackenzie intended. This was followed by the first green reconstruction by Maxwell at Augusta. This involved reducing the contouring of the third green. This also involved the alteration of the bunker on

The best-known renovations by Maxwell at Augusta are the movement of the greens on the seventh (above) and the tenth in 1937 and 1938 (courtesy of Mike Cirba)

the left side of the green. Maxwell created the peninsula nature of the left side of the green that is now an infamous part of the design scheme. This same "peninsula" concept was used by Maxwell on many of his early designs. The best example is on the eleventh hole at Muskogee.

The fifth green was on a plateau with a nasty bunker protecting the left side of the green. Beyond the green was a steep grade that resulted in many balls going into areas unfit for play. Perry altered the green undulations slightly to be more receptive of a good shot running in from the left and also added a bunker in the back of the green to prevent lost balls. The bunkers in front of the green and short of the putting surface on the left side were eliminated. Maxwell also altered another green on the course during his first visit on the sixth hole. This green was a major source of complaints from many of the pros in the Masters. Mackenzie had designed the green with a mound so large that it required the players to play around it instead of putting over the mound and towards the hole. The large mound on the right side of the green was recontoured by Maxwell and made much smaller. The green today is almost exactly as Maxwell rebuilt it in 1937.

The tenth is one of the most famous holes in the world. It is the start of the most famous back nine in tournament golf. The downhill tee shot to the valley at the bottom always left players with a short shot into the green Mackenzie created next to the beautiful fairway bunker. Unfortunately, drainage concerns created the necessity to move the green from that location. Roberts also felt the hole played too short for a championship course. The green was moved up the hill, closer to the tee for the eleventh hole. Maxwell also placed a bunker into the hillside to the right of the entrance to the green. As Jim Finegan called the hole in his fine article, "The House of Maxwell," it had to be one of the finest moves in the history of golf course design. It created a long par four that was unlike any other in the world. It was incredibly long, beyond the USGA standards at that time, for a par four and was strategic in nature. The fairway would allow for extra roll if you wanted to take the chance and go out to the right. Thus creating a shorter shot into the sloping green. Many of the strategic aspects of this hole have been mitigated, if not eliminated now, with the advent of rough at Augusta.

The following year saw several more changes by Maxwell to the course. The fourth hole featured one of the most contoured greens on the course. The green sloped so much that Roberts and several others felt the green needed to be "flattened." Even though Maxwell reconstructed the green to be more level than its predecessor it is still one of the steepest on the course from back to front. The seventh was originally a short par four with an odd shaped green fronted by a deep depression, modeled after the famous eighteenth hole at St. Andrews. Quickly, this hole was seen as a weak link by the professionals playing the course and it was thought that it should be a much more difficult hole for a quality tour event. It was determined to make it longer, but Maxwell was the one that decided to move the green to the current location and to surround it with bunkers, forcing an aerial shot to get close to the hole. This type of hole was used by Maxwell previously in his renovation work at Gulph Mills. The change was contrary to what Mackenzie had wanted the hole to play like.

Perhaps the one aspect of the original design that has been the most lamented was the loss of the boomerang green that Mackenzie designed on the ninth hole at Augusta. Perry redesigned the green in 1938 to be more of a standard plateau green sitting at an angle to the fairway. The green was also protected by two new bunkers created by Maxwell. The green is so steep, that over the years, many balls have rolled off the front of the green and many yards down the hill into the fairway. The green today is almost identical to the green that Maxwell created.

The seventeenth green is where Perry next worked on the course. The dominant belief was that holes in the closing stretch of a championship course needed to test the precision of players and too many greens with clear openings, such as those at Augusta, fell below this standard. It was decided to alter the entire green complex on the hole. Maxwell added three bunkers, one on the front right and two on the left side of the opening to the green. The first bunker on the left side has since been filled in. He also altered the green to be similar to the modern version with much more of a ridge dividing the left and right side while also having a steep slope from back to front. This hole did provide one of the most dramatic putts in Masters history. Jack Nicklaus sank the deciding putt in his final victory at Augusta in 1986 to win his sixth green jacket as a Masters Champion and to win his twentieth major championship.

The final hole on the course was also touched by Maxwell in 1938. The green alteration was perhaps the only one that resulted in Perry actually making more severe than the Mackenzie original. Maxwell first eliminated most of the tongue of the green that protruded between the two bunkers near the putting surface. The next step was making the green into a three-tiered monster that meant death for anyone that hit the ball above the hole. This was altered after the 1946 Masters when Ben Hogan three putted from twelve feet to lose the title. Robert Trent Jones commented later in an interview that he was directed to reduce the slope of the green only a few minutes after the three-putt occurred by Clifford Roberts and Bobby Jones.

Since Maxwell's work on the course, Augusta National has been touched by numerous golf course architects and would be architects. Maxwell made an impact on Augusta National just a few short years after his work at Pine Valley and it would cement him in history as being the only architect to work on both courses and would officially show the rest of the world that he was at the top of his profession. The significance of Augusta to the career of Perry Maxwell had many levels. Not only had he reached the top echelon of his profession by working at the top course in the country but he had also come full circle by being able to work on the two courses most closely associated with the two people who directed his vision in golf course design. With this work, there also was a sense of closure with the Mackenzie partnership. But as with many other jobs contracted during his career, Maxwell made a connection through Augusta that led to his greatest original work in the Deep South in between all of the great redesign work of the period.

The Old Town Links

The Old Town Club is located in Winston-Salem, North Carolina. The club to this day still does not have hole guides or items that are common to the pencil and paper set. As one person put it in preparing this text, "There are only members here and they know where to hit it and where not to hit it." The scorecard is an excellent example of the simplicity surrounding the atmosphere of the club. It is a white piece of paper with black lettering. No fancy course layouts or promotional advertisements are needed at this place. The origins of the club in the rolling foothills of the Piedmont actually date back to the course that was in the front yard of William Neal Reynolds. The "Reynolda course" was a nine-hole course laid out in the front yard of the Reynolds estate that is adjacent to the site where the Old Town Club would be laid out.

The Reynolds family headed up the construction of the first golf and country club in Winston-Salem. In 1912, Forsyth Country Club was founded and a nine-hole course was built. The course itself was soon replaced by a 1923 Donald Ross 18-hole design. The Forsyth Country Club was becoming overcrowded with golfers, and a decision was reached to start a new club within town to split the rounds up. Charles H. Babcock and his wife, Mary Reynolds Babcock, donated the land for the development of a new golf course.

Babcock was a close friend with another member of a prominent club in the Deep South. He quickly contacted his friend and asked if he was aware of an architect? His friend informed him of a man that was currently working on his home course and suggested him as a candidate. The architect was Perry Maxwell. Babcock's friend was Clifford Roberts, and the course was none other than the Augusta National Golf Club. Maxwell came up to Winston-Salem and began designing the course. The course construction began on January 1, 1939 and it opened on November 11, 1939 to rave reviews. The Old Town Club started with 100 transferred members from Forsyth Country Club and charged charter members a yearly fee of $1. Another large part of the opening of the course involved the hiring of Guy Paulsen as the golf pro. He was a noted teacher and professional who worked for Bobby Jones and Clifford Roberts at the Augusta National.

Years later, the Reynolds family became instrumental in the movement of Wake Forest University to Winston-Salem from the eastern part of the state. As part of the move, the university students and faculty were given access to the course at Old Town and were allowed to play for the paltry sum of $1. Due to the amount of congestion on the course, the offer was rescinded after ten years, but the course remains open to this day for the University's golf teams. This included such players as Curtis Strange, Lanny Wadkins, Scott Hoch, Jay Haas, Billy Andrade and noted architect Bill Coore. When reminiscing about the course Mr. Coore commented, "The greens at Old Town were the most exacting, undulating and subtle greens of any that Maxwell built. They were just so artistic in their approach of defending the hole regardless of how far the player hits the ball. They are a fine example of how to defend par and provide a challenge to the superior player in this day of 7,500 yard courses. The problem with reconstructing those greens is they had so many small little bumps here and there that it is impossible to rebuild all of those. The big sweeping contours are actually the easy part, but those little rises, that look like someone just pushed them up from underneath with an air hose, that's what created the intimacy that made those greens what they were."

In 1996, the club rebuilt the greens that Maxwell originally designed and tried to maintain the same character if not the same exact contouring through laser topographic simulation. The results were met with almost universal approval among the membership, but the idea of even tampering with the original greens on the course was a monumental decision. The club has gone on to add to the work. The club hired Bobby Weed and Scot Sherman of Weed Golf Course Design to oversee the installation of a new multiple row irrigation system and to help establish permanent fairway lines prior to sprigging them with a hybrid Bermuda grass, called Tifsport. Weed's work was performed with an eye toward restoring the Maxwell style and flavor. For instance, many trees were removed in hope of reclaiming the original fairway widths and broad sweeping vistas, which the course initially possessed. A couple of fairway bunkers, which are basically out of play, were revived to camouflage distances and provide visual orientation for the

97

golfer. Many areas will also maintain a more natural look, where native fescues will grow up in peripheral areas and seed out and go dormant in the summer months. The wispy, tawny type of look, is a Scottish style that was intended for this Maxwell design. While Weed attempted to recapture the original Maxwell style, he also endeavored to adapt Old Town Club to the modern game. Length, of course, is the additional ingredient. Weed, therefore, extended eight of the holes by constructing additional tees.

The Old Town Club was the chance for Maxwell to have a clean slate and design a course on a challenging site and combine the philosophies of the major inspirations in his designing career. The completion of Old Town also marked a turning point in his career and a culmination of all his talent and tutelage coming together on one course. The rolling terrain and meandering creeks characterized the topography. It was also one of the best examples of his talent at routing a golf course.

The Old Town Club uses many different approaches to the design of a golf course. Much of this was due to Maxwell's nature to try something once to help give the course it's own character. The routing is an amazing example of how to handle hilly terrain and to develop a course that just feels natural and makes use of all the wonderful features that were given to the architect to mold into a design of merit. Originally, the Old Town Club property resembled a sweeping meadow or pastureland. This area was where Maxwell laid out several fairways that merged together, but were loosely defined by a group of bunkers that were actually out of play. Some of those bunkers have been filled in as the fairways are much more defined by rough and trees today. An article written in the Winston-Salem Journal on July 20, 1939 provides some wonderful insight as to the value of the course and the approach to the design of it.

> The Reynolda course – officially named the Old Town Club, Inc.- marks a departure from ordinary golf links construction. Under way since December 6, 1938, it is scheduled for completion early in October. And its planners believe it will immediately take rank as one of the South's three great courses and as one of the nation's ten best.

> It is not a specialized course. Some courses are noted for their wide, long fairways, other for their hazardous and tricky traps, still other for their velvet-smooth greens. The Old Town course will have them all.

> ...A complicated watering system has been installed, and the links will be one of the few in America boasting watered fairways...Par? That nightmarish thing you'll be trying to break will be seventy, or 35 for the first nine and 35 for the last nine holes. If you find the course is crowded when you go out you can start from one of three holes.

> ...And there are many other minor innovations that added up together will make Old Town a great course. For instance, there will not be any power lines around the course. All electric and telephone lines into and around the clubhouse will be sheathed in underground conduits.

...After that – well, they're pretty certain that America's greatest golfers will be swinging down Winston-Salem way to spar a round with Old Man Par.[39]

Another quirk about the course involves the bunkering. Originally, the bunkers were designed with a natural ring of native fescue grasses growing around them. With the renovation projects by Bob Cupp, the grasses on the greens were switched to a new blend, called Crenshaw. To help protect the greens from poa annua infestation, Cupp surrounded the greens with zoysia grass to prevent the poa from encroaching. This zoysia is also now growing around the bunkers at Old Town and gives it a rugged textural look around the bunkers.

All the way through the round there are noticeable touches from courses such as Augusta National and the National Golf Links. But the primary influence with the merging fairways, the depressions around the greens, and the concept of greens within the greens all point toward this course being an ode to the course that Maxwell loved more than any other, St. Andrews. Having just completed work on his close friends course at Augusta, Maxwell must have decided to try

Aerial photograph of the Reynolds Park Golf Course (courtesy of Dunlop White III)

and complete his own version of an inland links in a similar setting. He even went so far as to refer to the course as "The Old Town Links" in several articles written about the Old Town course. Maxwell did not call even Prairie Dunes a "links" course. Maxwell also recognized the quality of the course as he labeled it "One of the three best in the South and as one of the seven finest in the nation." [40] This from the architect of Southern Hills and Prairie Dunes, who also had worked at Pine Valley, Augusta and the National.

The lack of notoriety of the course at Old Town is only somewhat disturbing in the fact that so many inferior courses get lauded with praise as the next great course, when there is a little secret in North Carolina that is far superior. But the fact that it doesn't get that attention probably suits the locals just fine as that leaves the course to them.

The Reynolds family was very much in the contributory mood in the late 1930s, as RJ Reynolds, Jr. followed the lead of his sister, Mary Reynolds Babcock, and donated land to a public golf facility to be known as Reynolds Park. He quickly nabbed Perry Maxwell during his construction of Old Town and hired him to do the original design of the course in Winston-Salem. The original design was built to conserve funds for the public parks system of Winston-Salem, so Maxwell actually implemented no fairway bunkers in the original design. The theme of the course revolved around minimal forced carries, open green fronts and numerous side hill, uphill and downhill lies. The routing and hole designs follow the lay of the land as Maxwell found it. The original routing is mostly in tact, with the major difference being on the part of the course on the opposite side of the road from the clubhouse. Originally designed with the stream not in play, the holes have been altered over time to have five holes cross the stream at some time during play.

Maxwell also received other contracts in the area. The first of these was to design and construct the first golf course for Duke University in Durham. The site had been selected and it is believed that Maxwell had developed a routing for the course. But construction was delayed initially due to lack of funds and then by the commencing of World War II. While in Durham, Perry also did a green renovation project at the Hope Valley Country Club.

The Gillespie Golf Club opened in 1941 as a nine-hole layout that was later altered by the addition of nine more holes. The course is most famous for a civil rights protest by a group of golfers in the 1950s. The course shut down after the incident and reopened as a nine-hole layout that was a combination of Maxwell's original holes and the nine holes added later by the city. The course has a fairly solid history as a regular stop as the host of the Gate City Open that saw many African-American golf legends play the course.

One of the myths about Maxwell's career has been his involvement with the Starmount Forest Country Club in Greensboro. Many have incorrectly attributed this design to him over the years. The firm of Stiles and Van Kleek, out of the northeastern United States, originally designed the course. They designed the course and oversaw the construction in the early 1930s. It has not been documented if Maxwell made any alterations to the course during his time in

100

North Carolina late in the 1930s or during his time working on the Gillespie Golf Club.

The completion of the course at Old Town and his other work in the Deep South, including Augusta, brought Maxwell immediate notoriety throughout the country. But much like the rest of his career, Perry had other projects going on while working in North Carolina. Most of these were located up the eastern seaboard as far away as Long Island in New York. Maxwell was accompanied by his nephew, Morton, on the trips back and forth between the two locations.

During the last few years of the Depression, Maxwell was also working so much that regular visits with his family were almost impossible. All of his daughters were on their own and were either married or pursuing their own careers. Dora would also go to Scotland in 1938, to visit Anstruther, much like her father did almost twenty years earlier. Press was only helping on jobs when time away from Dartmouth would permit it. Also, Dean Woods was beginning to be less active in the work by Maxwell as he would only work on one project at a time for Perry. The Depression was also taking its toll on Perry. His finances were sufficient, but the work was quickly dwindling in the country. Perry would take on one more major contract before the onset of World War II, which would prove to be a milestone in his career. But he would be fortunate in being the right person in the right place to handle a whole new crop of renovations due an unfortunate natural hazard in the Northeast portion of the United States.

The Hurricane Effect

Maxwell was heavily involved with renovation projects in the New York metropolitan area and primarily on Long Island in the vicinity of many of the oldest golf clubs in the country. As with the Philadelphia area, Maxwell quickly established a name. But unlike Philadelphia, much of the work on Long Island is difficult to recognize. It is believed that Maxwell worked on several courses in the area, but only a few have ever been officially mentioned in published works, and some of these are not correct. Much of this work was directly attributed to the referral of Charles Blair MacDonald after Perry completed his work at the National Golf Links a few years prior. Maxwell was seen as the only viable option to rebuild and restore many courses that were hit by the 1938 hurricane.

On September 21, 1938, a category two hurricane with sustained winds of 96 to 110 miles per hour raced across Long Island leaving devastation in its wake. Part of that devastation was done to the Maidstone Golf Links. The beach, dunes, cabanas, Hook Pond and both courses suffered severe damage. The courses were immediately closed and clean up began. In November of that year Perry Maxwell was retained "to make a study of the two golf courses...with a view to making changes that would improve the courses." In early 1939, Maxwell presented his proposal and it was misconstrued as a plan to create a "super golf course." Word of the Maxwell plan quickly spread through the membership and powerful member, Juan Tripp, quickly tried to squash the rumors.

101

Maxwell's proposals were presented by Tripp in January of 1939. There were three alternative plans, of which the first was the one adopted by the club. 1) Put both courses back in condition without making any material changes or improvements to either of them. 2) Reduce the East Course to nine and give up the seven ocean holes on the Further Lane property. 3) Reconstruct both courses and make "considerable improvements" in the West Course. The cost of the plans went from $10,000 up to $27,000. It was obviously the third option, which brought about the rumors of the "super golf course." In the end the work only cost the club approximately $8,800 and Maxwell was paid a $150 fee for his initial survey and report.

The proposal Maxwell submitted for alterations would have dramatically affected four holes of the course. Maxwell recommended the following changes as recalled by longtime member, Dudley Roberts, Jr. The plans would have involved moving the seventh green to the current eighth tee location and moving that tee to the top of the dune. Another major move would involve the movement of the ninth green to the fourteenth tee and thus creating a par five out of the most famous hole on the course. This would have required moving the thirteenth green and fourteenth tee. As can be guessed none of these recommendations were acted upon.

Jess Sweetser was appointed chairman of the green in 1939 and from records it appears that over his two years as chairman he made some noticeable changes to bunkers around the course. He began implementing bunkers with islands of turf in the middle, much like Maxwell had been using for several years in his designs. Whether these bunkers were part of the recommendations that Maxwell gave to the club is unknown. But it is noted in the fine course history by David Goddard, The Maidstone Links, that Maxwell also came back for consultation on some work to the ninth hole in 1940. Perhaps though, the most telling evidence of Maxwell's work on the course is the 17th green. The course history describes the green in this manner:

> The 17th, though, perhaps raises a question in respect to its authorship. Like the first and second holes it was on the old course (the original 5th on the Florence Quick Lot). It has some of the earmarks of a Willie Park design – two tiers and a slight fall-off at the back which he sometimes used. But, it is small, quite quirky in comparison to all others on the course, and bears some resemblance to a "Road" green as well. For the second shot the hole is setup to play like the 17th at St. Andrews. All the reward is on the right side of the fairway and the risk on the left.[41]

The location of the green dates back to the original course at the turn of the century but many experts, including noted architect Bill Coore, believe the green is actually of Maxwell design.

In the aftermath of the hurricane there were many clubs on Long Island and in the New York metro area that needed work. Maxwell was quick to jump on this but didn't want to sacrifice the excellent contracts he was also receiving in North Carolina at the time and was able to contact his nephew Morton Woods, Jr. to come out and travel with him for the summer between Rockaway Beach on Long Island and Winston-Salem in North Carolina. Morton would live with Perry during the summer as they traveled up and down the coast and made stops at clubs along the way. With Morton driving, Perry could concentrate on his work while riding in the back seat of the car. This was really Perry's preference as he had grown to dislike driving over the years. While on his trips he would leave Dean Woods in charge of the North Carolina work. Morton recalled one of the trips during that summer, "I was driving along and Uncle Perry was sitting in the back of the car drawing some holes on a legal sized envelope with this nub of a pencil and he noticed he didn't have his glasses on. Well, we looked throughout the car while I was driving and just couldn't find them. After about ten minutes of this he finally noticed that they were just sitting on top of his head the entire time." Morton did help out with a little of the work on the trips as well, but for the most part played the part of chauffeur. Morton recalled that Maxwell also worked on a few courses while in the Rockaway area other than the Rockaway Hunting Club.

The hurricane did massive damage to the course at Rockaway and Maxwell was hired to do restoration work to get it back to what it was before the hurricane hit. The work is believed to have included the fifteenth and sixteenth greens, but not many people are sure of the details behind the work done during this period, as records of the golf course were not a priority to the club at the time. The Rockaway course was just one of the more significant courses to receive attention from Maxwell during this period of work on Long Island.

Another high profile project during this stretch was alterations to the West course at the Westchester Country Club. The changes involved the first six holes on the course and the final hole. The largest part of these renovations revolved around altering the first hole and creating a new fifth hole. The creation of the fifth became necessary when the original second hole was eliminated from the routing. This created the need to renumber the holes in between and moving the tee on the sixth. The changes on the final hole were solely the addition of some bunkers near the green.

The hurricane and heavy rains took their toll on more than just the Long Island area. Many Philadelphia clubs had problems with excessive rainfall and Maxwell was called in by the Merion Golf Club to provide assistance. According to newspaper articles during the late 1930s, Perry Maxwell was involved with some green rebuilding at the Merion Golf Club due to the excessive rains from the 1938 hurricane. Details of the work were not mentioned in the article as to what particular greens, but it is clear from the information in the article, some work was completed by Maxwell. Over the years the references to Maxwell working on Merion have alluded to everything from a minor green rebuilding to a complete redesign of the entire 36-hole complex. Obviously, the latter of those two is incorrect, but Maxwell was involved in some type of project on the two courses at Merion.

For many years, the career of Perry Maxwell was identified more with his renovation work rather than his original designs. His work in the Philadelphia and New York metropolitan areas was seen as the epicenter of his design career with the exception of a few designs until recently. The work that took place in these two epi-centers of culture, along with Maxwell's work on other renovation projects are merely just another chapter of his career. Perhaps the greatest and most thorough redesign or renovation was of a course with which Perry was very familiar.

Return to Colonial

Since the completion of the Colonial course Marvin Leonard had requested that the USGA hold their annual Open championship at the course. Eventually he convinced them to come to Dallas and have the tournament at his course. They came out to inspect the course and made the suggestion that the fourth and fifth holes needed to be upgraded and made more of a test for the championship. Due to the assistance of Woods to the original construction and Maxwell staying in contact throughout the entire process, Perry and Dean were selected for the renovations to the course. The course was at its prime for the 1941 US Open.

The 1941 US Open program featured hole diagrams by Maxwell and Woods of each hole and brief descriptions of each hole. This may be the last record of what the course was like as it has been altered over the years due to drainage issues, changes made by the club and alterations to keep up with technology. The course in 1941, at 7,035 yards, would be just as much a test to the modern day player as the current course layout. The first changes to the course though were made strictly for the purposes of attracting the 1941 US Open to Leonard's new golf course. This was the first time an architect had been hired specifically to renovate a course for the championship and was a precedent for what would later be referred to as "Open Doctors."

Leonard purchased some remaining land adjacent to the boundary of the course. He reportedly paid the owner several times

A photograph of the medal received by Dean Woods for his work at Colonial (courtesy of Jerry Westheimer)

the worth of the property. He then brought in Maxwell and Dean Woods to assist with the renovations to the course. It was the beginning of what would become known as the "Horrible Horseshoe". The nickname for the third through the fifth holes came from the configuration and the difficulty of the three holes. The changes to these holes alone added 300 yards to the course and made it one of the sternest tests in golf. The development of this three hole stretch, dubbed the "Horrible Horseshoe" was made famous in Dan Jenkins book, The Best 18 Golf Holes in America, co-authored with Ben Hogan.

> In October of 1940, USGA boss Joe Dey made one of his inspection trips to Colonial to take a closer look and to recommend the customary USGA revisions that both toughen and enhance a course for an Open. Dey recalls that long after sunset Marvin Leonard said, "I want to show you something," and took him out to an area east of the 3rd green. Leonard proudly waved his arm through the darkness toward a vast tangle of large trees and dense underbrush. "I just bought it," said Leonard. "What for?" asked Dey. "It's going to be the new 4th and 5th holes," said Leonard. Joe Dey had sudden visions of being the only man in USGA history who ever held an Open on a sixteen-hole golf course. He retreated shaken toward New York amid the assurances of Leonard that Texas energy and Texas climate would have all well by the following June. Leonard was right. It took twenty-five men, mules, TNT and two weeks just to clear out the huge pecan trees and level and shape the land, but it was the best move Colonial ever made, for the two new holes helped form the three-hole "Horrible Horseshoe."[42]

This wasn't the full extent of Maxwell and Wood's work on the course. They rebuilt every green, rebunkered the entire course and added several new tees. This was a complete redesign from the original layout. Every green, tee and bunker was either redone or examined by Maxwell and Wood's prior to the event. It was perhaps the most thorough preparation for a major tournament up to that point in history, due to the extra scrutiny that Leonard gave to the Open Championship.

Due to the location of the course being so close to the Trinity River it has been prone to its share of flooding over the years, including the cancellation of the 1949 Colonial Tournament. This was eliminated due to some work in 1968 by the Army Corps of Engineers to reroute parts of the Trinity River to help with flood control. This created the need to rebuild nine holes and relocate two greens, the eighth and the thirteenth. The course did undergo a small renovation in 1999 when the greens were ripped up due to poa annua infestation. Keith Foster, a professed lover of traditional old-style tracks, was brought in for the restoration. "Colonial asked me to update the golf course, but foremost was to maintain the integrity of the tradition. At Colonial we tightened fairways, took some bunkers out, put some in, and re-did all the greens. It wasn't my job to put my footprint on Colonial, just do the job I was asked to do. We photographed elevations every five feet and ran a cross-section. We knew every contour of the greens, rebuilt them to today's specs and matched the contours exactly. We cleaned up the cavities and put the greens back like they were. We used a new strain of bent grass (A-4) and the all the new construction methods." All 82 of Colonial's bunkers were reconstructed to improve drainage, 68 new trees were planted and the east driving range was enlarged. This was the not the only renovation, but the most complete of the many done at the course.

The design of Colonial was from the start to be that of a championship level golf course. That is what Colonial has become. The championship history began with the 1941 US Open and the victory of Craig Wood. Wood almost left the tournament early though if not for the encouragement of Tommy Armour. Wood had just hit a tee shot into the gully on the fifth hole and was already three over when the USGA suspended play. Wood eventually would play even par throughout the rest of the tournament and won by three strokes with a final score of 284. As a side note after the completion of the tournament Dean Woods was awarded a medal for his work at Colonial by the club. The only other USGA championship hosted by the club was the 1991 Women's Open won by Meg Mallon.

Even with the extensive work done on the course over the years, the course has the feeling of the old, traditional course that Maxwell and Bredemus helped Marvin Leonard to create. But based on the amount of involvement by Maxwell in the early design plus his extensive re-design, the club's claim as a Maxwell design can be substantiated. The collaboration in 1934 was a stepping-stone for Maxwell to launch his string of national success, but was capped by the completion of the work in 1940 with the re-design of the course. This was also symbolic as the work at Colonial would serve as the end of what many people consider the "Golden Age of Golf Design."

One of the evident factors in the ability of Maxwell to garner work was by, what in modern terms would be called, networking. He developed a network of associates in Oklahoma based on his banking career. Then he became associated with developers and clubs in the Philadelphia area. Then through Clifford Roberts, Perry became associated with the "old boy" network in the Deep South. He also made great acquaintances in the New York and Long Island areas through his association with Charles Blair Macdonald. All of these associations contributed mightily to his receiving several contracts that led to his fame in the arena of golf architecture. Beyond this, he was a friend with other notable individuals and captains of industry. His pleasantness in manner and friendliness in demeanor made him easy to associate with and allowed others to feel comfortable enough to quickly entrust him with key elements of their lives. Perhaps that is why there is no account of anyone ever saying anything negative against the man. Perry's attitude towards life would pay benefits. The period of time from the start of the partnership with Alister Mackenzie to the completion of the Colonial project was one of the most prosperous time periods of any architect.

After the War

World War II was a tumultuous time that affected every person's life, including Perry Maxwell. His only son went off to fight in the war. Press was assigned to fly airplanes in the European Theater of the War. His career would be highlighted and he would be declared a war hero. Perry fretted about possibly losing his son. Perry also decided on developing a closer relationship with longtime friend Josephine Hume, whose husband had passed away. Perry also began having heath problems. The eczema that afflicted him earlier in his life had left him with an X-ray radiation burn that became cancerous.

Photo of Press Maxwell just prior to leaving for his tour
(courtesy of Dora Horn)

Perry continued to work through it all. Perry took on several small projects, including a five-year contract where he committed to renovating all the greens at the Clearwater Country Club in Clearwater, Florida for $600 each summer. The most promising project though was the beginning of a design at Lake Hefner in 1942 with Max Julian just outside of Oklahoma City. It was to be a public course but the design ran into roadblocks and many wondered if it would ever be completed.

Another project during this period was a solo design in Fort Worth, Texas called Walnut Hills. Walnut Hills was a design that quickly was shut down due to financial failure during World War II. Gaining other work for Perry was hit and miss, as almost no courses were doing any type of renovation work during the period, let alone any new designs. But the most noteworthy work during the war perhaps took place in 1944, at Saucon Valley.

Eugene Grace Calls

There were two main reasons the Saucon Valley renovation was noteworthy. One, the club was another of the premier courses in the country where Perry would add his touches and two, it was during this work that Perry lost his leg to an amputation.

Maxwell's leg was badly burned by a faulty X-ray to help diagnose eczema in the early years of his life. This burn was a constant source of frustration that eventually led to the development of cancer in his leg. During his trip to Philadelphia, in 1944, Perry went to Philadelphia to visit his family physician. The doctor performed an amputation, fitted Maxwell for a wooden prosthesis and released him to go rest at home after a few days and try to recover. Maxwell didn't rest for long. He was back in the field working in 23 days!

During his recovery, Maxwell was comforted by his youngest daughter Dora. The operation was conducted at a local teaching hospital and Dora even requested to observe the amputation, but was declined by the surgeon. Instead she watched other surgeries occurring at the same time. When Perry returned to work, Dora accompanied him to Bethlehem and met Mr. Eugene Grace. When Mr. Grace entered the room, Dora was amazed that her father immediately popped up onto his one leg, he had not received a prosthesis at this time, and balanced himself as if he had been without a leg his entire life. Though Maxwell felt at home in the field, he never did grow accustomed to the prosthesis and would at times hobble about the worksite or home with only a crutch.

For years there has been some discussion as to the actual work that Maxwell performed at Saucon Valley.

Press (left) and Perry working at Point Clear, Alabama after his return (courtesy of Dora Horn)

The discussion has varied from remodeling some greens to designing the Grace course for the complex. The Grace course was built after Maxwell was at Saucon Valley and opened in 1954, two years after Maxwell's death. The amount of work that Perry did at Saucon Valley is relegated to two holes on the Old course, the eleventh and the twelfth. He altered the layout of the two holes and completely redesigned the greens.

The eleventh originally was a par four and was changed to a par three and the twelfth was changed from a par three to a par four. The eleventh hole is a 175-yard par three named Turtle. The tee is elevated above the green. The shot is to a green shaped like a turtle's shell and surrounded by sand. It is the hardest green on the course to read. There is a flat shelf on the left side that holds the most difficult pin on the course. The use of the shelf was a common characteristic of Maxwell green designs during his career as he felt it created an ideal pin setting for maximum challenge. The design of the hole was based off the of the original Short hole design by Macdonald that Maxwell used on many courses over his career. The hole today is used as the seventeenth hole in most tournaments held on the course.

The twelfth is named Dogleg due to the true nature of the 400-yard par four that continually bends from right to left to about 150 yards out from the green. The tee shot is downhill, with a sweeping fairway that runs from right to left. The second shot can be semi-blind, depending on what side of the fairway the player is playing from. The green has characteristics of a Biarritz green, which again Maxwell pulled from his study of the National Style by Macdonald. There is a swale that bisects the green and leads to a reasonably sloped upper tier. The toughest pins are in front, although one can bump and run a shot into this green. The green is also protected by three bunkers, two on the right and one on the left.

Once Press returned in 1945 and the War was over, the work gloves were put back on and the Maxwells went back at it full force. After the return of his son, Maxwell seemed to take on a large number of projects. The work could easily be categorized into three groups. There were renovations, co-designs with Press, and jobs where Maxwell would layout a course and leave it for the members to construct. The period after the War was another period of solid work. This period of his career would be very reminiscent of the first part of his career prior to his association with Alister Mackenzie, where Perry created some lasting designs that were just a notch below the level of national recognition that Southern Hills had been earlier. Press Maxwell was also a different construction manager than Maxwell had in the earlier years of his career due to the retirement of Dean Woods. Maxwell also seemed to be stressing the involvement of Press in his designs. This was more than likely a way for him to introduce him into the business, as Press wanted to carry on the family trade. This was also evident as Perry proclaimed that several of the designs were joint efforts with Press. The one thing that surprises many was that Press was never given the level of partner in the family business. He remained Perry's "associate" until his death. The one point that seemed to be driven home with the courses during this period of Perry's career was that he was consistent. The War didn't end until 1945, but shortly before the return of Press, Perry accepted a commission by the Grand Hotel in Alabama.

The Hotel Grand

Point Clear, Alabama has been the home to one of the top resorts in America since before the Civil War. Known simply as the Grand, the resort has sat on the edge of Mobile Bay since 1847. The Grand made its way through times of turmoil, a Civil War, World War I and the Great Depression until it was purchased by the Waterman Steamship Company in 1938. The dream of the CEO of the corporation was to build an 18-hole golf course to complete the resort experience. Then World War II hit and the dream had to be put on hold. Eventually, the War would end and the dream became the center of the plans for the resort to go into the next phase of its development. Henry Slaton and J. Finley McRae, the directors of the resort, commissioned Perry Maxwell in 1944 to do the design.

Maxwell was amazed at the beauty of the site and the magnificence of the mature trees that inhabited the area. He even named the two sets of nine-holes upon completion after some of the trees that dotted the landscape, Azalea and Dogwood. The course was slated to open as part of the 100th anniversary of the resort, along with a reopening of the completely refurbished hotel, in 1947. The construction of the golf course included some interesting stories. Perhaps the most outrageous involved the draining of the swamp the course was to be located in. Before the construction could begin the swamp had to be drained. One of the largest expenses at the start of the construction was to hire men for the "unenviable task of patrolling the highway with rifles to kill the deadly water moccasins, which emerged from the swamp as it was draining."[43]

The design by Maxwell used several of his trademarks, including a bunkering style that was much more

Josephine and her daughter Jessie Hume
(courtesy of Jessie Hume)

110

reflective of his early work at Dornick Hills. The piece of land the course was located on contained some wonderful features. Though not necessarily a rolling site, the trees that inhabited the site were amazingly beautiful and Point Clear Creek ran through the plot as well. Maxwell though probably did not use this feature to its full capacity, as it only affects play on three holes.

There were two things of note about the work that Maxwell did at Lakewood. First, this was the most land moving he did in his career as they had to fill the drained swamp to get the course even in a workable condition. Due to this, much of the land is flat and very atypical of most Maxwell designs. The other main item of note is that this prohibited Maxwell from using his usual methods of finding green locations. He compensated by building push up greens. The fact that he adapted to this situation and designed a very solid course shows how flexible Maxwell was as a designer.

The signature hole of this Maxwell work is the mighty first. Contrary to Maxwell's typical opening hole, the first was a par five. It was routed around the creek that ran through the course. The hole is a 580-yard par five. From the tee the player gets a view of the Mobile Bay through the trees and must hit the tee shot over the creek to the angled fairway. A carry bunker marks the turn of the fairway as it doglegs along the line of the creek. The far side of the fairway is only yards from the road with trees protecting the player from out of bounds. The green contains all the Maxwell traits, undulations and tight bunkering. Three bunkers are very close to the edge of the green. This hole, is among the best long par fives Maxwell designed in his career.

The Maxwell course has hosted some significant events. Two USGA championships have been contested here and a promotional event called All-Star Golf was contested in 1959. This was a made for TV match play tournament. One of the more noted players was Tommy Bolt who had just won national fame the year before by winning the U. S. Open on another Maxwell course, Southern Hills. Bolt got all the way to the final, but lost to Dow Finsterwald, whose son would later become the pro at another course with a Maxwell connection, Colonial in Fort Worth, Texas. The Old Tradition course at the Lakewood Country Club is still much like Maxwell left it with only minor work done to it as a result of a hurricane.

Maxwell continued his frantic pace with a course in Springfield, Missouri. The Grandview Municipal Golf Course opened in 1946. It continued the trend of Maxwell designing lower profile courses. The course originally was designed for an individual in the Springfield area, but he allowed the public to play on the new links. The course was eventually purchased by the city of Springfield. During the work on this course was also when the Maxwells were working on the Executive Course at Excelsior Springs in a resort community. While in Excelsior Springs, Press would marry his long time sweetheart, Hodie.

In 1946, during the work in Springfield, Perry Maxwell had another major turning point in his life. He would marry longtime family friend Josephine Hume. They were wed in Princeton, New Jersey. Maxwell had grown quite fond of her, as he would visit often on his trips around the country. Josephine was also a classically trained pianist. She had attended the Julliard School in New York. Perry and Josephine shared the same interest in the arts and she would provide a great comfort to Perry in the last years of his life. Perry was quoted as saying at one time, "Has not God been good to me? Through His grace I have been permitted to live with two of the noblest women man could be given to know."[44] The new marriage would also have a dramatic effect on the career of Maxwell. After the marriage, Perry would have more focus on taking jobs in the area. The fact that his health was not what it had been in his prime and that he was tired of extensive traveling also made the decision that much easier. The remainder of his career would be spent working in the plains of Oklahoma and the surrounding states.

In 1947, Perry Maxwell was asked about the possibility of joining an organization of golf course architects. Included in the group was one person whose work he was familiar with, Donald Ross. Ross and Maxwell had met some years earlier while Maxwell was doing work on his Old Town "Links" in Winston-Salem. Though he had a partnership with Mackenzie, Ross was much more like Maxwell. They were both Scottish by heritage, both deeply religious and both getting rather long in the tooth by the time the American Society of Golf Course Architects was organized. The first meeting took place at Pinehurst in North Carolina. Maxwell was unable to attend, but a photograph was taken of the original grouping of architects. His son Press would also eventually join the organization and become the President of the ASGCA. Maxwell was not heavily involved with the organization, but he did attend the annual meetings until his death. This was not the first formal involvement by Perry in golf organizations. He served on the greens committee of the USGA in 1924 and was president of the Oklahoma State Golf Association the same year. He was vice-president of the OSGA three other times.

Following the privilege of being a founding member of the foremost golf course architect group in the land, Maxwell continued with his design business. By this time Maxwell was the best-known architect between the Mississippi and the Rocky Mountains, and perhaps the country, with accomplishments such as Colonial, Southern Hills, Prairie Dunes and Augusta National on his resume. While also returning to his traditional region of his work, Perry also returned to the original style that he used during his early days in Oklahoma. His greens would retain the famous "Rolls" but his bunkering became much less pronounced and simpler in style. His routings were still compact but the natural terrain of projects he took on was much less dramatic than some of the other sites he was blessed with during the Depression. Though these factors seemed to characterize this period of Maxwell's career, they did not mean that his courses were inferior. The changes in style made for a more consistent product. But even with this reserved approach two excellent designs would take place and they would be perhaps his last great works that he would see completed in Austin, Texas and Enid, Oklahoma.

112

Austin Country Club

The Austin Country Club has existed for over 100 years. In that time it has been located at three different locations. The second of these is now where the Riverside Golf Course stands. The Austin Country Club is one of the more historic courses in the state of Texas. The second home of the club was completed in 1948 by Perry Maxwell with the assistance of Press and is one of the better designs during this period of Perry's career. The actual work put into the course started as early as 1943 when Maxwell came to town to evaluate a possible site for a new course for the club. He handpicked the site where the course was to be built. Maxwell was selected when John Bredemus turned down the job, citing the lack of commitment he could make to the project because he already had two jobs going at the time.

While in Austin, Perry stayed with the club pro, Harvey Pennick. The stay at the Pennick home was not without incident. Tinsley Pennick, the son of Harvey, recalled a story told in the Austin Country Club history, "On one visit, Maxwell left his suitcases in the room where my sister Katherine slept, then went out to look at land with my dad. No one told Katherine we had a guest. When she came home from school, she was curious about the bags in her room and opened one. Maxwell, who had lost a leg to amputation...kept his prosthesis in a suitcase when not in use. As luck would have it, the case was the very one Katherine opened. She was half frightened out of her wits and went screaming through the house."[45]

The Club had sold the land where the original course was located to the city of Austin for $175,000. These funds were to be used to build the course, but they quickly ran over that figure, including the $8,000 fee for Maxwell. The course finally opened after five long years in the making in April of 1948. But the troubles weren't over. A herd of cattle broke loose from a nearby farm and ran through the course leaving hoof prints all around the course.

The course in its first incarnation was the home of some of the most famous players in history, Ben Crenshaw and Tom Kite. It also, more importantly, was the home of the most famous head professional this side of the Atlantic, Harvey Pennick. Pennick served as the head professional for the Austin Country Club for fifty years. The club decided though that the course wasn't up to their new standards and moved in the early 1980s. The course was run for a few years as a public venue, and then in 1985 the land the course is situated on was purchased by the Austin Community College. The future of the course is on borrowed time, as it currently is being leased and managed by the American Golf Corporation. But at any time the owners could decide the land would be more suited for a college dormitory than for a golf course.

The course underwent a renovation in 1999, due to a decision to sell some of the land the course was situated on. The result ended up keeping most of the course but not in the manner that Perry had designed it them. All but two of the original greens were preserved. Part of the renovation included a new irrigation system. Thirteen of the original holes still exist as Maxwell laid them out. The renovation also changed the order of the holes. The course though contains some wonderful holes from the original design, but eliminated the core nature of the routing that Maxwell had designed.

The original course contained several of the notable trademark Maxwell design traits. Elevated tee shots on the opening holes of each nine and uphill finishing holes for each side. Tight greenside bunkering was featured on each hole but one. Undulating green surfaces appear to also have been a prime ingredient, which would explain the amazing touch developed by the fine players the course has produced. The Austin Country Club was one of the more desirable assignments that Perry received at the end of his career. The club had already established an excellent reputation and history and had one of the prominent teaching pros in the country in Harvey Pennick. When the club decided to move Maxwell was somewhat of a surprise to get the contract, but the site was almost tailored made for his style of design. It even included an elevated location for the clubhouse. This led to Maxwell's favorite way to open the course with a hole that was slightly downhill and provided a good opening to the course as with almost every Maxwell opener. The hole doglegged to the left with a bunker protecting the front left portion of the green. The far right side was the preferred angle on this 400-yard hole into the putting surface and the width provided by Maxwell was the key to the hole. Without this width the strategy of the hole would not work because of the intrusion of a nest of trees.

The eighteenth was a typical Maxwell uphill finishing hole with an angled green and bunker set up similar in fashion to the final hole at Southern Hills. The hole was approximately 460 yards in length and featured a steep falloff to the right of the green. The left side of the hole was the ideal place to approach it from as the opening to the green was on that side. A bunker on the left side and one directly in front of the green provided most of the defense for anyone attempting an amazing recovery from the rough. The Austin Country Club contained one of the preeminent works of the late 1940s that was a semblance of what Maxwell could do if given the right circumstances in designing a course. The course itself is one of the more historic in the state, but due to the renovations done to it, it is just a faint memory of its former glory.

Oakwood Country Club

Located in Enid, Oklahoma, the Oakwood Country Club was the vision of a woman golfer known as Patty Blanton. Patty Blanton was a nationally known amateur champion. She was originally from Wichita, Kansas and played on several of Maxwell's courses in her career. When her and her family moved to Enid, she immediately wanted to help in the construction of a top-notch golf course and could think of no one better than Perry Maxwell. He was easily the most famous golf course designer in the state and she loved his designs. She invited Maxwell and his son, Press over to her house for dinner one evening to discuss the possibility of him constructing a course for her. Perry and Press went out and constructed a beauty.

The course featured undulating fairways with many of the famous "elbows," as Maxwell referred to dogleg holes, with an excellent routing in a tight area. The greens for the most part were tilted from back to front and were amongst the most undulating in his career. The only difference was that many of these greens were more like the push-up variety instead of his natural looking greens laid into the sides of hills or dunes. The course also featured two extremely impressive closing holes for the two sets of nine holes and a very dramatic opening hole with an elevated tee in the typical Maxwell style. Once the course was completed, the membership met with Maxwell to discuss his fee. They met at the same place that the whole idea had begun, in the house of Patty Blanton. He handed the club

The final hole at Oakwood (courtesy of Oakwood Country Club)

board an invoice for $10,000. When questioned about the amount of the invoice Maxwell replied, "The great artists like Shakespeare and DeVinci designed priceless masterpieces that no one would ever question about the worth. What I have given you gentlemen is a masterpiece." The members quickly opened their checkbooks and each paid their portion of the bill.

The course at Oakwood can easily be split in half as the front nine is mostly routed over flat terrain, while the back nine is over a much more rolling piece of land. The front nine is not overly dramatic but it is a solid set of holes with no weak link. It opens with a tempting par five of just over 500 yards that has three bunkers guarding the green. The green is a variety that is common on the course with a steep slope that contains two tiers and creates a very interesting putt if above a pin on the green. Ironically, the front side, though lacking in elevation changes has the better and more varied set of greens.

The front side completes with the ninth that also gives an indication of what the backside will provide. It winds through a couple of hills and the green is placed on top of a knoll short of the clubhouse. The hole is reminiscent of the ninth at Southern Hills without the bunkers. The gooseneck fairway shows the proper angle to come in from to attack the double tiered green but the shot with too much steam will roll off the back left as it rolls away from the middle of the green. The front side has nine solid holes that have a strategy dictated by the pin placement on the green. A strategy that was the keystone of Maxwell's hole design philosophy.

From this point on, the course goes through a stretch of five wonderful holes. The tenth is another mid-length par four of 420 yards. The tee is slightly elevated and provides a wonderful view of the fairway that winds between three hills and finally goes back up to the green cut hard into the side of a fourth rise. Two bunkers protect the front right and left of the green that slopes from back to front. This is the best hole on the course for many players due to the way it sets up the angle into the green. The natural terrain is used well by Maxwell on this hole. One can easily see how Maxwell saw this hole almost immediately after stepping foot on the property. The fairway was the only part that really needed touched and Maxwell added rolls that proceeded up to the green surface in a wave like fashion. The green slopes from back to front with a small tier on the back left.

The eighteenth is a great hole to finish the course on. From the tee the player sees a very narrow fairway with a hill cutting into it from the right. What the first time player doesn't know is that just beyond the hill is a 35-yard wide fairway awaiting the shot. The fairway then rolls up to the green with a gooseneck around the bunker protecting the front right. The green is another that slopes from back to front with two large rolls protecting the front portion at ten and four o'clock. Oakwood qualifies as a hidden gem that is appealing to anyone wanting to study Maxwell's work or for those who want to enjoy a very good course in a small town like Enid.

The quick tour taken of Maxwell's last two great courses strikes up excellent images of the early designs in his career at places such as Muskogee and Hillcrest. The use of the natural terrain to make undulating fairways and natural elevations to provide excellent green sites for natural drainage and air circulation was the hallmark of the early Maxwell style and these two courses provide several examples of that key component. After the completion of these two courses it became evident to Perry that he needed to slow down, at least temporarily, so he began to rely on Press much more over the next few years of his career. He had accomplished some amazing feats and perhaps felt that there was nothing left to do in his field and wanted to help guide Press to the next stage of his career.

After the completion of the courses at Oakwood and Austin, Perry took a much more limited role in the design of golf courses. The bulk of the work over the period from 1947 to 1950 was almost entirely from contacts that Press had developed while in the military during World War II. Other projects came along where Perry was involved with the design and layout of the course but the construction was left to the club or was completed by a different organization. It is believed that many of the unidentified Maxwell courses fall under this umbrella. In many cases the course is probably credited to the person who oversaw the construction or listed as a member designed course.

The Military Contracts

Due to his tour of duty and being a war hero in Europe, Press Maxwell made numerous contacts with notable people in the United States Armed Forces. Press used these contacts to help get his designing career off the ground. He and his father took on the contracts for multiple courses. Three of them would be at military bases in Texas, others were spread out over other states like Louisiana and Wyoming. The best of this group of designs by the Maxwells was the original layout of a course in Norman, Oklahoma.

In 1950, the Maxwells were commissioned to design an 18-hole golf course in Norman. The course would be the last original design work that Perry would see completed. The course was laid out southeast of the current University of Oklahoma campus. The local naval base contracted the course and allowed the use of the facility for the university golf team. The level of difficulty of the course was much higher than that of other teams in the Big 7 Conference, now known as the Big 12 Conference, so the University of Oklahoma golf team quickly showed the benefits by becoming the dominant team in the conference. The course routing was changed in 1972, due to the movement of the clubhouse, but this was not the last change to the course. Though the course was of a superior quality, over forty years of use it became dried out and decimated from lack of an irrigation system and improper maintenance.

In 1994, the University decided that they needed to get the course back into a useful condition, as it was becoming an eyesore. In September of that year, the OU regents heard plans about redesigning the course from Bob Cupp of Atlanta. At that time it was widely believed the site had great potential, it just needed to modernize but still maintain the feel of Maxwell in the end product. Cupp noted the prominent characteristics in his proposal; these included the rolling terrain, the potential for expansion and location of a creek running through the course. The estimated cost of the project was $5 million and funding plans would be decided once it was approved. Cupp expressed his pleasure of developing the new design, "Basically, you couldn't ask for anything more. Yes, there was a golf course here before, and it was "found" by a very well known golf course designer of an earlier era and we've preserved as much of that genius as we could. We're kind of using the best of both worlds here."[46] It was quickly decided the course would be closed in February of 1995 and reopen once the work by Cupp was completed. The course would not be the only new item in regards to the project. A new club professional was hired, Stan Ball, and a new name was decided upon, the Jimmy Austin Golf Course at the University of Oklahoma. Austin was the founder of an oil company based in Seminole, Oklahoma. After a brief inspection the course was quickly rewarded with a regional tournament for the 1997 NCAA Championships. Ball was quoted in the Daily Oklahoman about his impressions on the course. "Bob Cupp did an outstanding job. I'm the biggest Perry Maxwell fan around, I love Perry Maxwell, but we've got a better golf course."

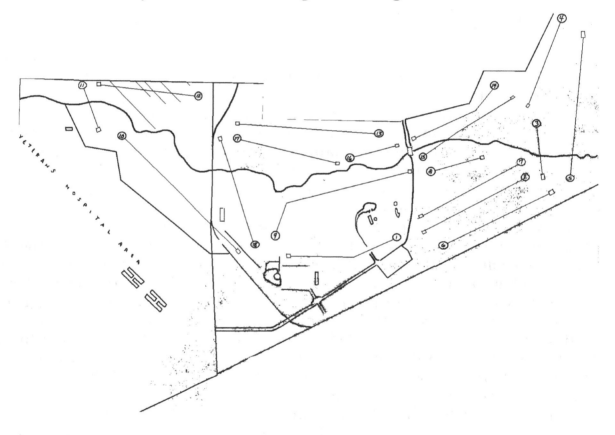

Line drawing of the original routing at the Norman, Oklahoma golf course.
(courtesy of University of Oklahoma)

The course was changed significantly by Cupp, but prior to his appearance, other changes had been made to affect the course. The hole sequence was changed over the years due to the change in clubhouse location. Also one hole was completely replaced with the clubhouse switch. The original clubhouse location was located at the top of the hill beyond what is now the thirteenth green. This elevated location was the key to the design as it provided a great view of the course over the lower elevations and the two creeks that ran through the course. One challenge in the design was the fact that a road was in existence at the time that ran into the campus.

A hole that will be sorely missed from the original routing was the fifteenth hole. From an elevated tee the player sees one of the best alternate fairway holes that Maxwell ever designed. A creek ran diagonally through the hole and Maxwell designed the hole with fairway on the right side that ran right up to the creek. On the opposite side of the creek the player could carry the ball to fairway as well if they so desired. The carry was approximately 220 yards to clear the creek and have a clear view of the green. For the player that didn't carry the hazard off the tee they had to carry the hazard the entire length of their second shot as the green was perched directly against the hazard at an angle from the player that require them to hit along the creek line. This was an excellent version of the "Bottle" hole concept that Maxwell learned from Charles Blair MacDonald.

The final hole of the original routing is the current 13th and aside from bunkering being added by Cupp at the corner of the dogleg it was untouched. This hole was a typical Maxwell finishing hole that ran uphill with the clubhouse in full view for the player. It also was unique as it is one of the only holes on the course that played with a prevailing crosswind. The bunkers added by Cupp create a risk/reward factor to the hole as they protect the preferred line into the green. The green features a steep back to front slope and is protected by a roll in the back portion of the green. Also, a false front comes into play as shots hit short from the uphill lie in the fairway will roll back down from the green. It should be noted that the original design by Maxwell did not include any fairway bunkers but did include a greenside bunker on the right side of the hole.

After the completion of the course in Norman, Perry continued to take on contracts. He accepted three contracts in 1951 while also taking on a project that had been thought to be forever a pipedream that would go unfulfilled. These would be his last set of contracts and only one of these would be completed before his death, the renovation of the Omaha Country Club.

Approaching the End

The last work that was completed by Maxwell is documented to be the renovation work at the Omaha Country Club. In 1951, Perry Maxwell was brought in to rework several greens on the course. It is believed he was brought in due to the association between the Omaha Country Club and Prairie Dunes.

119

Three holes involved the rebuilding of greens on their current location. The remaining holes that he worked on were actually redesigns of the holes by moving the greens in many cases forty to fifty yards. Five holes fell into this category. The par changed on three of the holes.

The fifth was perhaps the most dramatic change. Originally the hole was an eighty or ninety-foot climb from tee to green and was nicknamed, "Cardiac Hill." Maxwell changed the hole into a long uphill par three. This also allowed the sixth tee to be moved back and increased the yardage on that hole. The sixth hole work also involved the green being moved to the other side of a creek. The course as a whole fits in with the character of many Maxwell designs from his career. The terrain is hilly and provides wonderful opportunity to view the surrounding area. It was also the only work that Maxwell ever did in the state of Nebraska.

In 1951, during his work on Lake Hefner, Maxwell was diagnosed with cancer. Perry Maxwell passed away in 1952 as the malignancy from his original amputation came back and took his life. The last few months of his life were very difficult as the cancer, which afflicted him, had spread to his vertebrae and neck. His mobility was extremely limited but he was nursed this entire time by his second wife, Josephine, and her daughter, Jesse, in their Tulsa home. After Perry's death on November 15, 1952, he was buried alongside his first wife Ray in the Maxwell-Woods cemetery north of Dornick Hills. His death was actually attributed to pneumonia and other complications from cancer. Perry was a participating member of the Presbyterian Church of Ardmore and a 33rd Degree Mason at the time of his death. The memorial service was conducted in the same church he helped to build back in 1916 in Ardmore and news of his death was relayed in all the major papers in Oklahoma. Many of the clubs he worked at went so far to have their own services and a few even conducted memorial tournaments in his honor. Even till the day he died, Perry had a spirit of kindness that his family had seen in him since the beginning. His obituary appeared in over 100 papers in Oklahoma, Kansas and Texas and with his passing, also went one of the last members of a select group of people associated with a truly Golden Age

Upon his death, he had three projects that were not completed, River Hills, Oak Cliffs and Lake Hefner. The completion of the Lake Hefner and River Hills projects was overseen by family friend and attorney, Dickson Saunders. Saunders was quoted about Maxwell in his work after the completion of the projects, "When he died, as attorney to the estate, I took over and completed a course in Irving, Texas (River Hills) which was two-thirds through and the course at Lake Hefner. Perry was just extraordinary in a lot of ways. He was not very detailed when it came to financial matters; he ran a very large business just out of the stubs of his checkbooks. I'll tell you what he was not like. He was a very small man, but he did not have a Napoleonic complex. He was a pleasure to work with. By the time I got to know him he was not in robust health, by any means, but he had very strong ideas about how things should be done. He could be very forceful."[47]

The Unfinished Works

After World War II, Oklahoma City became a hotbed of golf. The city needed to expand their municipal golf facilities beyond the current courses. Max Julian, a local philanthropist, helped to arrange a lease agreement with the city for some land on Lake Hefner, located northwest of downtown Oklahoma City. The architect of choice was none other than Perry Maxwell. Julian and Perry had been working on the idea for the course for almost eight years at the time of the lease agreement being signed. Press Maxwell was also influential in the design. The

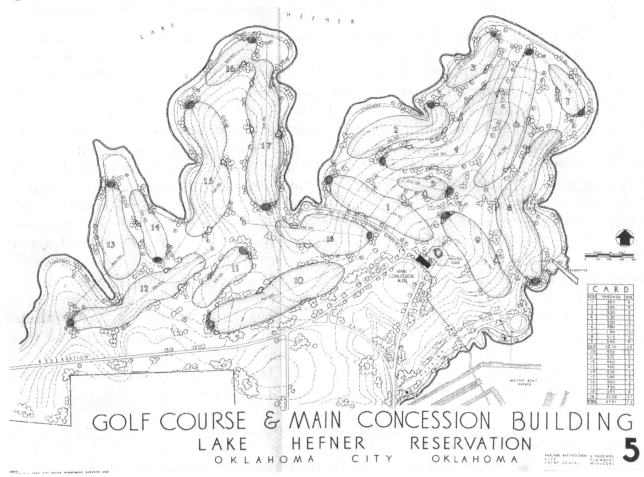

The original plan of the Lake Hefner golf course by Max Julian and Perry Maxwell (courtesy of Lake Hefner Golf Course)

construction of the course started in 1950 as an 18-hole facility for municipal play. Maxwell was very fond of the work as he told longtime friend, Charles Evans, on a tour of the facility. Later the Daily Oklahoman would call "the greens and the fairways created by Perry Maxwell... the finest they had seen in all their experiences." It is also believed that this was going to be the last design that

Maxwell would complete. His health was beginning to fail. Ultimately, he would not see the completion of the Lake Hefner design

The course itself harkened back to the old days of Maxwell design with small greens, tight bunkering, variety in hole design and doglegs. It was almost as if Maxwell's career had come full circle with the work on the course. He made the course on the hard red clay soil located around the Lake Hefner area and fashioned at that time a premier public facility. By the mid-1980s the course began to run into complications with keeping the Maxwell course in good condition. The original layout was scrapped and new course was routed, but many of the holes were laid out in almost the opposite direction from the original design.

The design of Lake Hefner would provide Maxwell something that he had not previously been given in his career. Perry had never received a contract for a course along the ocean, but at Lake Hefner he was given a piece of land that was surrounded by water with several small peninsulas. The routing of the course was also the prime example of Maxwell using the land to create the routing. It was an uncharacteristic routing that included seven par five holes, six par threes and five par fours. Only once did back-to-back holes have the same par. Twelve of the original holes were routed to have the lake in play at some time on the hole. The terrain from the water to the highest point only contained a small amount of elevation change so the challenge was to use the combination of water and subtle terrain movement to provide an exciting routing for the course.

In 1991, Tulsa native Randy Heckenkemper, was awarded the contract to redesign the Maxwell course to get the Lake Hefner courses ready for the "modern era" of municipal courses. As quoted in the Daily Oklahoman in 1994 for the reopening of the course, "This golf course was very short, in some cases the greens were less than 3,000 square feet...(Maxwell) never designed it for 70,000 rounds. You probably couldn't have more than 20,000 rounds and maintain it in the type of condition the public golfer demands these days."[48] The redesign increased the views of the nearby lake and also included a large improvement in the practice facilities and included a three hole teaching area. But the course that Maxwell left is gone forever.

The Dallas area was a burgeoning metropolitan area after World War II. Perry and Press both saw this and took two contracts for jobs in 1951. The first was River Hills. This was originally to be a new course for the Dallas Athletic Club. The course was laid out and construction had begun when Perry Maxwell became sick early in 1952. The work began to grind to a halt. After Maxwell passed away the contract was voided and the course became property of the Maxwell family. Press and his wife, Hodie Maxwell, oversaw the completion of the course and turned it into the first public upscale course in Dallas. An amazing story about the course was told by Hodie when reflecting about the course, "I was playing with Marion Pflueter, the River Hills pro, when a tornado whipped through Dallas. We watched the whole thing from one of the tees. While watching it, Marion goes, 'There went my house.' He went back home and the tornado missed

122

his house by about a block." The River Hills course was in the hands of the Maxwells until 1956 when it was sold to Bob Deadman, a local businessman. He converted the club to a private golf club and changed the name to Knollwood Country Club. The course quickly folded as the owner had financial difficulties and had to divest of all of his assets. Press also completed the course at Oak Cliff in Dallas.

Ironically, the Oak Cliff Country Club was originally organized by a group of doctors that belonged to the Dallas Athletic Club but wanted their own golf course to play. They were given the name of Perry Maxwell by the Colonial Country Club in nearby Fort Worth as a possible architect. Maxwell accepted the offer and came down to Dallas. He was impressed by the rough terrain and the rolling nature of the land. It also had a stream that cut through the plot and also has some steep cliffs that sloped down to the stream. This was perhaps the most diverse site that Maxwell had seen since his design of Old Town in Winston-Salem, North Carolina.

Oak Cliff was perhaps the best course of the late period of Maxwell's design career. Unfortunately, he only saw the routing of the course as the entire construction was started after his death. The trademark elevated tees by the clubhouse on the first and tenth holes along with the ninth and eighteenth holes running uphill all the way are just the primary components that people would associate with Maxwell's work.

The course at Oak Cliff was used as a PGA Tour stop in 1958-1962 and 1964-1967 as the host of the Dallas Open. As with many courses designed by Perry, the course was seen as a shot makers delight and rewarded those with excellent short games and control of their short irons. The course has recently been part of a renovation. The work eliminated much of Maxwell's work by moving bunkers and eliminating lines of play that Maxwell originally designed into the course. Until that time the course had only been slightly altered with one green being moved away from one of the cliffs on the course. Two tees were moved over time as well, one being a direct result of the green movement and the other to eliminate a blind tee shot.

Afterthoughts

Perry Duke Maxwell knew that his life on this earth was finite and that he could make a difference in the lives of others through his work, his church and through his example. To just sit back and discuss his philosophy of green design or some other golf related item would not do the man justice. He lived a life that was an example for others through community involvement and caring for others that should be what we take from his life as an example to us today. He had a gentle spirit that also was filled with child like enthusiasm. In the time between the return of Press and his death, Perry Maxwell designed or worked on about 25 more courses. Possibly to get as much exposure for Press as possible in the field and to get him well on his way to his own practice.

Below are the closing paragraphs from the writing of Charles Evans about Maxwell in the Chronicles of Oklahoma.

Through more than 65 years I watched his life, I never saw him perform a deed, or speak a word that was not as clean and pure as sunlight. He kindly but firmly refused to engage in, or listen to conversation seasoned with risqué stories or vulgarity. In Ardmore, he settled down as father, husband, and citizen, and was soon honored by positions of leadership in the Presbyterian Church and all moral and religious movements of the Community.

So, it was no wonder then in the Ardmore years he entered into every phase of church development and finally bringing about him many noble men and women of his faith, he drew a vision of a church building worthy of the splendid citizens of Ardmore. As his body rested there the other day I looked up and saw groined arches and sustaining beams, a small but beautiful presentation of the noblest of church architecture, and I said, "From foundation to the chimes above, this is one of the expressions of love for good he helped to give in the largest way to Ardmore." Out of this church the chimes he had placed there tolling, they took his body to the Dornick Hills and there where Ray has slept for 30 years, they placed him by her side, under the great oaks.

While it can be seen that this man was born well with clean Scottish blood in his veins, and was nurtured from his birth in an environment of wealth and high ideals, still it must be said that his life was greater than his heritage.

There was no cessation or period of vacant rest in this man's life. He early learned how to know that the best definition of rest is divine activity. He filled every day full to the brim. After a ceaseless round of labor which took him out into the fields and hills at the first dawn of light, he seldom stopped until the shadows falling eastward told him that the day as done. Then began some of his most wholesome and creative hours. If at home and near his library, he read, read incessantly, and there he talked with earth's greatest men and women. Maxwell was one of the best and most discerning readers that I have ever known in all my life. Whether it be a play of Shakespeare or the modern philosophy of Will Durant, whether it was a Tennyson or a Robert Frost, Maxwell often sat by my side and read and I came to know these thinkers of the world better because he often interpreted them far better than I could. His library was never large, perhaps, in number of books, but it was as large as all time in his choice of world wide and diversified authorship. He became such a man of learning that when he visited the great universities, the noted libraries of the world or found himself in certain centers of learning as at Harvard, Yale, Princeton, Columbia, Ann Arbor, all these welcomed him and made him a friend...

So ran the full stream of life for this fine soul. He built a home on top of the high rolling ridge not far distant from where he shaped, with Ray helping him, the beautiful Dornick Hills. But fate dealt him an all but killing blow in 1919 when it took from his side his adored wife. She had understood him when others thought him a visionary. She had given him faith, complete faith in all his endeavors. Her spirituality equaling, if not superior, to his, gave him always an atmosphere of refinement and culture, which his nature demanded. I heard from an old Oklahoma City neighbor of his severe sorrow and loss. I immediately took a train for Ardmore and I met him at the gate of his home. He said to me, "I knew you would be coming. I have told the minister that he could speak of the church life of my wife but that I wanted you to tell of her loved ones, and of our home life. I am going to place her form out yonder on the Dornick Hills golf course which we shaped in love and I shall build an archway there, perhaps a nameless one, but it will tell of my silent and everlasting devotion." So on that June day, I stepped to the side of the grave and with a number of those who loved her, stood beneath a wonderful blue sky and great green oaks, and with God's open spaces reaching far out to the top of the Arbuckles, I told the story of the life of two fine souls I had seen mate and pass from my school room out into the world. I have experienced many occasions in a long life where I was called upon to interpret the deeds of men and women. Never had I known an exultation surpassing that, wherein I felt that every word I said was used in defining two lives as good as any I had known...

So the story runs of his wonderful life. Let no man or woman who may read this think for one moment that anything said here smacks of overemphasis. I end this brief offer of my love to Perry D. Maxwell as I began it. He, in truth, was one of the greatest men Ardmore has ever known. The entire home, school, church and cultural life of Ardmore, out to the very edges and on through the state and nation has been enriched by the work of this man.

Ruskin says, "The finest of all fine arts, is the art of right living." If this be true, and it is, this man was one of the cleanest, noblest artists I have studied. High aims, walking only with those of clean thoughts and worthy living, sought by men of low and high estate alike, it must be said of Perry Duke Maxwell, he met every test Tennyson sets forth in his Knights of the Round Table, where he says:

> *"His glory was redressing human wrong;*
> *He spoke no slander, no, nor listened to it;*
> *He loved one only and he clave to her."*

Charles Evans was perhaps the closest friend Maxwell had, other than his first wife Ray Woods. The words written by Evans may have been the hardest he ever had to write, but it more than likely flowed from his fingertips like music came from the hands of Chopin and Mozart. Every person that knew Maxwell in more than a passing manner truly respected and loved the man. The sanctuary of the Maxwell's home church in Ardmore was packed at his funeral. The town never forgot the man and still carries his name proudly as a local hero. Over time the stories of a man like Maxwell seem to fade away, but due to the love and devotion of his family many of these stories can be relayed in other ways.

This impression was not only made on the people that were close and knew Perry intimately. Even those who just knew him briefly were impacted from meeting him, even in a chance opportunity like that presented to Verle Simpson of Salina, Kansas. Perry was hired by the Salina Country Club to make some renovation plans for the course in 1944. This was just prior to the amputation to his leg, so Perry was having problems with mobility at the time, so the club brought in a 14 year old Verle to serve as Maxwell's "errand boy," as it were. In the world of a 14 year old, Perry Maxwell was an unknown and the concept of hiring a golf course architect was completely foreign. But what Verle took away from the opportunity was the fact that an immediate bond was formed as they talked on the benches by the tee boxes of the Salina Country Club while Maxwell designed the renovations on four holes over a week. Verle remembers Perry appearing in khakis, a double-breasted suit coat and a Stetson hat. He also remembers how Maxwell treated him instantly with respect and as someone beyond his years. It was also that chance meeting which sparked an interest that

The Ardmore First Presbyterian Church with the bell donated
by Perry Maxwell appearing on the left side
was the site of the funeral ceremony in 1952.

exists to this day in golf course architecture for Simpson.

The life of Perry Maxwell was one of an extraordinary individual making the most of extraordinary circumstances. He was the product of a broken home when his father died and he was the young age of nine. He overcame a devastating illness that took the lives of numerous people. He moved his wife and her family to an unknown and wild area of the country that had not even achieved statehood at the time. He got past the early death of his beloved wife and raised four children to be wonderful citizens in their lifetime as well. He saw two World Wars and survived the Great Depression. If he did no other thing, that would be a full life for any man. But that was not all that Perry Duke Maxwell did. He would become a leading citizen in his town and become a high-ranking official at a local bank. He would then become one of the leading golf course architects in the world and the most accomplished in a time of no economic growth in the country. He would not only design masterpieces on his own, but he would work on the epicenters of the golfing world. He touched the courses at Augusta National, Pine Valley, the National Golf Links, Westchester and Saucon Valley. He was an innovator in the design of greens across the country, including the building of the first grass greens in the state of Oklahoma. He would design and work on golf courses in twenty states. He would work with perhaps the greatest golf course architect in the history of the business, Alister Mackenzie. He was also asked to design courses for the epicenters of learning that he so loved. He would also help his son get into the business he loved. All of this while maintaining a love of the arts, his children and his God. What more could be asked of any man.

The Legacy of Perry Maxwell

Perry Duke Maxwell's career ended shortly before his death in 1952. It all began in 1913 with the breaking ground on the original four-hole course on the site of Dornick Hills in Ardmore. His career lasted roughly forty years and during that time he completed a large number of projects. It has been noted in several publications that Maxwell believed the totals to be approximately seventy new courses and fifty other remodeling projects. It can be documented currently to be closer to fifty new courses and thirty other remodeling projects. During that time he worked on several courses that still spark conversation to this day. Prairie Dunes is often listed as one of the most beautiful inland courses in the world. Southern Hills is known as one of the most difficult courses in the United States. Crystal Downs is seen as a museum piece of golf course architecture. This doesn't even touch upon his great courses at the Old Town Club, Twin Hills and Oklahoma City. The career of Maxwell did reach its peak though right before World War II. His renovation work at Colonial and the new design at the Old Town Club are what many consider the end of the greatest period of golf course design in history. He was a dominant figure in his field for a period of twenty years. Mackenzie, Ross and Tillinghast were all great architects in the 1920s but not one of them was as dominant a force as Maxwell during the Depression. After the onset of the Great Depression, Ross and Tillinghast effectively shut down operations. Mackenzie was still active but had serious financial difficulties and died in 1934. Some of Mackenzie's best work during the last few years of his life was with Maxwell, in their partnership. Maxwell was the only one left standing in an era where most courses were built through the use of WPA funding and manual labor. But even with this status, Maxwell was still relatively unknown to the vast majority of people in the golf industry. But his contemporaries knew of him.

The work he created was some of the best ever, including his famous greens and his talent for routing a course through extreme sites. So much so that he was in demand by some of the best courses in the world. Pine Valley and Augusta National hired him to do work and until recently he was the only architect to have worked on both sites. He was seen by the best of many eras as being among the best ever. Mackenzie is quoted as saying, "Mr. Maxwell speaks of my ability to make a good fairway or develop a worthy green, but I wish to tell you that in laying out a golf course and to give it everything that the science and art of golf demand, Mr. Maxwell is not second to anyone I know."[49] He was personally asked by Donald Ross to join the American Society of Golf Course Architects as a founding member. A fact he proudly proclaimed on his business cards and advertisements for the rest of his career. He was also the only architect C.B. Macdonald allowed to touch the course at the National, while he was alive, and then referred him to other courses in Long Island due to his successful work at the course that inspired him to go into the design industry. Robert Trent Jones was asked to make alterations to Southern Hills and stated, "You've got one of the greatest golf courses in the world. You'd be a fool to let anyone make any further changes."[50] This was great praise from a man who was never afraid to alter classic designs. Floyd Farley, perhaps the most prolific architect to ever come out of the plains, called him a major source of inspiration in his design and would often note that one of the few things he should have done differently was to work under Maxwell. Maxwell's own son Press, was there to observe much of the greatness and in a letter to a relative, years later, comments on how his courses lacked his father's genius. Current design icons Bill Coore and Ben Crenshaw are quoted as saying they think, "Maxwell hung the moon." So obviously he is in high regard from many in his field past and present.

Maxwell was also an innovator. He was the first person to develop grass greens in Oklahoma, even though no one thought it possible. That experiment allowed him to develop his ideas on green design and to eventually shape the path of golf in the state of Oklahoma for the next fifty years. He developed the concept of the first documented stadium course in the United States at Hillcrest in Coffeyville, Kansas. An idea that until recently was acknowledged as being developed by a group of TPC style courses from the late 1970s and early 1980s. He was also one of the partners in one of the most powerful combinations of talent in golf course architecture in America, with Mackenzie. Often Mackenzie was seen

128

as the driving force then leaving Maxwell to construct the courses. It appears through studying his early work in Oklahoma we can find evidence of the same hole concepts before he even met Mackenzie indicating that Perry may have been more of a driving force than first thought in the partnership. Much of this information is lost due to a lack of recognition of his work. Some of this was by the lack of action by Maxwell, and his willingness to just do the job and not trumpet his accomplishments. That does not mean he didn't speak the lingo to sell himself and get jobs. He, much like any other architect, spoke several times of how a piece of land was intended to be used as a golf course. Maxwell was a

Photo of the Maxwell Cup (courtesy of Southern Hills)

salesman, but often would just do what he needed to do and leave it at that.

The question can be asked whether his courses can stand up today. The answer would be yes. Much of this can be directly linked to his techniques used during design. Often you hear of how a course is strategically sound from tee to green, in the case of Maxwell he approached that strategy in reverse, from green to tee. He would locate green sites in ideal locations and then develop the strategy for the hole using the terrain to shape

the layout. The strategy on his courses seemed incredibly simple, hit from point A to point B then to point C. If your shot to the green is exceptional you might score well, if not then you should be happy with par. Even on his greens though a two putt was not always automatic. His greens are often the great neutralizer of power in the game. The greens dictate what the player can and cannot do. His designs do not care if the player drives the ball 300 yards off the tee, but if they play their shots from the correct positions. His courses reward the accurate player, the shotmaker. To this day, the courses he designed have held numerous championships. Maxwell courses have hosted 26 USGA events, 4 PGA championships, numerous PGA and LPGA tournaments, 14 NCAA championships and several other national tournaments, including the Trans-Mississippi Amateur 15 times and the Maxwell Invitational each year at Dornick Hills. His courses have and still provide an excellent test to the best players on all levels. Perry would often travel back to his courses to watch tournaments to see how the players were playing on his courses and to see the type of shots they played on them. All in an effort to design courses that were manageable distance wise but still a difficult test. Perhaps studying his designs more would help us to figure out a way in this day and age of long golf balls and high tech equipment to still

129

challenge the player while not having 7,500 yard courses. Maxwell was a genius at routing courses to test every facet of a golfer's game. His designs still are challenging today due to their original nature to test the drive and to test the short game. His courses still do that, regardless of the length of the hole.

The true test of any architect's greatness though is his influence on those that follow after him. If Maxwell's concepts went away once he died in 1952, how important would they really be? Maxwell had two obvious disciples from his career, Floyd Farley and Press Maxwell. Farley tried to implement the same concepts as Perry but used his own style in designing a course. Press tried to use both the style and concepts that his father employed. Both paths led to successful careers for both. But they were both voices in the wilderness when compared to the influence that was dominant in the industry during three decades after Perry's death. The course at Southern Hills was an immediate and dominant influence on architecture in Oklahoma until the opening of the Oak Tree Golf Club by Pete Dye. Until that time every course was compared to Southern Hills and in many cases was patterned to look almost like the famous work by Maxwell. Until the work by Dye and other more recent works by Tom Fazio, there was only one course to pattern after in the state. This was very similar to the same phenomenon that you could find in North Carolina in regards to Pinehurst #2. Every course in the area was compared to it and many strongly resembled it and the Ross pattern of design. Luckily Maxwell did not design more than a few courses in Oklahoma after the completion of Southern Hills, so he did not face these issues in his later work.

Today's architects are just as influenced by these ideals. A group of individuals subscribe to the minimalist theory of design, of which Maxwell was a strong proponent. These include people such as Tom Doak, Gil Hanse and the team of Crenshaw and Coore. Their credo is that the land shall shape the character of the course. The land will dictate the holes and little earth will be moved unless absolutely necessary. This often results in quicker results with less expense. Another of the core ideals of Maxwell's design philosophy. Other less well-known designers have also used the concepts of Maxwell successfully in their work as they have drawn from numerous projects on Maxwell original designs. These architects would include Tripp Davis and Jerry Slack. These concepts seem to be growing in popularity and begin to hearken back to the principles of Maxwell and so many other early architects.

The legacy of Maxwell has not been lost on his courses either. Courses such as Twin Hills and Hillcrest in Coffeyville, Kansas have recently gone through restoration projects. The Old Town Club has just recently finished a sympathetic restoration by Bobby Weed. Maxwell's own home course at Dornick Hills is also preparing to undergo a restoration of the original nine holes designed by Maxwell. Clubs like these have known how special their course was for years but have recently gone through steps to document the original aspects of the design. Some are even trying to bring those old design traits back to life. Other courses have tried to tap into this sense of nostalgia through other programs.

The Colonial Country Club, Southern Hills and Prairie Dunes each year hold a club match between the three clubs known as the Maxwell Cup. This is a Ryder Cup style of competition between the three clubs that often evokes strong competition and emotions. Right now there are no plans to expand the competition to other clubs, but in an offshoot program called the Maxie Cup a similar concept lives. The Maxie Cup is a junior version of the Maxwell Cup that also involves Dornick Hills in a program to give kids a chance to play these other courses and provide an opportunity for teaching and learning about the architect that links all of them together. But perhaps the best example of building a sense of nostalgia is the Maxwell Invitational.

The Maxwell, as it is usually referred to, is the top collegiate invitational tournament in the country. To many programs it only falls behind their conference and NCAA Championships. It is a team event that also involves a huge program for community involvement. The program was the concept of Ardmore citizen and Dornick Hills member Terry Harris. Mr. Harris developed the idea of having a top-flight competition to provide an example to the community and young golfers in the Ardmore area. The intent was to help children see where they could go and what opportunities present themselves through the game. One of the most important aspects is the commorodity that is built between the players and the local youth. During the tournament a group of children are assigned to a team for the week and get to be with the team for many functions during the week and get to build a real relationship. Many noticeable accomplishments, such as area teams winning state championships and area golfers receiving Division I scholarships to play golf have come about due to the program. It has also provided the community a chance to get involved in a cause that benefits it and the club. The Invitational along with some other programs have helped to solidify that Dornick Hills remains in existence and can continue the tradition of Maxwell's philosophy.

In recent years, there has been an increase of interest in the career of Perry Maxwell within the golf course architecture community. A sign of Maxwell's recognition within the golfing community was the announcement that his top two designs, Southern Hills and Prairie Dunes, hosting the top tournaments on the Men's and Women's professional tours, the US Open Championships, within one year of each other. All of these items are indicative of the impact that Maxwell has had on the world of golf and is why his legacy will live on way past his years. The legacy of Maxwell is one that has been overlooked in golf course design and golf in general. He did not design the best golf course in the world, but designed the best golf courses he could with his method and beliefs.

After all of his work and after his life had expired Maxwell was remembered by his loved ones as a compassionate father, friend and husband. His golf course design work for many years had been his life and, aside from his children, from where he drew his pleasure. At the time he embarked on a new career he probably felt the least able to do so due to the recent passing of his wife. But if not for the encouragement of his first love, the things that we now associate with

131

Perry Maxwell would not exist, so we would not be able to feel some connection to the great man that had done not only so much for golf, but for his community and his family as well as we play the game that Perry grew to love and feel passionately about thanks to that day he read an article in Scribners Magazine in 1909. With that we can only thank Ray for her encouragement and Perry for his hard work to provide a lasting legacy for them and their families to be proud of and for so many others to enjoy. Cheers to you both and may you rest in peace until the King comes back again.

Part Two: The Work

Tenets of Design

When Perry Maxwell first laid out the basic four-hole routing of his home course in Ardmore, Oklahoma few would have guessed that Perry had only read one book on the subject matter and studied from afar the wonders of the new National Golf Links of America in Southampton, New York. He would sustain this simple style over the duration of his career. Minimalism was not just his approach to golf course design but the basis of his way of living. Maxwell was humble, almost to a fault, about his thoughts on design and did not document them in the fashion of someone such as A. W. Tillinghast or George C. Thomas, both prominent architects from the 1920s. Little would be known about Maxwell's philosophy if not for the 1935 interview in American Golfer magazine. From the interview it was apparent that Maxwell held steadfastly to his beliefs and was not afraid to express them, often in long flowery sentences. Maxwell obviously had achieved a solid understanding of both the technical aspects and the artistic side of golf course design and construction.

Maxwell had three main tenets that he felt needed to exist for a golf course to reach its ultimate potential. "The minimum of expense was the first consideration, that and the importance of creating a course that would be a legitimate tax upon the skill of the players. It is my theory that nature must precede the architect, in laying out the links. It is futile to attempt the transformation of wholly inadequate acres into an adequate course. Invariably the result is the inauguration of an earthquake."[51] These statements would be the outlines of the basic philosophy of Maxwell. He championed economic design that tested the player and fully utilized the land while appearing completely natural. Every part of Perry's design philosophy revolved around these basic thoughts.

Even when he began his career, Maxwell saw the impending issues of cost keeping the game away from the masses of potential patrons. Today, this issue is still prevalent. Maxwell saw economical course construction as being the key component to keeping the game affordable for public consumption. When asked what caused him to take up this pursuit he replied, "Frequent visits to Scotland and among our home courses have convinced me that the time is ripe for a stupendous revision looking toward a saner and simpler plan for turning the good earth into playgrounds for those who follow through."[52] Perry would even be willing to go to extremes to often get a job at a lower cost, partially for the reason of his beliefs and partially to make sure he had work during the Depression. Dora

Harrison, Perry's daughter recalls, "Father would often just drive up to New York or Philadelphia and go from club to club asking if they had work. He often made trips to the area, so each time in passing through if he saw a club, he checked to see if they had work. Obviously, during the Depression, not everyone was doing something at the time he would come through, but he worked on many clubs just by stopping and bugging them about doing work." Another relative of Maxwell's shared how he would bid on jobs, "Perry would go out and find out what the lowest bid was on the work and go lower. He would sometimes go over his budget, but he would still come in at less than what the next lowest bid was and the club would still get a deal." The feelings of Perry can best be summed up by his own statement, "Millions of dollars annually are wasted in devastating the earth; in obstructing the flow of rainfall; in creating impossible conditions. Don't blame all of this on the architects; the guilt lies primarily with the influential misguided club members who take sadistic joy in torturing the good earth. As a result the majority of American golf clubs are in the red, gore of the steam shovel, blood drawn by the mound-builders. We have learned nothing from Scotland and England where the ancient and honorable game can be enjoyed on marvelous links at one tenth the admission fees, dues, green fees, etc., that prevail in the land of the free."[53]

The second consideration by Maxwell concerns the challenge to the golfer. The main approach by Maxwell to provide this challenge was to use the terrain provided and create a variety of shot and skill requirements throughout the round. One way he did that was through the use of template holes that he borrowed from Charles Blair Macdonald and also those that he created on his own. Though not as rigid as the formulaic approach of a Macdonald or Raynor in having four particular types of par threes on each of their courses. Maxwell did have a selection of holes that appeared over and over on his designs. But in most cases, these holes appear incredibly natural on the landscape, the 8th at Prairie Dunes being a perfect example. The amazing thing about Maxwell was that his designs took on a different look as you went from course to course. Southern Hills always appears much more dignified and pristine, while Dornick still appears to be as if he laid out greens and tees in the landscape. The original design of Old Town included a wide open area where several fairways met together, separated only by bunkers that seemingly were out of play but framed the holes accordingly. Prairie Dunes is on a flowing landscape surrounded by plum thickets, yucca plants and wild fescue. Variety was what Maxwell was about as he stated, "...it will have its own character, distinct from any other course in the world."[54]

The last tenet can be drawn from the statement by Perry in the 1935 interview dealt with the selection of the land and the use that the designer attempts to get from the land. Maxwell was aware of the fact that to have ideal golfing terrain, the land itself must have some character. Using this character to its fullest capabilities was what Maxwell did on almost every course. It was also his belief that each piece of property provided a separate identity for each course. "The site of the golf course should be there, not brought there. A featureless site

135

cannot possibly be economically redeemed. Many an acre of magnificent land has been utterly destroyed by the steam shovel, throwing up its billows of earth, biting out traps and bunkers, transposing landmarks that are contemporaries of Genesis."[55] The other prime component of Maxwell using the terrain to its fullest was knowing the needs of his client. Projects of larger scope such as Southern Hills and Old Town seemed to befit the property they were situated on. Maxwell also knew when to keep his designs low key to benefit the client. Understanding what his client wanted would not only accentuate all of his theories on design but would also eliminate the club from running into extravagant costs later on.

View from the tee of hole 13 at the University of Oklahoma in Norman
(courtesy of Matt Cohn)

Through all of this, Maxwell was attempting to keep his thumbprint off the land. "We can't blame the engineers, surveyors, landscape experts and axmen for carrying out the designs in the blueprints, most of which come into existence at the instigation of amateurs obsessed with a passion for remodeling the masterpieces of nature. A golf course that invades a hundred or more acres, and is actually visible in its garish intrusion from several points of observation, is an abhorrent spectacle. The less of man's handiwork the better a course."[56]

Through his developed style, Maxwell was able to be a prime contributor in the partnership with Alister Mackenzie. Mackenzie is often seen as a prime influence on Maxwell. To a degree this is true, but it could be argued that Maxwell had some influence on Mackenzie during their shared enterprise. One thing that cannot be argued is that Maxwell's greatest works occurred after his association with Alister. Perhaps the area that Maxwell gained the greatest from Mackenzie was in adding a touch of flair to his designs, specifically in the area of bunker design. Even though his career was influenced by these two paragons of design, his work is easily identifiable in comparison. In an interview with University of Oklahoma golfer, Matt Cohn, he describes Maxwell's courses, "His courses sometimes are labeled short, but small would be a much better description. They start out with small yardages in hole length, and then go down to small widths of fairways, then to small greens with numerous small undulations within the greens themselves. This provides the player small areas to play shots into and from and a small chance of recovery if they fail." His strategy was simple.

Of all his contemporaries, Donald Ross is perhaps the one architect that is most easily comparable to Maxwell in style and in persona. The two held similar beliefs of a personal nature, including the fact that both were members of the Presbyterian Church. They also had very similar beliefs in the design of golf courses. Both were known for efficient and intelligent routings that made great use of the land. Both used a similar theoretical structure by using the highest points on the property to hold green and tee complexes. Maxwell's style used fairway bunkering less often, very little of the early work by Maxwell in Oklahoma even used fairway bunkering. For an architect without a so-called discernable style, his method of operation was rather evident when compared to others from this era in American golf course architecture. Though his work cannot be identified through thirteen points like his friend Alister Mackenzie, general guidelines can be identified to lay a sturdy groundwork from Maxwell's body of work.

The career of Perry Maxwell also saw a vast change in the style of his work from the early courses at Dornick Hills and Twin Hills through the end of the Great Depression. Then after World War II his style fell back in step with what he had done earlier in his career as he refocused on local courses in Oklahoma and other southwestern states. This "evolution" in his style was evident in all aspects of his designing: inspiration, routing and green design. After his tour of the National Golf Links and meeting Charles Blair Macdonald, his designs reflected the classic hole designs presented by Macdonald at the National. Examples of this are located throughout Oklahoma and prominently at Dornick Hills. The inspiration for much of Perry's work early in Oklahoma can also be traced directly to the Old Course at St. Andrews. From touring this course during his trip to Scotland in 1919, he was able to note how courses should incorporate the surrounding terrain with a minimum of movement of the land to create strategically challenging holes. Maxwell then used this expanded knowledge to

137

create many excellent works in Oklahoma that many of this generation of elite golfers have never seen. These are not just hidden gems in the wilderness of Oklahoma, but courses that have hosted national and major championships. The list includes Twin Hills, Muskogee and Oklahoma City. Maxwell also evolved in his use of hazards. Early in his work, Perry was reluctant to create mandatory carries off of the tee and for approach shots into green sites, specifically over water. Examples of this are at Dornick Hills and Twin Hills. At Muskogee Maxwell began to experiment with the strategic use of water hazards. Maxwell would eventually begin to use these hazards in his designs. He even went so far as to go back to Dornick Hills and move the 10th green across the creek that ran behind the green previously. But the area where Perry would "evolve" the most would be his green design concepts.

The Maxwell "Rolls"

Several experts, including noted architect Bill Coore, have called Maxwell the best green builder in the history of golf course design. His style was a mix from studying the greens by CB Macdonald, the putting surfaces at the Old Course in St. Andrews, some of the work of Alister Mackenzie and of what he originally developed during his early years in Oklahoma. The contours that Maxwell implemented on his greens were an omnipresent factor on every hole he designed. In today's game of long drives and flip wedges, these greens still hold fear and still make the holes an adventure. The shortest shot into many of Maxwell's greens is not always the preferred attack. Bill Coore, who played several years on Old Town, has said, "The big sweeping contours of the greens at Maxwell's courses are the ones that scare you from the fairway, but today's player often doesn't notice the little contours that ebb and flow between the large sweeping mounding." It is often these contours that begin to push the ball away from the intended target and then the large contours eliminate any hope of holing a birdie putt. These little contours have been equated to ripples of water or to someone pushing up the green with an air hose from underneath in several locations.

The greens are very artistic. The flow from one contour to another is so smooth that each undulation appears to be alone and secluded but each mounding is intertwined to form a web of subtle shifts in elevation that help to confound and force decisive play by the player. Maxwell selected his green sites based on two main factors. They usually were on natural rises that allowed for excellent drainage and air circulation. Maxwell also was the one responsible for grass greens finally making their way to Oklahoma. The grass of choice was Bermuda and to compensate for the decreased green speed, Maxwell designed his dramatic greens with contours that at today's green speeds almost defy gravity. They became known as "Maxwell Rolls." Before putting them on the ground though, he would shape them as clay models, obviously an ode to his love of the

138

arts. The National Golf Links provided Maxwell with the inspiration to use a concept that Charles Blair Macdonald used at the National. He began to develop greens with quadrants, or small greens within the larger green complexes, to them that were instrumental in maintaining the challenge of Maxwell's greens even to this day. The best example of this can be found at the Old Town Club in Winston-Salem, North Carolina. He used his experiences in Scotland as a way to incorporate the green sites into the landscape and make them feel and look as if they were naturally there. Mackenzie helped him to realize that dramatic contouring was possible on greens. He had implemented this in his early designs in Oklahoma, but dramatically enhanced the contours after his experience with Mackenzie at Melrose. The artistic nature of Maxwell's courses is often overlooked. Unlike the dramatic bunkering of Alister Mackenzie's courses like Cypress Point and the Valley Club, Maxwell used a simple formula that relied on nature, whereas the artistry of Maxwell was in the contouring of his greens. But this skill in design did not just happen overnight. It matured and evolved over time.

The course at Dornick Hills was a testing area for Maxwell to develop his undulations on Bermuda grass greens, the first in the state of Oklahoma. The slower grain grass would allow Maxwell to begin the development of his undulations in a mild form on his first course. Maxwell would later come back in the mid-1930s and add to the undulations on the greens at his course. It is believed by many of the older members at the club that the greens at Dornick rivaled those of the more famous Prairie Dunes and Southern Hills.

The rolling green on the seventh hole at the Old Town Club
(courtesy of Dunlop White III)

After the completion of the course at Dornick, Maxwell then began to experiment with the development of sloping greens. The course at Twin Hills in Oklahoma City features many greens that don't have the typical rolls or mounding found on many Maxwell courses but greens that slope fiercely in one direction or

139

another. The "rolls" that do occur on the greens at Twin Hills are often mild and provide more of a change of pace from the flatter green surfaces on the course. The other primary component that Maxwell fine-tuned during this period was his ability to locate a green site that provided proper air circulation and drainage.

The first set of excellent greens that Maxwell would design would come almost seven years later in Oklahoma City at the Nichols Hills Country Club, now called the Oklahoma City Golf & Country Club. Since the work at Twin Hills, the green designs of Perry had slowly evolved and at Oklahoma City the first dramatic change in his green design became evident. Maxwell oriented the slope of the greens with the prevalent wind on the course. The other part of the design of the greens involved the location of many of the sites. Maxwell created a number of greens of similar nature to the greens by Charles Blair Macdonald on his famed course. So the combination of green location, undulation and slope can be traced to this course. The other new feature that Maxwell began to implement, inspired by the greens at the National, would be the sectioning of the greens into separate areas within the greens. This was like miniature targets within the larger green surface. One other noticeable change also was the inclusion of false fronts to some of the greens at Oklahoma City. Almost all of this was possible, due to the use of a new tile for drainage that was particularly effective in the clay-based soil of Oklahoma.

Maxwell began working with Alister Mackenzie at Crystal Downs in 1928. Mackenzie and Maxwell co-designed this museum piece of architecture with Maxwell overseeing the construction over a period of three years. Perry actually lived on site to watch over the construction and was involved with the detail of each green. The course contains some Mackenzie designs such as a modified Redan and a boomerang green on the seventh hole, but many of the greens are reflective of the style of Maxwell. It was at this course that he really began to create a web-like design of the contouring on many of his green sites. Until this point, the dominant large elevations were the primary part of the design, but at Crystal Downs Perry began to tie these large undulations together with smaller and subtle bumps in the greens. All of this while maintaining the slope and undulation that would have been characteristic of his earlier greens. Due to the sand based soil, Maxwell was also able to build these greens with additional contouring because drainage was less of a concern. The other major change in Maxwell's design was that he began to include multiple rolls on his greens, where on prior courses he would design the green with one dominant undulation and work from there for the rest of the green site.

After the work at Crystal Downs, Maxwell was involved with two projects that involved the use of bent grass greens in environments that had never been exposed to the strand. The first of these was a collaboration with Marvin Leonard at the Colonial Country Club in Fort Worth, Texas. After the completion of that work, Maxwell was intent on having the first bent grass course in Oklahoma and this would take place at Southern Hills. The greens at Southern Hills were an experiment in using this new grass to determine if the same undulations were possible using a faster strain. The results were successful, as the bent grass seemed rather resilient in the Oklahoma summer heat with the proper amount of irrigation.

Perhaps the most renowned set of greens by Maxwell are those at Prairie Dunes and one can easily see why. The greens at Prairie Dunes epitomize what Maxwell was envisioning with his web-like pattern of design with many large and small undulations on the green sites at the course in Hutchinson. There are many instances around the course where putts over ten feet will break in two directions and depending on the speed applied on a seemingly straight putt it could break to the right or the left. The greens at Prairie Dunes often draw comparisons to those at Crystal Downs but they are slightly better in that the large undulations are even more dramatic than the ones at its cousin in Frankfort, Michigan.

Though many consider the greens at Prairie Dunes to be the top level of Maxwell's abilities, that honor actually must go to the Old Town Club in Winston-Salem, North Carolina. The Old Town course features the most complex and complete set of greens in the entire Maxwell portfolio. The greens feature the large undulations that are present at Prairie Dunes while also containing the subtle contouring found at Crystal Downs. Many of the greens are on ideal elevated sites such as at Twin Hills. But the one thing that makes them complete is that Maxwell continued to evolve his design as he also included the concept he used at Oklahoma City with the sectioning of his greens using ridges to make small greens within the large putting surface. The strategy necessary to play to each part of the green could vary daily as well, depending on the wind and the pin placement. Maxwell also used extensively two other concepts as an exhibit of his tutelage from the Old Course at St. Andrews. Many of the greens employ a swale that helps to defend the putting surface, much like those found at the Old Course. The ultimate compliment to St. Andrews though was the creation of a double green for the eighth and seventeenth holes. All of these factors pulled together make this the epitome of what Maxwell envisioned when he began designing courses just twenty years earlier at his home course in Ardmore, Dornick Hills .

The greens by themselves are quite remarkable, but when you throw them into the context of the entire design concept by Maxwell you realize how different his work was from any other architect. The green was the center of his strategic design of each hole, but it was just a part. Maxwell would design holes that would use the layout to create a challenging shot to the green from the fairway due to the lie the player had and the undulations that player would face from that angle of approach. The shot from the preferred spot would have a much more favorable if not flat lie into the putting surface. The difficulty was also in getting to that shot as Maxwell was notorious for using rolling and undulated fairways and to get into the ideal position and would require a shot that was shaped just right to account for the flow of the land. So it could be argued that Maxwell designed his holes from green to tee instead of in the opposite direction. This concept by itself was quite innovative and should be no surprise to come from a man that was able to

141

take inspiration from Charles Blair Macdonald and Alister Mackenzie and to create his own style that was perhaps the best in his era.

This evolution though seemed to conclude at Old Town. Much of this can be directly related to his health and the loss of a leg, but also to a change in the construction of the courses. Press was brought on to oversee the construction of Perry's designs after his return in 1946 from World War II. WPA funding was also gone from the equation. So large numbers of workers were not always possible. But the other apparent fact is that Maxwell made a conscious decision to go back to his original concepts that he found so popular early in his career. The larger scale projects at Southern Hills and Prairie Dunes were wonderful creations, but it appeared that Maxwell was willing to settle for designs that were much smaller in scale.

Aerial view of the routing of Twin Hills. Note the axis routing around the clubhouse
(courtesy of Twin Hills)

Axis Routing and Minimalism

Perry Maxwell's "Rolls" have been referred to as one of the greatest concepts in golf history and the attention his greens have received over the years has often left some of his masterful routings as a forgotten treasure. The basis of the routing was the position of the clubhouse. In most cases this was positioned at the highest point on the property. Once this was identified, he would go about the property with a sketchpad, or even perhaps long letter envelopes to draw up routings and sketch holes. He would often walk the property for hours or, in some cases, days. He would do this to identify the higher points of the property to locate tees and greens. It is rare on a Maxwell course to find consecutive holes that do not have either an elevated tee or green. The elevation of the tees provided the player an excellent view of the hole they were about to play, and in some cases would provide excellent views of the course and the course surrounds.

Early on in his career, Maxwell also learned the importance of green positioning to help with drainage and air circulation during his study tour of early

American golf courses. Elevated green sites became commonplace on his designs. Maxwell would then use the central elevation factor, the clubhouse location, to locate numerous elevated greens and tees to provide a core routing with the first and tenth tees in close proximity of the clubhouse and the ninth and eighteenth greens within yards of the clubhouse as well. In many cases he would also have other holes radiate out from this location in a fan or axis like pattern. This strategy would also allow Maxwell to be flexible in the number of the holes he would design at one given time. Maxwell would often come in and design eighteen holes for a club but only be contracted to construct nine holes. This was often thought to lead to Maxwell coming back at a later point in time to construct the remaining nine holes. The reasoning for this was due to the lack of financial backing due to the Great Depression at the height of his career. The Palmetto Country Club contracted Maxwell to design 18 holes and have him oversee the construction of the first nine holes. It is believed the Prairie Dunes Country Club originally hired Perry to design thirty-six holes, but the eventual goal was for him to design and build nine holes and to return for the second nine when the funds were available. Maxwell kept all of the notes and details about the remaining construction. Nine holes were built twenty years later by his son, Press Maxwell. The Arkansas City Country Club can provide another example. Maxwell designed 18 holes originally with the full intention of him returning once the club had funds to construct the second nine. The club didn't acquire the funding until after Maxwell's death and thus constructed a front nine that bears little resemblance to the Maxwell plans.

Another prime component of his routings would often be the use of the prevailing wind. Professionals and those who often don't have the best interest of the game at heart often see wind as an unfair element in the game of golf, but in Oklahoma and Kansas, the wind is a major factor in play. Much like Maxwell's ancestral home of Scotland it directly affects play and from hour to hour could create a different course on the same layout in the same day. Maxwell would often use the wind to its fullest depending on what type of hole he was designing. He often had a penchant for designing long holes to play into the wind and shorter holes to play down wind. This would require the player to hit truer shots and would also help to emphasize the ground game nature of golf. He would often orient the slope of the greens based on the prevailing direction of the wind. An example is provided by the Oklahoma City Golf & Country Club course. The course is laid out on a narrow strip of property that has several holes going in one of two directions. He would often have holes that were going downwind slope away from the players and greens playing into the wind slope towards the player.

The last major factor in the development of Maxwell's routings were the natural land features found on the site. Maxwell made a point to try and only select sites with natural features such as rolling terrain, twisting creeks and small lakes on the plot. The Hillcrest Country Club in Bartlesville, Oklahoma provides a good exhibit to use as the selection of a proper site by Maxwell. He surveyed two sites and selected the one with the creek and rolling terrain. Maxwell was a master of finding a dominant feature on the site and using it in a variety of ways around the course. It would affect the tee shot on one hole, the approach on another, be a green side hazard the next time you saw it and so on.

One of the finest routings that Maxwell ever put together was at the Old Town Club in Winston-Salem, North Carolina. The Old Town Club uses all of the attributes of the plot to its full extent. The site contains a few creeks and several elevation changes. The course also uses some tree-lined areas to help with the ambiance on some of the holes. The flow of the holes also masterfully allows for many of the players to play a quick three holes as the third hole comes back to the clubhouse. Many of the holes also use the elevation change to provide interesting lies as approaches to the greens are often on side hill lies to the natural green sites. The Muskogee Country Club in Muskogee, Oklahoma is another fine routing that Maxwell used in a redesign of the course. The course uses the rolling terrain very well, but the mastery of the routing is the use of the small lakes on part of the course. Maxwell used the lakes to affect the shots on four of the holes in that stretch at different times on each hole. One affects the approach to the green, another is a hazard the complete length of the hole, the next is a cross hazard that could come into play for longer and shorter hitters and the last in the sequence is a forced carry from the tee with a increased degree of danger depending on the intended line of the player. The work at Southern Hills used the large hill on the south side of the plot on many holes. Seven holes use the hill as either the location for a tee or a green. Maxwell was even capable of tying in drastic elevation changes as with the courses at Dornick Hills and Twin Hills in Oklahoma City. The Dornick Hills course was lined on the north edge of the property with a steep cliff that Maxwell was able to tie into the design of four holes. Maxwell also used a dramatic land feature of two large hills on the eighth hole at Twin Hills.

The bunkering at Old Town had artistic edges and natural appeal.
(courtesy of Dunlop White III)

Maxwell Trademarks

Apart from the use of the elevated tees and greens that come into play on many of the opening and finishing holes that Maxwell designed, there were other consistent themes to the type of holes he laid out. During the "Golden Age" other designers followed a formulaic approach to the design of individual holes. This has been referred to as the "National School" of thought led by Charles Blair MacDonald often used the theoretical structure of particular holes as the basis of the individual hole design. Very often the courses under this style had the same type of holes from course to course, such as the Redan, Eden, Cape and Road holes. This style was the main influence on the conceptual hole designs of many Maxwell courses. Early in his career, specifically with the first nine holes at Dornick Hills, Maxwell used very similar hole concepts to the ones found at the National Golf Links and other Macdonald courses. What Maxwell found early on in his career though was that many of these concepts were repetitive and he began to compile his own inventory of conceptual copies to use over his career. When added to the number of holes from Macdonald's Ideal Course theory, the sum of "template" holes was considerable in number. The use of conceptual copies was a key component to the design philosophy of Perry Maxwell. The difficult part was using the correct "template" with the nature of the land. The use of these "template" holes helped Maxwell to cut down the time and expense of laying out and constructing the course, as opposed to the possible experimentation that could happen and result in having to double efforts if the experiment failed. If he found a similar landform to something that he and his crew had encountered before, he would just refer to a prior course and hole and they would construct a similar hole.

Another hallmark of Maxwell's strategic design was the challenge from the tee. If you hear anyone describe his work, you almost always hear the courses described as a "shot maker's course." The approach to the green is often the key to this type of design. Approaches on Maxwell courses almost never have level lies. The ball is always above or below your feet with possibly an uphill or down hill lie also affecting the shot. The lie in most cases would help with the shape of the shot into the green. The approach areas of many Maxwell fairways also seemed to have "rolls" in them that were similar to the rolls in the greens on his courses. Maxwell would have his crews use their horse drawn plows and fresnos to create some rolling fairways, such as those found at Prairie Dunes. This was often tedious work, but the end result was well worth the effort. This effort paid off as the player would have to contemplate on the tee as to not only the spot to aim towards but the shape of the shot as well.

The most widely used hazard by Maxwell would have been the greenside bunker. The greenside bunkers built by Maxwell have over the years taken on the term "clamshell" bunker. The term "clamshell" refers to a bunker with a somewhat oval in shape and would have a concave bottom to the bunker with a sand-splashed face to it leading into a slope of some type and in most cases was built into the base of the elevated green site. Maxwell's bunkers originally were not like this in many cases. This is a modification from years of maintenance practices and misguided renovations of the green sites. As with the variety exhibited in the general layout of his courses, his bunkers also varied from location to location. Originally many of those bunkers were flat-bottomed with roughed out edges that blended much more into the landscape than their modern day counterparts. The bunkers at Southern Hills are perhaps the farthest removed from what Maxwell originally designed. The bunkers at Prairie Dunes and Crystal Downs are much more reflective of what Maxwell would have done in his career, with some grass tufted edging but still maintaining their own individual style. Most of his courses did not originally have an extraordinary amount of fairway bunkers. Even at Prairie Dunes Maxwell did not design a large number of these. Most of the holes with fairway bunkers were laid out by his son Press. Bunkers were a particular source of aggravation for Maxwell, as he saw it as an unnecessary expense that added to the maintenance cost of the course down the road. In his American Golfer interview he was quoted, "Far too many exist in our land. Oakmont, Pittsburgh, where the National Open will be played this year, has two hundred. Other courses famed everywhere average one hundred and fifty. From twenty to twenty-five, plus the natural obstacles are ample for any course."[57] One other characteristic of his bunker designs, especially those in the fairway, which could be attributed to his exposure to Alister Mackenzie, is that his bunkers seem to almost disappear once you reached the green. The bunkers at Southern Hills provide the best example of this. Standing on the greens at this course, you will hardly ever see the trace that a fairway bunker actually exists. This is due to his using the natural landscape to provide the location for these bunkers and he would build them into faces of slight rises in the terrain.

If one were to reflect back to Dornick Hills though, this would reveal a side of Maxwell's early design that was heavily dependant on hazards. This would be the only course that he would design this way, but the use of hazards was worthy of mention. He used some excellent tight bunkering around the greens, but he also had a variety of hazards that he used throughout the course. The sixth hole featured a large Hell's Half Acre imitation that came into play on the first and second shot. A cross bunker unlike anything seen on any of his other Redan style holes was a dominant feature on the eighth hole. The tenth and eleventh hole featured a large carry bunker that protected the best line on both holes. The thirteenth featured deep bunkers along the right side of the hole paying homage to the Road Hole. The seventeenth also feature a deep pit on the left side of the hole that had wooden walls, much like some of the bunkering still found in Scotland.

Several courses in this day and age are overrun by trees or have had strategic play affected by trees that have grown to full stature, Maxwell often allowed for trees to be involved in the direct line of play. He originally designed

146

several holes of note with trees in play. Though it was not an occurrence on a large number of courses, it is worth noting that Maxwell did use trees in his design. The first hole at Muskogee is an example of this as the hole doglegs from right to left, but the player who cuts the fairway will be faced with a shorter approach that must clear a nest of trees, while the player with the longer approach will have the clear view to the green from the right side of the fairway.

Typical Three Pars

The par threes on many Maxwell courses, often are the most overlooked group of holes due to the natural way they use the terrain. In most cases, these holes were the first found when doing the routing by Maxwell. In almost all cases they were where the terrain slightly rose above its surroundings creating a type of plateau to create the green site. Very often Maxwell would put bunkering tightly around the green to one side or the other but allow for the other side to be open as

The natural greensite of the second hole at Prairie Dunes was a version of
one of Maxwell's template par three designs. (courtesy of Peter Herreid)

another approach. The two par threes from the original nine holes at Prairie Dunes are excellent examples of how Maxwell did this. The current second hole at the course plays from the tee to the green site placed into the side of a dune about 160 yards away. The greenside bunkers create a menacing look from the tee as the player realizes that he must hit the correct tee shot. The tenth at Prairie Dunes, labeled by Maxwell as the finest par three of his career, plays across an area of scrub to a green laid across the top of a rise with a steep falloff in the other direction. Oftentimes, Maxwell would lay out the par threes in differing angles, so the wind would affect each hole differently. The length of the holes did not necessarily matter to Maxwell as he often used his par threes as ways to bridge parts of the course together. He designed very few short par threes, those under the 150-yard range, and only a small number of long par threes over the 220-yard mark. Most of his par threes play as medium length shots that take the wind and the natural terrain into consideration. But one could possibly identify four particular styles of holes that appear in numerous cases on many Maxwell courses.

One of the most visibly pleasing and dramatic of these types was the drop shot par three. Maxwell would often lay out a drop shot style par three on his courses to connect one elevated green site to a hole that he wanted to lay out a short distance away. Very often these types of holes were modified versions of the famous Short hole at the National by CB Macdonald. The best examples of this hole are the seventeenth at Dornick Hills and the fourth at Twin Hills. Another favorite of Maxwell's was the modified Redan. This particular hole seemed to carry some special significance to Perry as he used this hole on several courses. Several excellent renditions exist including the third at Crystal Downs and the fifteenth at Old Town. The original eighth hole at Dornick Hills was also an excellent version of a Redan.

Perhaps the most overlooked were the holes where Maxwell used a natural water hazard to provide a diagonal carry. Many excellent examples exist including the eleventh at Oklahoma City and the twelfth at Oakwood. Perhaps the best example was the original eighth hole at Colonial. But the best of the bunch was often Maxwell's own version of the Short Hole. The Short hole, much like the Redan, was inspired by the National Golf Links and Maxwell would often use this in combination with one of the previously mentioned styles. The green would often have the front angled so that one side would be a slightly longer carry from the tee. The green would also contain spines in most cases that would divide the hole into smaller sections. Maxwell almost always designed this hole with five bunkers surrounding the green. The second at Prairie Dunes and the second at Old Town are prime examples of this template.

Perry's Par Fives

The par five portfolio of Maxwell on the other hand is much more diverse. His view on the number of par fives on a course also was diverse as the number varied from course to course. Maxwell did, more often than not, design only two par fives on his courses. Whether Perry thought this was ideal is difficult to determine. To take this a step further, in most cases, his par fives on these courses were similar in length. He would have two short par fives in the case of what was designed at Iowa State or design two very long par fives in the case of Nichols Hills, but they would offer completely different strategic options.

Most of Maxwell's par five holes can easily be classified among three different categories. The first category would be what most would call the reachable par five, or a par five that can be reached with the second shot by a large number of players. The most famous of these would be the seventeenth at Prairie Dunes. In most cases, Maxwell wanted the player to attempt to reach the hole and would often only use natural terrain as the main obstacle. He felt that if the player wanted to attempt the play he should have a good chance at birdie even if the shot was slightly off, but these holes often had one of the most severe green complexes on the course, thus making the player earn a birdie if it was to happen.

The second group would be what is termed the mid-length par five. This group of par fives often made use of a dominant natural feature of the course, such as a creek, lake or some other facet of the land. The ultimate example of this design thought is the famous "Cliff Hole" at Dornick Hills. Maxwell implemented the hole with a green atop a forty-foot stone faced cliff. The hole is the ultimate in intimidation. Many have tried to carry it to the green, but to only be rejected and end up with a large number on the card. Even laying up isn't the entire answer. Laying up in the right spot is the most difficult part of the hole. You must be close enough to get on top of the cliff, but not so close that your shot hits into the cliff on its upward flight. This grouping is probably the least used by Maxwell over his career, as he only seemed to use it in rare circumstances

The fifth hole at Oklahoma City

when he was presented with a unique landform.

The third group of three-shotters would be the long par fives. The quality of these holes is not up to the standard of the other two groups but some interesting holes have been laid out by Maxwell over the years, such as the fifth at the Oklahoma City course. The approach was to a blind second unless one carried their second over the mounding some fifty yards short of the green. For those that carried the hazard they were shown the punchbowl green setting that was vexing to all that tried an aerial approache to the green that runs slightly away from the player. Usually these holes would contain some movement in the terrain with the approach being contested with a tightly protected green testing what was usually a short pitch into the green. Maxwell often used a bunkering scheme around the hole with three bunkers protecting one side, while pinching in the opening to the green with one bunker on the front of the opposite side of the putting surface. This set up required the player to hit their second to the correct side of the hole to have a clear shot into the green.

Famous Four Pars

The heart and soul of most courses are the par four holes. These make up a majority of the holes on every course and often make or break the design. This

The seventh at Crystal Downs

was just as true in all of Maxwell's designs, but this was also where his genius truly was. Maxwell was able to imagine so many ways for players to approach a green from the tee and would often design holes to create many alternative routes to that end. He created holes that could be driven from the tee or require full wood shots from the fairway. The shorter range of these holes was a particular favorite.

Perhaps the best of these is the tenth hole at Twin Hills in Oklahoma City. The drive to the green is protected by four bunkers short of the green, but with just enough room between them to get on the green if the shot was hit accurately. The lay-up from the tee was often uncontested but the challenge on the approach was difficult due to the bunkering short of the hole only allowing an aerial approach. Every course designed by Maxwell featured at least one hole of this nature. The course at the Melrose featured numerous short par fours.

The short par four may have been a favorite, but the mid-length par four was perhaps the hole that Maxwell was his finest at designing. These holes often feature numerous options from the tee with the difficulty of the approach being defined by the wind and the pin location. The player could encounter a different hole each day of the week depending on these two factors and the proper approach to the green would be determined from the tee. The wrong decision or poor execution would almost always result in a bogey. The Old Town Club in Winston-Salem features perhaps the finest example of this type of hole. The seventh hole featured numerous options from the tee. The tee shot could land short of the cross bunkers for the weak hitter. The player who thought he might run into the bunkers could play to another route along the right of the hole and the daring golfer could attempt the 200 yard carry over the cross bunkers. The player who wanted to aim straight down the middle was forced to make a decision on the tee as a large tree separated the fairway into two distinct halves. The angle into the green was usually the best for the player who carried the bunkers. The valley short and the large hump in the green complicated the uphill approach. The shot from the right side must go directly over the bunkers short and deal with the hump. The eighth at Prairie Dunes was originally designed as a 385-yard hole with dunes along the left the entire length of the hole. The correct tee shot will try to hug the dunes with the wind blowing your shot towards native fescue rough and the slope of the fairway pushing you even farther that way. If the drive plays to the safe side, the approach is extremely difficult to the extremely well bunkered green.

The most famous holes that Maxwell designed are arguably long par fours. They were often difficult and many times would play directly into the wind or uphill. The twelfth hole at Southern Hills is perhaps the most celebrated hole in the history of Maxwell's career. A dogleg left with a fairway sloping away from the player is compounded by the fact that the correct approach to the green requires a controlled draw with the ball above your feet. A sectioned stream runs between the player and the green, which is located on a shelf and has bunkering on one side and a severe slope running away from the green and down into the stream.

151

The use of the highest point on the course to locate the clubhouse automatically creates the opportunity to create some of the most exciting views on the first tee. An elevated tee on the first hole often sets the tone for the entire course as the player looks over the course and views its full splendor. These holes have become somewhat of a trademark of many of the Maxwell courses. Often the opening tee of the course would not only be elevated but would be situated so as to take in a natural skyline, as with the first at Southern Hills or a view of mountains in the distance, as with Dornick Hills. This trend continued throughout the career of Maxwell even in his later designs.

Another by product of the location of the clubhouse and opening tee includes the creation of some terrific closing holes that run uphill and the most difficult of both nines on the course. In many occasions these holes would run parallel to each other and the ninth would be slightly shorter than the eighteenth. Again, Southern Hills provides a wonderful example of this as the eighteenth is the most difficult hole on the course and the somewhat shorter ninth runs parallel to it. The Old Town Club also provides a great example of this as the ninth and eighteenth dogleg in slightly opposite directions to seemingly converge at the green. Both holes are equally difficult with side hill lies producing dramatic approaches into undulating greens.

Perhaps though, Maxwell's favorite hole was a template hole of his own design. Early in his career, Maxwell found a site with a particular peculiarity that he found a unique cure for. He often located tees to give the player an open landing zone and allow the player to drive out to the end of a plateau. Once at the end of the plateau the player was provided with a dramatic view down to the green site. In some cases, like the seventh at Crystal Downs, the length of the hole allowed the player to possibly drive to the lower elevation short of the green. In others though, such as the fifth at Oakwood, the low area would have a hazard in the form of a creek flowing through it. Other noted versions of this same hole appeared at Hillcrest, Hardscrabble and a doglegged version at Dornick Hills.

Very often Maxwell is underrated as a strategic designer. A favorite technique to input strategic play into a particular hole was the use of a dogleg. Many of Maxwell's courses feature a large number of dogleg holes, which he referred to as "elbows." In most cases today, dogleg holes often go into the slope of the land. Maxwell used the standard style of hole but also constructed many doglegs so that the land actually flowed away from the player, thus creating a greater need for the player to control his shot in a particular fashion. This would also often create downhill, side hill, uphill and at times combinations of these lies for the approach shots into his contoured greens. Maxwell also made use of what is referred to as a reverse-dogleg, which "cons" the player into thinking the best play into the green, is over a hazard or to cut the corner of a dogleg hole. Another added effect that would be created due to his influence from Alister Mackenzie was to use the "Line of Charm" to fool a player. The 1st hole at the Old Town Club provides and excellent example of this. The player from the tee would think the preferred line would also be the safer line straight out from the tee, but the learned player will place the drive near the bunkers to get the better angle into the green.

Grass and Greenkeeping

Easily the most overlooked aspect of Maxwell's career was his expertise with the growing of grass in climates where it was not thought to be possible. Maxwell not only constructed the course at Dornick Hills, but until 1921 he was the unofficial greenkeeper of the course. He planted the grass that proliferated greens and fairways and made sure that it stayed healthy through the early years of the club. Maxwell was seen as an expert in the field and was invited to speak to the United States Golf Association Green Section on January 5, 1924.

Maxwell began his study before he even built his course at Dornick Hills. He originally toyed with the idea of sand greens like those that were in north Texas, but felt the game was lacking. He then made a study tour of courses in the South from Houston, New Orleans, Atlanta and in Florida and determined that he could only use Bermuda grass in Ardmore. He had difficulty at first until he realized that the key to growing grass in any region was the selection of the right strain.

During his study he also found the best way to propagate Bermuda was via the vegetative method, by taking roots from one location and transplanting them to another. This was before seeding was a real possibility. Even the USGA was amazed that he was able to grow anything in Ardmore. They responded in a letter to Maxwell, "We are afraid you are a little too far south for bluegrass and too far north for Bermuda."[58] Maxwell himself made the assertion that they "were between the devil and the deep blue sea."[59] After the propagation method was determined, the use of creeping grasses like Bermuda was complimented with a healthy mixture of manure and sandy loan with a clay subsoil.

The fact that Maxwell studied so thoroughly the details of greenkeeping before his attempt at golf course design and construction was a key reason for his success. He had the experience of knowing what it would take to maintain a course after the construction and what facets of a design would be most affordable to construct or maintain and help the clubs to stay within their respective budgets and was a large factor in his style of design.

The style of Maxwell in this day and age of "rape and shape," movement of millions of cubic feet and creating the golf course would obviously be different. Would he survive today? Without a doubt. Maxwell was an excellent salesman and would often get a job when it was thought impossible. He knew what to say to clients. He could build an excellent course with a limited budget, unlike the multi-million dollar monstrosities created today. Would he be at the top of the profession? That is debatable. He may have created a niche for himself along with names like Tom Doak, Coore and Crenshaw and Gil Hanse. But something suggests in this day and age where golf gets more expensive and "Country Clubs

153

for a day" are the fad that Maxwell would have delighted in being a daily fee public golf course designer with the simple man in mind. His skills and philosophy would have been exactly what would be needed to build fine municipal courses. The end of his career saw him go more and more towards this as he probably felt this was what would be necessary to grow the game, something Perry always had at the core of his thoughts about the game he grew to love.

Aerial of Pennsylvania Golf Club after the course was abandoned circa 1938
(courtesy of National Archives)

The Masterpieces of Maxwell

The career of Perry Maxwell spanned over thirty years and he designed and laid out reportedly seventy courses over that span. He was the dominant architect in the Southwest United States. Many of his designs were of a superior quality. The following pages run through the top tier of the courses that encompassed the career. The narrative does not go into detail on every design by Perry but only those that deserve special recognition. The complete list of his work as known today is provided in an Appendix following this section.

The career of Perry Maxwell did not have one distinguishable look or style. His first and last designs featured a design methodology that was similar to that of Charles Blair Macdonald and the National School of Design. Much of his early work in Oklahoma featured a simple style that was very unimposing on the terrain. It appeared that Maxwell returned to this style later in his career when he focused again on Oklahoma and Texas after World War II. Then there was a brief period where Perry was much more artistic in his design, some of this was undoubtedly from the influence of Alister Mackenzie. The courses that are reviewed in this portion of the text are a cross-section of all these periods and styles and should provide a clear view of the morphing style of Maxwell from one era to another.

Though he has often gone mostly unnoticed as a designer by many in the sport, his career spanned more years than many and produced as many quality layouts as all but perhaps the most notable names of Ross, Mackenzie and Colt. His portfolio features some of the greatest courses in the country with three courses in the top twenty in most national rankings and another course that is often on the list as well. He also has significant layouts that are of almost equal value littered throughout Oklahoma and the rest of the country. But the course that Maxwell would always have an affinity towards above any other was the one that he designed in his own backyard and that is the course where we will begin the trek through the masterpieces of Perry Maxwell, his own beloved Dornick Hills.

Dornick Hills Country Club
(1914-1923, 1936) Ardmore, Oklahoma

The course at Dornick Hills was not only the first design by Maxwell, but is was perhaps his most prized. He continued to tinker with the design for twenty years as he lived adjacent to the course on the southwest corner of the original plot of land the course was laid out on. As mentioned earlier the course was originally a four-hole design that was laid out in 1914 that was without bunkers. After taking a tour of golf courses in the Southeast United States, Maxwell began to implement changes to the course eventually creating a complete nine-hole course which necessitated the elimination of the original fourth hole. This first nine holes had a very distinct flavor that resembled many of the designs of Charles Blair Macdonald. After the death of his wife, Maxwell again went on a study tour. This time to Scotland where he studied courses such St. Andrews. When he returned he promptly laid out a new nine hole design which had a considerably different flavor than the original nine holes which incorporated untried design concepts that Maxwell would later use as his own template holes in his career.

For the first effort by Maxwell, Dornick Hills was a bold design that was unlike any other in the Southwest. It featured large and intimidating hazards but also provided ample room for the less skilled player to make their way around the course. The use of grass greens and canted fairways were new to the players of the region as well. The use of the canted greens with Bermuda grass was to help facilitate surface drainage and to deal with the extreme Oklahoma heat. Maxwell also perfectly routed the course in and out of the valley that featured the natural creek and pond on the property. He also made excellent use of the cliff on the northern edge of the property and the rise at the southern edge of the site. Maxwell also routed holes to run along the edges of the rises and created canted fairways unlike anything else seen on the flat courses of Oklahoma. Dornick Hills was a pet project to Perry and his heart was in the design and it can tell when someone reviews the course in detail.

Of all his courses, Dornick Hills has perhaps the greatest variety in hole design and is one of the best routings he ever laid out with the use of the highest points on the property and the use of the creek on many holes as a parallel hazard. The original set of par three holes that Maxwell laid out at Dornick Hills was one of the strongest that he ever constructed as they tested different skills and were quite different in look and play. Most of Maxwell's par threes fell into a group of template holes as mentioned in the previous chapter on design tenets. Many of these templates were originally conceived on the terrain of Dornick Hills. As with the par threes, the two-shot holes on the course were a combination of the templates of Macdonald and the newly devised template holes by Maxwell that would be used throughout his career. The diversity of the holes show the thoughts of Maxwell and that he could design a hole of any length and was willing to use the terrain as it was presented to him. Maxwell often only designed a pair of three shot holes on his courses. One was often reachable in two and the other involved some natural hazard which made it a true par five in design. Perhaps the best two he ever designed were on this very first course of his career.

Hole One – 400 yards

The original first hole has been eliminated from the current routing due to the alterations made by Black and Nugent. The original tee gave an elevated view of the first fairway which had two distinct options on the tee. The player could decide to try and hit down into a valley and have a blind approach up the hill to a skyline green or to lay back off of the tee and have a visible, but difficult shot into the green with a long iron. The green was protected by a lone bunker on the back side and sloped from back to front. A practice green remains today at the far end of the practice range and it can easily been seen how difficult an opening hole this was.

In the renovation that altered the front nine, the tee was moved slightly forward by about twenty yards and the greensite was placed adjacent to the natural pond that protected the second hole.

Maxwell later would add a bunker to the front left of the green to provide further protection. One of the overlooked elements to the hole was the carry hazard that Perry placed short of the fairway. This was more than likely something that he picked up in his travels and having seen several Donald Ross courses in the Southeastern United States.

The first at Dornick Hills

Hole Two – 175 yards

The second hole at Dornick Hills was perhaps the most beautiful of the group. It featured a diagonal tee shot over a natural pond to a green that jutted

157

into the water. The bunkering by Maxwell was a generous buffer for those that were just short of the green. The difficulty of the green grew as the pin placement went further to the right. The hole was eliminated in the renovation to the front nine as the green was moved further to the left and the tee moved to create a hole that was all carry to the green over the pond. This was one of the great losses on the course. The original tee remains today with two trees between it and the green. One can easily imagine the difficulty of the hole from this angle and can also envision hitting a clear shot to the green if these trees were removed.

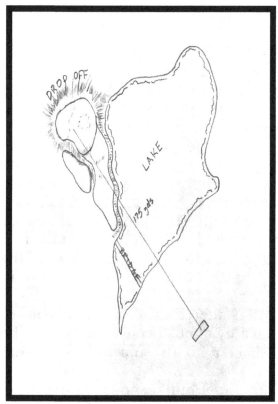

Hole Three – 425 yards

The third is a dogleg that runs at the base of a hill and provided great danger on the approach as Maxwell laid out the hole to have a fallaway green that would send approaches that were too strong into the creek behind. The green was slightly moved and the bunkering changed in the first massive redesign on the course. The landing zone for the drive featured a bottleneck fairway that was most accepting of a running draw to use the slight slope off of the hill. The bunkering on the hole was of little notice for those in the fairway, but was of obvious concern for those who left their approach short. Perry left the area directly in front of the green open allowing anyone to play short and bounce their approach into the green and make use of the natural flow into the putting surface.

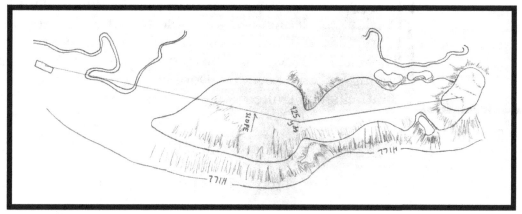

The second and third holes at Dornick Hills

158

Hole Four – 190 yards

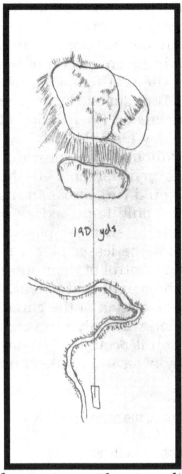

No hole at Dornick Hills is as maligned as the fourth. This is mostly with the disdain that elevated greens on par threes receive today. There is some fascination with being able to see one's approach hitting on the green. But those fixated with this fail to see the wonderful feeling of anticipation as one walks up a hill to see the final results of a well-struck shot to a skyline style green as was constructed at Dornick Hills. The hole itself was originally constructed to be a simple shot up the hill to a skyline green. Those that were just short were given some relief as a bunker was built into the slope to prevent balls from rolling all the way back down the hill. The green originally sloped slightly back towards the tee. Today the bunker in front has been eliminated and two traps have been added that flank the green and the green is almost two-tier in design.

Unlike most of the course, the fourth hole was most receptive to an aerial shot that was a well struck and reached the target. Anything short would roll back down the hill to the large bunker built into the hillside. Thankfully, Maxwell constructed a large green that could receive almost any shot that cleared the rise. The beauty of the Maxwell's routing is revealed with this hole as the player was easily taken down to the lowest spot on the front nine without realizing how much they had traveled downhill from the first tee. The shot up the hill on the fourth reveals the true elevation change that has gracefully occurred on the prior three adventures. Maxwell also used the fourth to return to an elevated green and tee location, a recurring trait throughout the back nine holes.

Hole Five – 390 yards

Maxwell was quick to adopt template holes in his career and the fifth at Dornick Hills is a prime example of one. The drive is out to a plateau that then provides an elevated view down to the green that is perched perilously close to a hazard. In this case the creek runs behind the green and a bunker was built fronting the green. So a solid pitch or short iron was necessary from the fairly flat lie. Maxwell also gave the player the option to try and cut off as much as possible by creating a dogleg. The hole has been mitigated by technology and tree growth. There are no real options for the average player as trees protect the inside of the

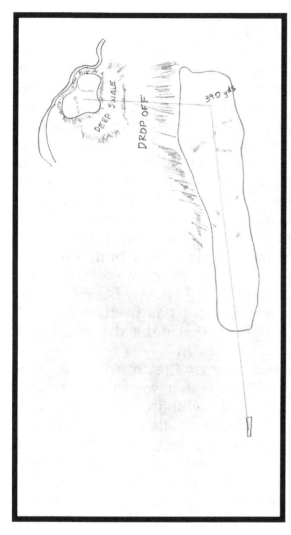

dogleg. Technology though has made it so that today's Herculean drives can clear all the drives and attempt to drive the green.

This was the original version of this hole that Maxwell would use on several of his designs and is possibly the first template hole of his own design. Thought it lacks the catchy name of the Redan or Eden holes of his mentor, it was an easy formula to follow. Also the terrain of Oklahoma often provided the chance to use this style of hole in the routings that Maxwell would run across in his life. Today the hole has only improved as it plays as a tempting hole to stronger players and provides a chance for the lesser player to still compete if they have control of their short game and do not have the length that is found all to often in the modern version of the game. The original plateau green was only protected by the precarious position it occupied. Today the green is protected by two sand bunkers on the left and back right.

Left: The fifth hole at Dornick, the original Maxwell template hole
Previous: The uphill fourth hole

Hole Six – 510 yards

The only par five on the front nine holes was the sixth. Though most can attempt to reach the green in two, it would be a bold and careless move. With out of bounds on the right and a creek to the left, the need to hit the tee shot into the correct position is most important. The sixth was perhaps the most strategic hole on the course, with three different paths to the green. The player that wanted to lay back could do so, and on their second clear the waste area without much challenge but still be faced with a delicate short approach into the green. Another option was to go to the left side and still play long enough that an approach to the green on the second was possible, but had to carry the creek and the swale short of the green. The last option would be to try to stay in the strip of fairway that ran along the side of the waste hazard. This would set up a much simpler approach into the green and could provide an easy shot at birdie.

The strategy of the hole provided so many different paths of attack it was truly and stellar hole in design. In some ways it bore a strong resemblance to a famous hole design that was used by Charles Blair Macdonald at his much acclaimed Lido design. Macdonald had developed a hole concept that he called the greatest three shot hole design in history. It was named the Channel hole due to the use of a waterway that divided the hole and provided an island to land an approach on and have much shorter shot into the putting surface with the waterway crossing again in front of the green complex. Though Maxwell lacked the waterway, he did have some naturally occurring swales on the sixth hole that provided similar danger. Instead of an island he used a thin strip of landing area that was pinched by the hill on the right and the deep hazard on the left hand side. Anyone able to keep their ball in this region was able to attempt the carry to the green over the swale and bunker short of the green. Those that played to the wider left side of the fairway were only allowed to lay up and have a testing pitch into the steeply sloped putting surface. This was an excellent adaptation of the Channel hole concept by Maxwell in a circumstance that did not have the obvious look for such a hole.

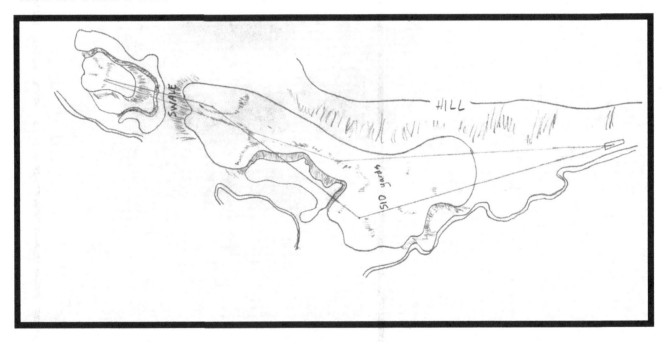

Though not having all the usual trademarks of the famed Channel hole Maxwell created a reasonable replica in the form of the sixth at Dornick Hills.

Hole Seven – 360 yards

The seventh hole was laid out at the base of the hill where the Maxwell Cemetary was placed. The drive is semi-blind over the crest of a hill with a push-up style putting surface. The best part of the hole was the wonderful hazard that was laid out around the green and was a hazard that impacted the tee shot on the left side of the hole. The hazard was eliminated in the first renovation of the course. Other than the change to the hazard the hole is very much like what Maxwell laid out. The hole is perhaps the least notable on the front nine, but with the technology of the game in this era it has now become a testing short par four with a steeply sloping hill. With the cemetery overlooking the hole, it is best perhaps that so little has been done to the hole. The club would probably not like to awake the ghosts of Maxwell by stirring with the land right below his resting place.

The slope from the crest down to the green creates a testing pitch into the green that slopes over six feet from back to front. Anyone going long has no chance of recovery due to the pond behind the green. This just makes the agony quick, but the original bunker prolonged the pain for the player as their next shot was from a deep pit that was unforgiving.

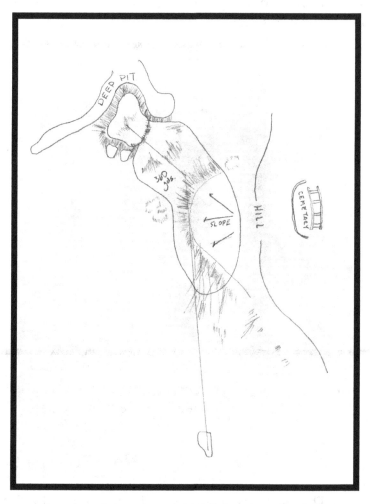

Drawing of the seventh highlights the role of the
bunkering behind the green.

Hole Eight – 225 yards

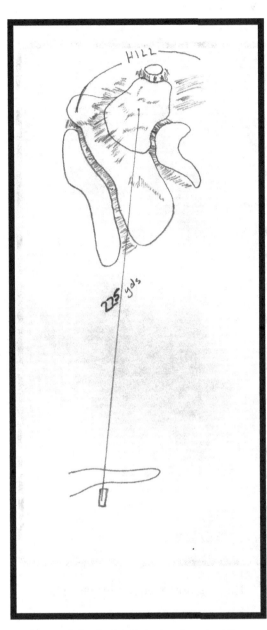

The original eighth hole showing the impact of the large waste bunker short of the green on the longest par three at Dornick Hills

The difficult 8th hole has been shortened from the original length of roughly 225 yards. The bunkering on the hole has also been drastically changed and the terrain of the hole has been altered beyond recognition. The original hole was constructed as a long version of the Redan hole only running from left to right. A bunker ran almost forty yards in length as a carry hazard from the tee. The green also sloped from the front left to the back right side of the green with another bunker protecting this right side of the green. Maxwell designed the hole to have the ideal landing spot just beyond the furthest tip of the carry hazard. For those that didn't want to challenge the hazards and bail out to the left, the slope of the green made many pitches difficult to stop near the hole. The difficulty of the hole would have been truly monumental during the era it was laid out. It also took a conceptual copy by Charles Blair Macdonald and altered it for a new hole that did not fit directly into the "Redan" template that he preferred.

Strategy was also in play on the hole. A player could lay up in the front half of the fairway and have a somewhat easy chip onto the putting surface that would allow him to even roll the ball to the back right corner of the green. The hole allowed for the daring shot and the conservative shot, with the reward being their for the best executed plan.

This was the first course that Maxwell would design this style of hole and it would become one of his favorites over the years. Many similar holes would be laid out throughout Oklahoma and also one would appear at Old Town in North Carolina. It was truly the beast of his template holes. The hole at Dornick Hills has since been cut down in length by forty yards and the green has been tempered. This was Maxwell's first great par three design.

Hole Nine – 410 yards

Perhaps the best remaining example of Maxwell's design is the wonderful 9th hole. The drive is uphill to a hog's back fairway that has severe penalties if you fall off of the fairway. Any shot to the right and the left create a much more difficult approach into the angled green. The wonderful green also reflects some excellent Maxwell "Rolls" that create a difficult putt from any location. Former University of Oklahoma golfer, Matt Cohn, describes the hole in the following manner, "This is a classic Maxwell hole. Its 406 yards are uphill and into the wind, making it play like 440 or more. The hole seems to steer players right of the fairway, from where a player will not have a shot at the green. One of the hole's defenses is the green, which slopes steeply back to front (except just over the front-right bunker, where a small mound makes back pin positions even less accessible!) Any putt on this green can cause trouble, and up-and-downs from long or left are almost impossible."

From the tee the player sees the uphill nature of the hole and the pattern that Maxwell would use throughout his career. The best example of Maxwell's reverse-dogleg is also perhaps in the construction of this hole. The player that hangs to the right side of the fairway and does not attempt to cut some of the length off of the hole is rewarded with a much better angle into the green and perhaps a flatter lie as they would be atop the hog's back feature in the fairway. Also from the tee, the player does not see the one thing that has changed drastically since the original layout, the bunkers up by the green.

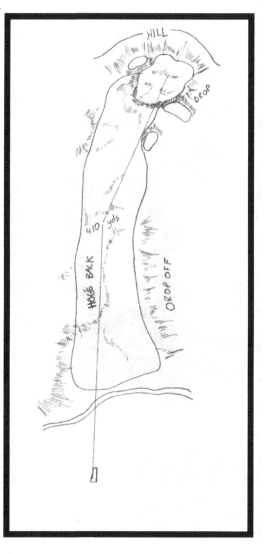

The original layout of the ninth hole

The bunker configuration that Maxwell laid out provided a much more open front of the green and still provided someone on the right a chance to get on the green surface. Today the bunkering almost makes that impossible and only provides a narrow opening in the front of the green that is partially blocked by a bunker short of the green on the left. As with much of the course, the ninth is a microcosm of what has happened to the course.

164

Hole Ten – 283 yards

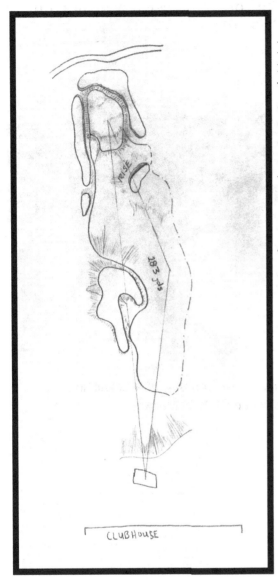

Maxwell perched the tee of the tenth hole on a highly elevated spot overlooking the immense rolling terrain of Primrose Hill. The view was inspiring. The player could see almost the entire site with only minor disruption from trees along the creek. The cliff on the other side of the property and the bluff overlooking the back corner provided excellent vistas in the distance. The green was not in sight of the player as it was placed short of the creek that marked the base of the valley and behind a rise on the left side of the fairway. The width of the fairway was "immeasurable" as described in a newspaper article from the period which allowed the player to choose their preferred line from the tee. Despite this width, the fairway still contained two well-placed hazards. Perry placed a carry bunker on the left hand side to protect the best angle into the push-up green complex. The player that attempted this route was rewarded with a much easier approach to a green. Maxwell placed the other bunker into the face of a slight rise fifty yards short of the green. The player that stayed to the safe side was given a testing approach into the green and also had to deal with the hazards around the green. There was a bunker that ran completely around the green complex. The rough edging of the bunkers seemed to fit nicely with the rough terrain and steep walls ensured that any recovery was to be a challenge. The putting surface was somewhat flat but did have a slope from front to back with rolls in it that resembled waves.

The green was moved by Maxwell in 1936 to the other side of the creek. This move was made simply out of response of seeing players compete at the 1935 PGA Championship in Oklahoma City at his own Twin Hills. He felt this would increase the difficulty of the course for the top players of the era. The green was later rebuilt to the left of that location by Jeff Brauer. Restoring the original carry hazard on the left and the original greensite would make the hole much more interesting. The hole was the first template style hole that Maxwell would ever lay out. The tenth was a version of the "Sahara" hole created by Charles Blair

165

Macdonald. The basis of the hole was to attempt the carry of a vast hazard to a blind green beyond or lay up into the visible portion of the fairway and have a much more difficult approach into the green. This original design was much more unique than anything that existed this side of St. Louis.

Above: Original photo of the tenth hole from the tee circa 1914 (courtesy of Max Williamson)
Previous: Layout of the first hole ever designed by Perry Maxwell

Hole Eleven – 400 yards

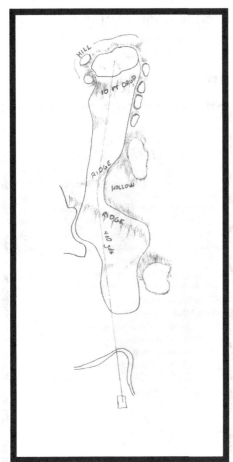

The original second hole and current eleventh was much more strategic in nature than its current version. The best approach to the green was from the left side, which was protected by a bunker that separated the original first and second holes. Also adding to the challenge of getting to the preferred landing zone were two ridges that forced the terrain in opposite directions. Landing between the ridges was the key to having a shot into the green that did not have to avoid the bunkers on the right side of the hole. The bunkers ran along the right side of the hole all the way to the putting surface in a stair-step manner. The original bunkers would have been grass bunkers. Early photos of the course do not show sand bunkers from the tee. They were later converted to sand by Maxwell. The player had to hit an approach shot uphill to the green perched precariously atop the knoll and stuck between the first and third tee boxes. The lesser player was given the chance to lay up, as the area below the

Photo of the eleventh hole circa 1914 (courtesy of Dora Horn)
and to the left is the hole layout from the original design.

167

putting surface was completely open. The second featured a larger green than the current version: it was almost twice the current size but it sloped considerably more from back to front. The green at that time featured a ridge running through the middle of the green, creating two distinct sides.

Hole Twelve – 420 yards

With the design of the twelfth hole on his course, Maxwell again went back to his study of the National Golf Links. This time he built a replica of the famous bottle hole. The bottle hole concept is derived from a famous hole at the Sunningdale Golf Club in England. The player is provided two distinct alternatives from the tee, one of which often requires a much riskier shot, but then provides a much simpler approach to the hole. Perry's version was somewhat tame in comparison to the Macdonald beauty, but it had all the key elements. There were two distinct fairways, with the one having the preferred angle on a slightly lower level than the other. The player would either have to use the terrain to get the ball to this lower level on the right or carry it over two bunkers on that side. The deterrent on the left side of the fairway was a tree fifty yards short of the green. This was the first indication of the impact Maxwell thought trees could have in the design of his holes. The alternative fairway could be reached with a daring carry over two bunkers on the right hand side while also being protected by the steep slope that split the fairways. The green was also protected by a swale short of the green and had a false front much like Macdonald's version. For those who went right of the green, there was a vast waste bunker that made saving par difficult, as the green sloped away from the hazard. The preferred line into the green

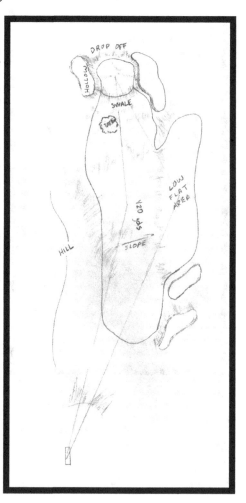

The twelfth hole by Maxwell

was made much simpler when Maxwell moved the tee boxes forward in 1936. The tee boxes were also lowered and this created a semi-blind tee shot. This, along with the lack of an irrigation system probably led to the eventual demise of the double fairway; as it was seen as unnecessary with the shorter hole and with the blind drive the player would not see the options from the tee.

Due to maintenance practices the right side of the fairway has been largely eliminated making the tree the primary focus of the hole. This was the first hole that Maxwell laid out with a canted fairway. This was also the first hole that Maxwell laid out that would draw the chagrin of many players. The natural slope of the fairway creates a lie where the tendency is to fade the ball, but the player must play a draw around the large tree.

Early construction photos of Dornick Hills. The top photo is of the twelfth hole during construction And the bottom is from the site of the clubhouse. The man standing in the photo is Perry Maxwell overseeing the work going on down the hill in the previous photo. (courtesy of Dora Horn)

Hole Thirteen – 445 yards

The original four-hole course featured another excellent hole of roughly 400 yards. From the description by Dr. Watson and the layout at the time of the 1926 design, it can be surmised what the hole was like. The tee was positioned so the hole would play across and along the creek all the way to a green location just west of the second tee. Two carry bunkers provided the hazard in getting the preferred line into the green; this was away from the natural line the player would choose at the tee, which was along the creek. The player then had to deal with the hazards surrounding the green. On the right was the creek and to the left was a deep bunker or swale. These two made for a demanding approach. This hole was eliminated when the course was expanded to nine holes. The current turf and tree nursery is near the location of the original green.

With the first expansion of Dornick Hills, Maxwell created his own version of the Road Hole on the long par four thirteenth that featured a tee shot out to the fairway from the same tee location but along the western boundary of the property. The fairway on this hole was shared with the fifteenth and sixteenth holes and was actually split by small hills and bumps created by Maxwell during the construction of the holes. The approach was very difficult as the left side of the green was protected by a deep pot bunker and the right side was protected by two long bunkers that were created to symbolize the famous Road at St. Andrews. The green was also well-defended as the slope of the green ran almost six feet from back to front and three significant tiers. With the expansion of the course, Maxwell also rebuilt the first three greens on the course to have grass greens. The use of a bermuda strain of grass that could sustain the hot summers in Oklahoma.

The natural slope of the land in this case was used in this case to help the player place their tee shot on the correct side of the fairway. The narrow opening to the green was best attacked from the right side of the fairway and the player that shaped their shot accordingly had the best chance of staying on this half of the landing zone. But the player that hit an inaccurate approach would be penalized heavily as all the remaining hazards were along the right side, with the exception of the pot bunker short and the bunker placed directly behind.

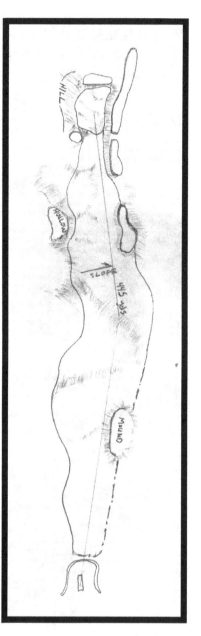

Maxwell's ode to the Road Hole at Dornick Hills.

170

Hole Fourteen – 275 yards

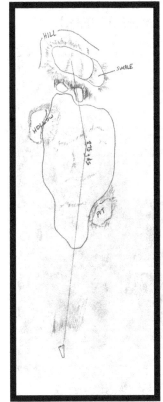

The shortest par four followed the longest and was a great hole that was amply protected by deep hazards short of the green and was also well defended by a steeply sloping green. It gives the longer player a true advantage, but they must execute their shot perfectly or they will be in a worse position than the player that lays up in the fairway. This was Maxwell's version of the "Knoll" hole where he had deep hazards short of the green that was perched on a rise.

Width was the key component of the hole as the fairway was almost forty strides across. The deep bunkers in the face of the hill were a force to be reckoned with if any approaches lack the strength to go up the hill. The best angle into the green was from the right side as the player would also be able to hit into the slope of the green and possibly stop their shot before going to far beyond the hole and be faced with a difficult down hill putt that could easily end up in the swale off the right side of the putting surface. The steep putting surface was altered in the renovations by Jeff Brauer and perhaps for the better as the modern green speeds would make this hole impossible for almost anyone to play unless they could defy gravity.

Hole Fifteen – 400 yards

By this point in the routing the player was put onto the dominant feature of the southern edge of the property. A steep forty foot cliff provides a dramatic elevated tee that is used first on the fifteenth hole. Another prototype hole for Perry Maxwell was the fallaway hole which featured a green that sloped significantly from front to back and away from the player. The 15th was such a hole. The large shared fairway was pinched by bunkers on the left side. The approach to the green was what would truly test the mettle of any player. Short of the green was a swale on the right side accompanied by a mound on that

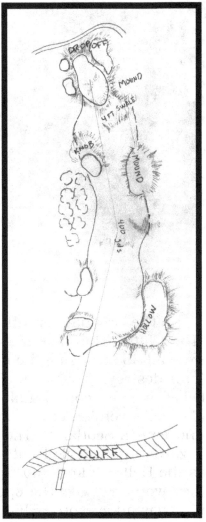

Left: Hole 14 drawing
Above: Hole 15 drawing

side. This mound would provide the impetus for the dominant slope of the green as it would slope away from the player. Maxwell also provided the player some reprieve with bunkers that would keep balls from going into the creek behind.

Photo of the famous Cliff hole (courtesy of Jerry Westheimer)

Hole Sixteen – 530 yards

The original seventh hole, the most famous at Dornick Hills, is known as "The Cliff." This hole more than any other signifies what Perry Maxwell designs were all about: using the natural features of the land to make a golf course rather than destroying what is already there. The hole is further testimony to Perry's belief in the conceptual copy theory of Macdonald. This hole represented Maxwell's version of the Long hole. The Long hole is the famous 14th hole at St. Andrews in Scotland. The sheer length of the hole made it difficult but the use of hazards in strategic locations added to the peril, especially the hazard referred to as the Hell Bunker. Most players would object to a modern hole like this because they wouldn't have the opportunity to get home in two shots, or that the granite wall was an eyesore. That would be our loss, as this is one of the truly great par-five holes by Maxwell. The hole plays at 532 yards from the tips, and the green can only be reached in two with a tailwind. The rough and the trees to the right are the primary danger, but the key to this hole is where you put your second shot. The green sits atop a forty-foot cliff and is extremely difficult to hold. It was also one of the more insidious on the course: it featured three mounds and ridges

172

that dominated the contours of the green, making putting an adventure if the player ends up in the wrong portion of the green. There is no safe spot if you need to bail out on the approach, as out of bounds is behind and to the left, and short is the rock face. The original hole layout also featured some bunkering that would add much interest to the hole again, if not for the abundance of trees around the hole. This bunkering seems to have been set up to force a player to make a decision on the second shot. If they laid up they would have a long approach into the narrow green that may not stay aloft long enough to clear the rock wall. If they tried to get as close as possible to the green, they would have to get the ball up quickly and have a delicate touch to stay on the green. Maxwell also presented another option with the shared fairway to the left side that allowed the player to

have a short iron approach into the green but from an angle that allowed the player to use the entire length of the green. From one side to the other this portion of the fairway would have been almost eighty yards wide. Not only was this hole as natural in appearance as Maxwell could ever hope, but it presented the player with multiple options due to the width of the fairway and the excellent use of hazards. Though the hole was wide Maxwell also designed it to have penalties for the player who strayed too far to the left of the conservative line, as he designed many ripples in the terrain that created uneven lies and only added to the frustration of the player who was errant off of the tee.

Hole Seventeen – 150 yards

The last one-shot hole, the 17th and the only one on the original nine holes was a fearful examination of the players swing and his courage. The elevated tee called for the player to hit a shot into the Oklahoma winds and play against the prevailing breeze. It also required the player to navigate around the hazards, including the deep pit to the short left side of the green. The pit itself was about six feet in depth and had a wood wall to support the green. The green was a smaller version of the "Short Hole" green found at National Golf Links and had very clear undulations that split the green into three distinct portions. The hole has been severely altered overtime with the most recent changes being a reconstruction of the green and the

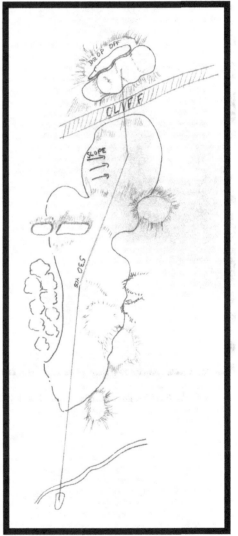

Drawing of sixteenth hole

173

elimination of the bunkers on the left side with a retention pond.

The green and bunker complex was also the basis for one of Maxwell's most used templates. There were several version of the green contouring used throughout his career where he would divide the putting surface into three distinct sections using ridges and slope. The bunker complex was also similar to what he would later do throughout his career. Instead of having the one long bunker on the left side he would split it into two hazards and add one more to the right, thus surrounding the putting surface. Other versions of the hole would be found in the form of the second at Prairie Dunes and the second at the Old Town Club.

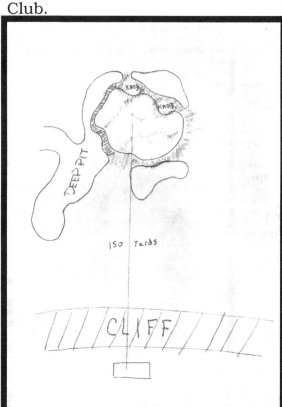

Drawing of original Dornick Hills
Short Hole

Hole Eighteen – 380 yards

The typical Maxwell finishing hole is an uphill par four. Dornick Hills was the first of these. The tee shot is the most difficult part of the hole. It runs dramatically uphill to a fairway that almost seems to be a staircase. The fairway in the original design, sharing the fairway with the first hole, contained a noticeable hazard. Anyone who strayed too far to the right side would roll down the banking into the first fairway and have a much more difficult approach from a lie with the ball below their feet; but the left side of the fairway was a challenge to reach from the tee, as a large hazard protected that side. The green itself was a three-tiered monster. It was protected on the left side by two bunkers and was extremely large and sloped steeply from back to front. The most difficult pin position was the one tucked behind the bunker protecting the front of the green. The design of the hole gave the player an awkward lie that would induce a particular shot, such as a fade, into a green that really preferred the opposite shot, in this case a draw.

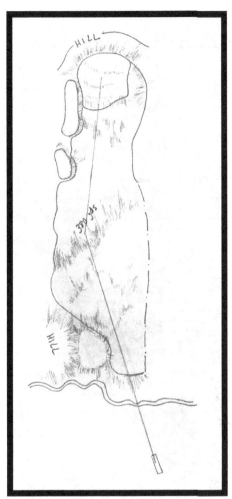

It is easy to see the innovation and bold character that Maxwell put into his initial design. The course would go decades with only the slight tweaking that Maxwell himself would make. Unfortunately, some of his work has been altered beyond recognition. The natural routing of the course from one elevated section to the other and back again with the winding creek serving as a dividing point, worked wonderfully to provide an ideal setting for Maxwell to implement his style of routing. Though it was early in his career, there were few mistakes that were evident. The only one being that he may have used the creek differently if he had been further along in his career when he created the course on his property. The amount of inspiration from the National Golf Links is evident throughout the course and provides excellent proof that Maxwell's early style evolved from that of Charles Blair Macdonald. He would provide one of the best examples of the National School of Design in history, and in his own backyard.

Drawing and photo of the final hole at Dornick Hills with the clubhouse in the background (courtesy of Jerry Westheimer)

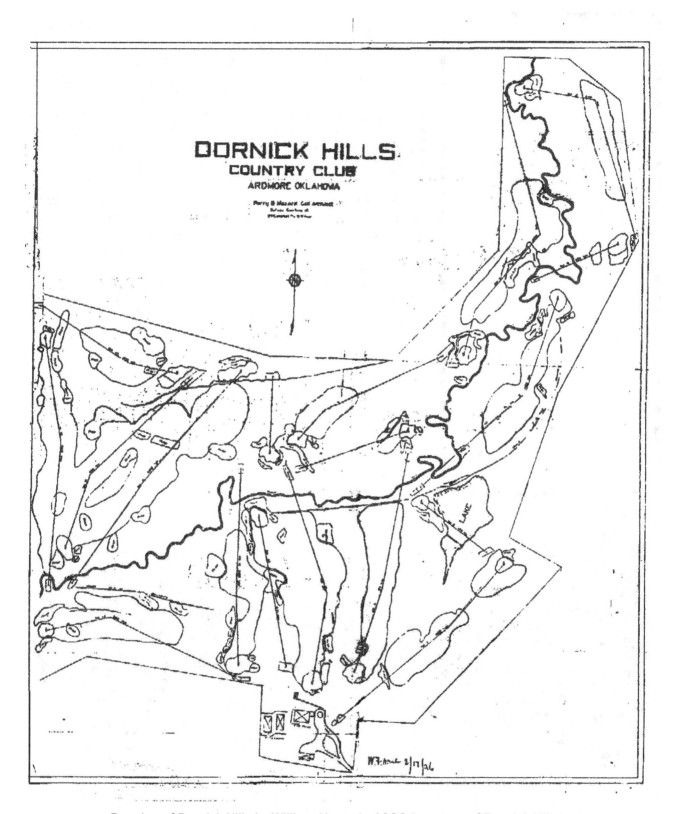

Drawing of Dornick Hills by William Hume in 1926 (courtesy of Dornick Hills)

Twin Hills Country Club
(1919-1923, 1935) Oklahoma City, Oklahoma

Twin Hills was the first contracted job by Maxwell. With the design, Maxwell was fairly conservative in the layout of the course. The style of the design was a vast contrast with Dornick Hills and lacked many of the large bunkers at his home course in Ardmore. The design has a typical country club feel to it with a nicely compact design on a rectangular plot. But the pedigree of the course is matched only by a few west of the Mississippi. The club hosted a major championship in the form of the 1935 PGA Championship. Just prior to the championship Maxwell came back to Twin Hills to make some minor changes to the design. During the competition he carefully watched the competitors to make note of how they played the course. He would use this knowledge later in his career to layout a true championship course in Tulsa that would become the famous Southern Hills.

The routing of the course, though only the second of his career, was perhaps the best in his portfolio. Twin Hills does not have design traits that stick out at first glance. But when one looks at the individual holes, it is obvious Maxwell had a touch of genius at this early stage of his career. The simple designs used mostly simply tilted greens to provide the best defense on a course that has mostly subtle terrain movement. As with the clay soil in Ardmore, the greens at Twin Hills needed to have sufficient slope to provide surface drainage for water runoff. The most dramatic thing about the course is the way that Maxwell laid out the course on the rectangular plot with several holes returning to the clubhouse as if it were the axis on a wheel. Five holes finish near the clubhouse and provide many opportunities for the player to play a short round late in the day. The course was laid out on an area that was originally heavily wooded and required the clearing of many trees. This alone makes it even more amazing that there is only one tree in the line of play on the entire course. A discussion of the course is presented by grouping the holes together based on their par orientation. The analysis will begin with the one-shot hole variety.

177

Par Threes

The one shot holes at Twin Hills were of a different nature than their predecessors in Ardmore and used a vastly different terrain. Basic single bunkers aligned on one side of the green created preferred angles into the holes and force the player to either shape their shots correctly or have aerial shots that land softly on the narrow, but wide greens. The first such hole presented to the player is Twin Hills' own version of the Cliff Hole in the form of the drop shot par three fourth. The green was placed at the top of a knoll with the shot coming from the top of another hill about 140 yards away. The slope of the green and one bunker in the front of the green and one in the back left corner. The open space around the hole makes the shot very susceptible to the wind. Even today the hole, in spite of its length, still presents a stern test of the short game of any player. The shot can require any number of clubs from the tee depending on the force of the wind and the direction.

The longish seventh is another hole that Maxwell laid out without moving any terrain. The seventh green was placed at the base of the hill that the eighth and fourth tees occupy. The creek to the right does not come into play, but the

The view of the seventh from the tee shows the slight slope of the terrain.
(courtesy of Twin Hills)

slope of the green is slightly away from the player with a bunker protecting the left side of the green. This is also the only hole on the front nine that does not have a significant change in elevation from tee to green. It is fine hole that is sandwiched between two of the best on the course.

The best par three on the course, the eleventh features a potato chip style green with a bunker on the front left. The tee shot is again across a valley, but is slightly uphill from the tee and about forty yards longer than the fourth. Even Alister Mackenzie was impressed with the hole. A simple tee shot if one has the ability to stop it quickly on the green and the nerve to carry the ball over the bunker on any flags cut on the right side of the putting surface. The green today is almost identical to the original design with the added difficulty coming in the form of a sand bunker in front of the right side of the putting surface. The front half of the green was slightly lower and served as a collection spot of shots that could not stay on the back half of the green due to backspin or not having enough strength to reach the higher tier. The number of trees surrounding the hole also added to the tight feel of the tee shot. The last par four on the course, hole fourteen, was somewhat less dramatic than the others but is well protected with a multiple of bunkers surrounding the green tightly.

Above: View of the fine eleventh hole from the tee
(courtesy of Twin Hills)

179

Par Fives

Maxwell again laid out the course with a variety of three shot holes. Holes five and thirteen are possibly reachable in two shots while the second and sixteenth require three solid strikes of the ball. The second hole runs along the northern edge of the property and runs dramatically down hill after the two hundred mark from the tee. The green is located at the lowest point on the course and the place where all water drains towards throughout the site.

The fifth green is placed on a plateau across a dried creek bed and requires a long shot from a slightly awkward lie with the ball above the feet of the player. The fairway slopes dramatically from right to left and creates a definite problem as the boundary of the property runs along the right side of the hole. The thirteenth is another hole that runs downhill. For the second shot the player is given the chance to hit to the tiny green that has a steep falloff behind it into a dried creek bed. This is an instance where a hole has actually been improved over the years as two bunkers were added, but left a wide enough opening to hit a shot into the green. The other remaining par five is the sixteenth. The sixteenth may be the best of the bunch as the green is nicely placed at the base of a slight hill and features a chance for the player to run their shot into the green using the terrain. An often overlooked component of the hole is perfect placement of the fairway bunker approximately one hundred fifty yards from the green requiring the player to make a decision of direction and length on their second.

Left: Photo of the thirteenth green with the eighteenth fairway in the background (courtesy of Twin Hills)

Par Fours

The heart of the course at Twin Hills is formed around the excellent variety of the par fours. The majority of the great holes are on the front of the course but some are on the back side of the course as well and all provide a stiff challenge to each of the tiger golfer and the hack. The elevated first tee looks out over a creek bed and provides a wonderful view of the wide fairway. As the fairway climbs back up on the other side it has a slight cant towards the creek and actually helps to shape the approach into the longish green on the first hole. The opener is a solid starting hole that gets the player comfortably away from the clubhouse.

One of the best mid-length par fours of Maxwell's career was the beautiful uphill par four third hole. The drive must run up the hill to the fairway that cants from right to left. The left side of the green is protected by a large tree. The green was also cut directly into the hillside and presents a target that appears it is barely being held into place at the edge of the rise. A large pimple in the back side of the green clearly divides the green from right to left. The sixth is another fine

mid-length par four that goes from the rise at the southern edge of the property and into the lower portion of the course where creeks are the dominant feature. A creek runs parallel to the fairway on the right and creates the perfect hazard as the player must hug that side as the cant of the fairway will push the ball the opposite direction. Again a narrow green is the target from the landing zone.

The hole that provided the name for the course was the great eighth hole. The tee shot went from one hill, the highest point on the site and was hit over the rise that was approximately one hundred yards away and into the fairway that drastically sloped from left to right and downhill. The approach would be from a hanging lie in the wide fairway to an Alps-like green with a slight rise short of the hole and to a green that ran from left to right. The hole was one of Maxwell's best but the original rise was flattened in the 1960s as was the rise short of the green. Bunkers were placed around the green to supposedly increase the challenge. From behind the hole it is readily apparent the natural terrain was used to create a truly beautiful and natural hole. The concept that Maxwell used on the hole was borrowed from the National Golf Links like many of his other great holes in his career. The hole features all of the danger on the right side of the hole until one hits it into the deep pit that sat behind and to the left of the green. This presented an impossible recovery for any player.

Previous page: Third at Twin Hills from the tee
(courtesy of Twin Hills)
Below: Tenth at Twin Hills from fairway with skyline behind
Following page: Eighth at Twin Hills from behind the green
(courtesy of Twin Hills)

Another of Maxwell's finest holes was the short par four tenth at Twin Hills. The tee shot was struck into the wide fairway that sloped from left to right. But the player had the option form the tee to try and carry the ball all the way to the green if they could avoid the minefield of bunkers on the right side of the hole. The green was also defended well by its slope from front to back. Players who hit pitches or drives into the green would have to be aware of the slope away from their shots and the deep ravine behind the green. Today the green and bunkers are surrounded by deep rough and large trees protect the right side of the hole so any drive at the green would be truly foolish. So another green strategic hole is relegated to one path of attack.

The twelfth is a great dogleg par four with and elevated tee shot. The challenge of the hole is try and carry the depression of a dried creek bed in the fairway or lay back off of the tee, thus affecting the difficulty of the second shot. The green is also defended by well placed bunkers on the front right and a green that has several interior contours to provide backstops for pitch shots placed accurately or to push away shots struck just a tad bit loosely.

The finishing hole at Twin Hills carried the brief tradition of Maxwell courses by finishing with a uphill par four that was a difficult finale. The tee shot ran down hill slightly and short of a dried creek bed. The second though has to be struck from a slightly hanging lie and uphill towards the green. This shot is perhaps the most difficult that any player can hit. But Maxwell thought of this and provided ample room on the other side of the creekbed to land the shot and have an easy pitch into the putting surface and a chance to hopefully save par. Twin Hills is probably the one Maxwell masterpiece that is the most often overlooked by people who look at his career. Any course that has hosted a major championship and was an early dominant design in its region should be studied regardless of the architect. The wonderful combination of holes and the masterful routing should be a requirement of any that are wanting to eventually becoming a golf course architect. Though the course has been slightly modified over the years, it truly represents much of the early style of design that Maxwell implemented in Oklahoma in the 1920s.

Oklahoma City Golf/Country Club
(1926-1927) Oklahoma City, Oklahoma

Oklahoma City is one of the greatest courses that Maxwell ever laid out and is worthy of a complete study from the first tee through the last green. The course was a clear mark as the end of the first part of Maxwell's career. The course drew much of its inspiration from the National model much like his first course at Dornick Hills. It was also contracted as part of the Maxwell and Mackenzie partnership and would officially launch their partnership and make the transition to the second part of Maxwell's career as a golf course architect. This was also perhaps the best eighteen hole loop design that Maxwell ever created. Unlike many of his early works, the course originally referred to as Nichols Hills did not have two sets of nine hole loops and return to the clubhouse throughout the round. The only hole that finishes near the clubhouse is the last, a long par four that runs alongside the clubhouse facilities as members can watch the action from the tee to the green from within the confines of the large building. As with the earlier tour of Twin Hills a study will begin with the short holes from the course.

Par Threes

The one-shot holes on the course were not necessarily the best of Maxwell's career but they were each unique from each other and provided different challenges. As with most of the layouts in his career, there were four par threes on the course. The two particular holes of note were the third and the current eleventh hole. The other two were less stellar. The sixth featured a notable mound short of the game that played havoc with a low running shot, but the green is only defended on the flanks by two bunkers. The original fifteenth was eliminated shortly after the opening of the course due to drainage issues on the greensite that was placed hard against the large lake to the right. The original green was near the back tee marker on the sixteenth hole. This created a difficult shot with water threatening the entire length of the hole on the right side.

The third hole has a dramatic tee shot as the player tees off over the finger of a lake and hits the shot towards the hidden green. The putting surface is hidden by the bunkers that are close to the front edge and run all the way to the right side of the green. The left portion of the green is less protected and is a much less intimidating target. The putting surface is a difficult one to figure out as the dominant slope is from back to front, but it interrupted by a prominent pimple in the back half of the green. A player that hits their tee shot on the wrong side of the green is presented with a very difficult two-putt.

The eleventh, originally the thirteenth, features a creek that was used by Maxwell to intimidate the player. The wandering creek on this hole often makes the player think of the trouble to the right, but the real key is to staying below the hole at the green location. The green uses the flow of the land from right to left to create a steep slope from a slight hill behind the green down to the water. The right side is also protected by a deep bunker. Directly behind the bunker is a shelf for a great pin placement. This was a derivation of a template hole that was used by Maxwell on many courses in this career, including the original second hole at Dornick Hills.

THE OKLAHOMA CITY
GOLF AND COUNTRY CLUB

Above: Routing of the Oklahoma City Golf & Country Club as it appeared in the 1953 United States Amateur Championship program.

Par Fives

Maxwell continued drawing from his early study of the National at the first par five on the course. The fifth is a long par five of almost 600 yards. The landing zone rolls from left to right and is extremely wide. The green is hidden from view until fifty yards away due to large mounding short of the green. The green was built into the base of a hill and slopes off of it from front to back. This hole was obviously inspired by the Punchbowl hole at the National. The punchbowl hole is defined as a green complex situated in a natural hollow that funnels the ball towards the green. In most cases there is bunkering short of the hole. Maxwell did not use bunkering short of the green, instead he used the natural mounding as a defense. The putting surface also slopes from front left to

Top: Photo of the fifth punchbowl green from 1953 U. S. Amateur Program
Bottom: Photo of the undulating thirteenth green at Oklahoma City G&CC

back right off of the hump that is in the front left of the green. Two bunkers did serve as defense for the putting surface and affected the player from the right side of the hole as they would have to keep their approach between the two bunkers and on the green. This is one of the top par fives that Maxwell ever designed. There are also some similarities to the fifth hole at the St. Louis Country Club that was designed by Macdonald. It can be surmised that Maxwell would have seen the notable design by his "mentor" prior to the construction of Nichols Hills.

The other par five on the course was a long double dogleg design that is the modern thirteenth. The long hole is shaped with a creek bed running the entire length of the hole with the fairway sloping from left to right. The best feature of the hole though is the wildly undulating green that is hard against the creek on

186

the right. The rolls short of the green provide a defense and also opportunity for attack. Hole locations directly behind the front right bunker can only be attacked by running a shot through the hummocks short of the green as they will naturally feed the ball just past the bunker an into this small hollow on the putting surface.

Par Fours

As with the other major course by Maxwell in Oklahoma City, the par fours are the greatest feature to the course. Unfortunately, the curse of the course at Oklahoma City was that the most ordinary holes on the course were the first and the last. The first is a nice dogleg hole to the left. The last is a straightaway hole that runs up to the clubhouse and has a large green with some nice rolls in the putting surface. But in comparison to the rest of the course, the two holes that most often leave a lasting impression pale in comparison.

The second presents an uphill drive to the crest of a ridge and then presents a downhill second to a green that slopes away. In the fairway are many rolls and humps that play havoc with any lie. Two bunkers pinch the opening to the green slightly. This is a throwback that would not be constructed today. It is one of the most unique greens anyone could find. This hole is an example of how length alone is not a sufficient defense against the long player. The strategy of the hole requires the player to pick a side of the fairway from the tee based on the pin location. The outside of the dogleg is the tougher to stay in due to the number of small rolls. So right side pin placements are treacherous on the hole. The green is two tiers with the second tier falling away from the front half of the green. This forces the player try a lower trajectory shot with more spin to stay on that portion of the green, but the entrance actually rolls down to the green so any chance of staying on the front part of the green relies on the firmness of the putting surface. Also if the player pulls or pushes the shot to the green, they will more than likely slide off the green as there are steep fall offs to take away any near misses. In a phone conversation former architect and peer of Perry Maxwell commented on this particular green, "It seemed to run down almost ten feet from front to back. It was the best green out there."

The fourth features a drive over a dried out creek bed to a fairway that elevates to the crest of a hill. The fairway up to the halfway point of the hole, 220 yards, is full of small hummocks and hollows that will funnel a ball in different directions. The player that can carry these will have a much better shot down the hill to the green that is placed near the lake. The green all flows from front right to back left and off of a prominent roll in that portion of the green.

The only par four under 400 yards from the back tees on the opening nine holes is the short eighth. Maxwell's design of 280 yards plays all uphill. The fairway flows from left to right with bunkers at the top of the hill. Behind the bunkers is the hidden green. This hole was inspired by the famous second hole at the National known as Sahara. The Sahara concept calls for a hidden green to be located just behind a rise or hill and still be reachable for the longer hitter and dare them to attempt to carry to the green in one shot. This is yet another sign of the influence the National had on Maxwell's designs. The player can try to carry the ball all the way to the green, but few accept the challenge and even fewer succeed. Those that elect to lay up can use the fairway to shape the shot. A little nook short of the green is the ideal spot to land short of the green. An uphill chip is much more easily negotiated than a sand save from the bunkers short of the green, which runs away from the player. This is an ingenious use of one of the old concepts in golf.

The best hole on the course is the ninth. The tee shot must clear a lake to an uphill fairway that has a crest in the landing zone. The right to left slope of the fairway is helpful though for the downhill approach. At 150 yards from the green, a valley begins to slope down to the green. In windy conditions the more experienced player will use the mounding out to the right of the hole to help run shots up to the green. A bunker on the front left penalizes anyone underestimating the affect of the lie on the ball. The green features a back to front slope with two tiers. The second tier slightly slopes from left to right. Any shots that go over the green are looking at one of the fastest greens on the course.

The Eighth and Ninth holes at Oklahoma City

188

Holes ten, twelve and fourteen are all impacted by the creek running through this portion of the course. The tenth runs along the high portion of the course and the green is placed on the opposite side of the creek and features a lovely view of the green that slopes from back to front. Shots short of the green have a high risk of ending up in the hazard. The twelfth is a unique hole that has the creek crossing the hole twice. The length of the hole is only around 330 yards and requires a player to basically split the hole with his tee shot. The demands of the hole are unique and are open to some criticism. The fourteenth is an offshoot of a Maxwell template hole. The drive can either be hit to the flat part of the fairway or the player can risk have a downhill lie and try to carry all the way to the bottom of the hill with their tee shot. The slope of the fairway could give a player as much as fifty extra yards with fast and firm conditions. The green is perched just over the creek and near the road that splits the course into two sections.

The next holes all run in the same direction, but have different demands. The sixteenth is split by a gulley in the fairway and features a beautiful greensite that is split by a spine in the middle. The seventeenth features a tee shot that must clear a valley to be able to see the green on the second. The green is two-tiered and runs from right to left. This green design and use of bunkering is the early template for what Maxwell would use for his famous redesign of the seventh hole at Augusta National later in his career. The hole location is the prime indicator as to how to play the hole and dictates which side of the fairway to play an approach from.

With two courses only fifteen minutes apart, a comparison only seems natural to see how Maxwell evolved as a designer from his first for hire project, Twin Hills, to the last course he would complete in Oklahoma before the Depression, Nichols Hills. Both courses feature two of the better routings that Maxwell ever did. He used the narrow land of the Oklahoma City club to provide a strong and varied routing, which was one of the few non-core routings that Maxwell laid out. The course at Twin Hills used almost every square inch of the 160-acre rectangular plot that was filled with more drastic elevation changes than the course at Nichols Hills. The main difference in the routings is the use of the water at Nichols Hills was more directly in the line of play than at Twin Hills. As Maxwell matured as a designer he was willing to use forced carries to challenge the player at times during the round. The greens at the two courses are drastically different. By the time Maxwell did the course at Oklahoma City he had fully developed the idea of using rolls, his trademark, in the greens. The Twin Hills greens though seem to be much more simplified, using two tiers and back to front slopes. But to be fair, the Twin Hills course has seen much more work by the club and other architects.

The area where it appears that Maxwell had changed the most between the two courses was his development in hole design, specifically in the area of par five and par three holes. The par three holes at Twin Hills were all somewhat downhill and two of them feature the same shot. The par five holes also were repetitive with uphill or semi-blind drives with downhill approaches to the greens. But at

Twin Hills, they did vary in length and did present different problems based on that length. The par three holes at Nichols Hills are much more different than their cross-town counterparts and provide more variety. The par fives at Nichols Hills that Maxwell originally designed were both around 600 yards, but Maxwell used the terrain to make the holes play much different in nature. What can be gathered from the two courses is that Maxwell knew how to design a short par four from the start of his career, as both courses feature two of his best, the tenth at Twin Hills and the eighth at Nichols Hills. Both courses contain some of his best long par fours as well, the eighth at Twin Hills and the ninth at Nichols Hills being prime examples. So it appears that Maxwell did somewhat evolve over the early part of his career and was using many techniques and concepts early and exhibited a strong understanding of the concepts that Charles Blair Macdonald used at the National Golf Links.

The early part of Maxwell's career is where you find the blueprint of his philosophy about golf course design and what it was all about. He made courses out of land that previously was dirt and had no other value to anyone. Maxwell's most significant contribution during this time was not necessarily the courses he designed, but the fact that he brought something to Oklahoma that it did not have before. He dramatically changed the course of history as golf became a dominant part of the sporting culture in the state. Maxwell took a land full of brown sand greens and developed it into a land full of contoured Bermuda greens. The rolling greens reflected the nature of the land and provided an enjoyable experience to all that wished to play the game. During this time, Maxwell also had perfected his own style of design and it would turn out to be a strength that would place him on a national scene in a time of turmoil. It would also set him up to become one of the preeminent golf course architects of his generation and the 20th century.

Crystal Downs Country Club
(1928-1931) Frankfort, Michigan

      Crystal Downs was relegated to almost a confidential secret among a select group of golf aficionados until the last ten years. In that time, it has risen from a level of obscurity to a cult favorite among architectural groupies. With great reason as the entire experience at Crystal Downs is breathtaking from the moment you set foot on the opening tee. The course is a complete test and features what many feel are the best short to mid-length par fours in the world when viewed as a set. These great holes are accompanied by some excellent world-class long two-shotters and a top notch par five. The one weak spot one might find is with the one-shot holes, but that is for one that is too preoccupied with trying to find a weak link and not satisfied with near perfection.

Thirteenth green at Crystal Downs is set in a natural amphitheatre

Par Threes

The critic that is wanting to find something to pick apart could possibly find some fault with the one-shot holes at Crystal Downs. But that is only if they want to find anything. To those wanting to enjoy a fine round of golf, there is nothing to complain about. The third hole features a wonderful green complex that flows directly with the terrain from right to left and many balls that land in the middle of the green will slowly trickle to the left portion of the green. On days when the greens are slick, the ball may even roll into a bunker if the player is not careful.

The infamous ninth features a unique setting of a par three that is very uphill. The player will be required to hit an extra club from the tee and make sure it is short of the hole. The beauty of the ninth is that it provides the player a view of the entire front side of the course and allows them to soak in what they have just gone through again. Many courses would do well to try and match this view on their layouts. Anything above the hole is difficult to save your par on. But the ninth is almost like a tabletop in nature when compared to the steeply sloping eleventh.

The backside features a more secluded and wooded setting and uses a bluff that runs along Lake Michigan. The player is taken into the more wooded section of the course and is given a beautiful introduction to this portion of the course in the form of a classic par three. The eleventh takes full advantage of a valley that runs between the tee and the green with two large blowout bunkers behind the green. The green here features one of the more severe back to front slopes on the course. Any shots above the hole are full of fear and unless the ball happens to find the hole you are more likely to be chipping back up from the fairway than to be putting again. The green features three tiers and with the modern day green speeds is almost beyond what most players would like to even attempt to putt on. This green was the source of many

The view of the eleventh green from the tee
(courtesy of Jeff Reel)

frustrations in the only USGA Championship to be contested on the course as several players putted off the surface when the pin was located on the front tier. The secret is not to putt directly at the hole but admit that a three putt is likely and try to get into position so that you can either have a chance at par or be close enough that no worse than bogey is part of the equation. To find this green site was an incredible work by Mackenzie and Maxwell and helped to create a perfect transition to the set of holes that run along Lake Michigan. The green complex bears a resemblance to the eleventh hole at Oklahoma City, which Maxwell laid out just a few years before.

After having visited Pine Valley, the impact of the course was probably immediate on Maxwell and some reflections of that can possibly be found in the fourteenth hole at Crystal Downs. A short par three, reminiscent of the tenth at Pine Valley, over a large amount of scrub to a small target surrounded by peril with a wondrous view of Lake Michigan in the background and the Sleeping Bear Sand Dunes off in the distance to the right. The green is less canted than it appears but is surrounded by several deep bunkers that if found on the tee shot, the player has almost no chance of saving par unless a miracle of some minor magnitude takes place. The comparisons to the tenth at Pine Valley even go beyond the hole's design. The pot bunker short of the green is referred to as an unmentionable part of the Devil's anatomy. One almost has the feeling that the routing of the course in this direction was for the sole purpose that the player would have this wondrous view.

Par Fives

Crystal Downs was only designed with two long holes on them, but Maxwell and Mackenzie did not relegate themselves to potentially long par fours. These holes will almost always require three shots and they must be solid shots or the chances of success disappear rapidly. The eighth hole is the last in this amazing sequence of holes on perhaps the finest front nine in the

The eighth hole with the green in the distance circa 1933
(courtesy of John Stiles)

United States. A long par five that plays off of a large hill in the fairway and then plays back down hill and then up to the severely sloping green. The amount of subtle elevation changes that exist on this hole are truly amazing and they run from the start of the fairway to the green. This is perhaps the finest par five that Mackenzie ever laid out. The construction of the fairway contouring was a marvel as Maxwell and Dean Woods headed up teams of workers that used fresnos and horses to manually create the contouring that accented the natural flow of the terrain. Due to the "rolls" in the fairway, this may be the most intimidating tee shot on the course. If the player does not reach the elevated area, the ball would roll down the fairway as if it was being repelled like a climber on the side of Mt. Everest. The preferred landing areas of the eighth hole almost give the impression of a target style of design to the hole. If the player is not on the flatter portions of the hole, then a severe lie creates an incredibly difficult shot. Much of this is illusion as there are many locations that provide flatter lies at the base of the plateaus in the fairway. The only limitation associated with the low areas are the blind shots that are created due to the terrain. This idea also works up by the green as the approach area almost creates a diagonal carry to the right side of the fairway to get a clear shot at the green. The green is then perched hard on the edge of another hollow and slopes severely from back to front. This hole from tee to green was definitely a Mackenzie design but the construction created by Maxwell took a well-conceived hole design and made a masterpiece. The residence that Maxwell and Woods stayed at during construction was located on the road that winds through the course. Due to its proximity one can only wonder how many late evenings Maxwell was working on this hole just prior to turning in for the night.

The other long hole on the course is the sixteenth and it is the last hole along the plateau that runs parallel to the Lake Michigan coast line. It is a slight dogleg that is very flat until you get within 50 yards of the green. The ideal approach is from the left side of the hole into a green that is setup much like many other Maxwell par fives. It is a green with bunkers protecting the front right and that run along the left side of the green, leaving the front left open for low running shots. Maxwell used this green design on several courses. Prior to Crystal Downs a prime example could be found on the final hole at Hillcrest in Bartlesville, Oklahoma.

Par Fours

The first hole has one of the great vistas in golf. The first fairway and most of the front nine holes are visible. In the distance you can also see Crystal Lake and off to the right you can see Lake Michigan and more than likely with a wind in your face. The first hole plays with a bunker along the right hand side that is shared with the second hole. The hole takes advantage of the drop in elevation as the slope flows from the left down to the fairway which has rolling features that keep the player off balance on their second shot. The farther left the player hits their tee shot in the fairway the more roll they will get off of the slope. The fairway then dips and goes back up a slight rise to the green with three blowout style bunkers. The bunkers are even more fearsome when right beside them and the player realizes that the first bunker rises almost ten feet from one end to the other and into the hillside. The green slopes steeply from back to front with three tiers and is a perfect opening hole as it gives you the feel for the entire course. The hole also encompasses the standard Maxwell trademarks of his preferred opening holes, an elevated tee with an excellent vista while also providing a strong challenge. This same style is also reflective of Mackenzie; as he preferred elevated tee shots that provided interesting vistas over the property.

The second hole takes you back towards the base of the large dune where the round began. The tee shot appears to be straightforward but it all depends on the location of the pin. If the hole is on the left side of the green, the large fairway bunker must be flirted with. If it is on the right the player will more than likely have to play from a lie with the ball above his feet, if not from the rough as the ball will roll with the slope of the terrain. The green is deceptive as it is placed into the side of the hill and slopes much more to the left than it appears from the fairway. The terrain actually flows down to a flatter portion of the putting surface on the front left. This particular pin location is also well protected by one of the bunkers in front of the complex. The opening to the green is much wider than the bunker placement and ridge short of the hole would lead the player to believe as well. The second is one of the more underrated holes on the course due to it being preceded by an all-world opening hole.

The first two holes provide excellent examples of the two styles of green locations that Mackenzie used most. Mackenzie preferred the plateau or

View of the front nine from above the ninth green (courtesy of John Stiles)

punchbowl variety of green complexes that used the terrain in a natural manner. This method was similar in some ways to Maxwell in regards to the plateau style green. Maxwell's alternative was more often than not a push-up style of green complex that would be graded out almost fifty yards from the putting surface to hide the imprint of his crew and their work.

The dogleg was an instrumental part of both Mackenzie's and Maxwell's careers. A solid example of this is found on the fourth at Crystal. The carry bunker on the front right actually marks the direction the player wants to go off the tee, but they should use a cut shot to get to that position. The approach then from the fairway reveals a sea of ripples in the fairway all the way up to the green. Often overlooked the 4th is one of the most solid but simple holes on the course.

The fifth hole is one of perhaps the best-kept secrets in the world of golf. It is the start of a stretch where the influence of Alister Mackenzie is most evident at Crystal Downs. From the tee the player is not sure where to hit. All the player sees is a blowout bunker to the left, the three sisters, a group of bunkers in the fairway, and a large oak tree to the right from the elevated tee. The safe route is over the tree in the valley. The far more adventurous can attempt to carry the hill with the vast bunker in it. But the smartest route is over the last of the three sisters, as this will set up a pitch or short iron into the green from the most level lie anyone could find on the hole. Once the player clears the crest, the fairway creates numerous small basins for the ball to roll into. The closer the player is to the green the flatter is the lie and less uphill is the approach. This was clearly an idea by Mackenzie to accentuate the differences between the more daring line from the tee. The green is well protected with many deep bunkers that prevent the player from going out of bounds to the right. Obviously, this was one of Mackenzie's attempts to prevent lost balls and supported one of his underlying principles of design. The slope of the green runs from back left to the front right and a downhill putt in this direction could easily end up in the bunkers to the right of the green.

The fifth at Crystal Downs is a testimony to creating a hole that must be discovered, rather than the fully visible hole that has the route prescribed for the player before he even takes off his head cover. One of the concepts that Mackenzie explains in his last book, The Spirit of St. Andrews, is the "Line of Charm." This concept would be influential into the design career of Maxwell later on as well. It basically states that the player is more inclined to play a shot along what he perceives to be a straight line from tee to green than to play another route if the alternative is not placed clearly before him. The fifth at Crystal Downs is, in a manner of speaking, the ultimate foil to the "Line of Charm" as there is no perceived lines of play to any player. The fifth is an excellent example of how width can still be a factor in the design of any golf hole. Without the width that currently exists the design intent of the hole is lost. If the fairway were narrowed it would eliminate the various avenues of play and take away the mystery of the hole. The fifth also was a master stroke in routing the course as it was placed in the corner of the property so there would be no wasted land.

The sixth is another hole in this fascinating stretch. It is a simple dogleg right, but again the question is where do you play to. The famous "scabs" are along the right side and two other little pots are directly behind it, along with a tree to provide a deterrent for anyone wanting to cut length off of the hole. This was obviously intended to be a test of accuracy off the tee, as opposed to the wide fairway of the preceding hole, this hole features a very narrow landing area. The approach can be deceiving with a mound on the left side, which helps to make the green appear closer to the player. The approach shot is to one of the best greens in the world. The green was sculpted out of the dirt to resemble the rolling waves of the ocean with the back right flowing down to the front left. Within this flow is a large "wave" in the middle of the green. This technique effectively creates multiple tiers in the green while also not providing a flat portion to the putting surface in any of the 7,700 square feet. This is the largest green on the course and it creates almost a double bowl due to the undulations. Behind the green is a fairly steep runoff that creates a tough chip that goes back down the slope of the green. The wild undulations and the bunkers protecting it create a wonderful green complex, which is a perfect mix of Mackenzie and Maxwell. This is probably the poster child of the green complexes at Crystal Downs with the number of rolls and tiny bumps throughout the surface.

The seventh hole is also a museum piece of architecture. The drive, though not incredibly fearsome, makes the player decide his strategy from the tee for the hole. The player can either lay up and play from above in the fairway or try to boom his drive into the valley short of the green. The green though is the story on this hole. The green was designed to snake around the mound and bunker that exist on the right side. To be able to putt the complete surface Mackenzie designed it to have significant slopes feeding into the middle of the green. The back portion of the green is fairly flat but slightly downhill. The front portion of the green almost forms a punchbowl. The trick is to approach the green from the left edge as anything on the right will bounce into the bunker and create a difficult bunker shot, especially to anything on the back half of the green. The original boomerang style green that Mackenzie used later at the University of Michigan course in Ann Arbor and at Augusta National was originally implemented here. This hole has often been attributed directly to Mackenzie's direction on the design. But based on studying early works by Maxwell the same hole design, with the exception of the green, was used previously on many courses.

The second half of the course provides a different feel than the front nine. Mackenzie was heavily involved in the layout, but Maxwell made some significant changes to those plans when he felt it was needed. The construction of the back nine began during the second summer of Maxwell's stay in Frankfort and was constructed over that summer and during the third summer on the premises. The front side of the course flows through a great deal of uneven terrain and provides many more dramatic green and tee locations but the back has a section of much more even terrain. That does not begin at the tenth however. With the tee just a few steps from the pro shop window, a tee shot hit into the valley below can be viewed by many onlookers and the pressure can be intense. The approach up the hill to the plateau green can be difficult as well. The big mouth bunker protecting the front right is a menace to be avoided, but the green is the real defense as it slopes dramatically towards the front of the green.

The first hole on the plateau setting is the twelfth. It is perhaps the least noticeable hole on the course. The tee shot is out to a wide fairway when aimed at the lone tree on the interior landscape of the plateau. The second is then hit to the flattest and one of the largest greens on the course. Perhaps Maxwell constructed the hole as a contrast and relief from all of the other greens on the course that require the ultimate in skill. The natural tilt of the land though is most evident when one looks at the hole from the fairway.

Maxwell built the thirteenth hole using the slope of the land and nothing else. The slope of the terrain on this hole feeds off a rise on the left side. The flow of the terrain takes everything off of this rise and down to the treeline along the right side of the hole. There is ample width to use the terrain to work shots from left to right. The left side of the fairway was constructed by Maxwell to create natural drainage tracks from the left side and in the process created ripples of land that mimic the movement on many seaside links courses. The hole leads down to a green that slopes away from the player. The front part of the green is like the hood of a car, then once you cross the ridge in the front third of the green, it falls away with a slight slope from the left side down to the right. This hole, along with the second green at Oklahoma City, are the best examples of this type of "fallaway" green complex that Maxwell ever constructed. This hole perhaps more than any other on the course personifies what Maxwell's design style was all about. Incidentally, several of Maxwell's early courses have hole designs similar in nature to what Maxwell perfected at Crystal Downs in the form of the thirteenth.

The short par four fifteenth hole has a large number of dips and dives similar to the fourth and thirteenth holes. These small constant changes create a situation where an uneven lie is invariably going to happen for all players in the fairway. The challenge is what do you do with the pitch shot remaining. The undulations and rolls in the fairway are more severe on the left side of the hole and

Postcard of the third hole and photo of the seventeenth (following page)
(courtesy of Jeff Stiles and Jeff Reel)

make it apparent that the right side is the preferred angle into the green. The green, an obvious Maxwell creation, has a large hump on the left side. Anything coming from that angle will surely go offline and leave a long putt on a very contoured green, that could even result in a three putt and a bogey on a hole under 350 yards. No wonder the locals refer to it as "Little Poison." This hole again bears more than a striking resemblance to another Maxwell creation in the eleventh at Muskogee and with the original ninth at Hardscrabble. The layout and bunker location are identical to other holes that Maxwell used as a template in his designs earlier in his career.

The seventeenth hole on the course is possibly the most famous on the course. How often do you hear of players laying up on a 311 yard hole? Well, it may very well happen here, as the distance of the hole is misleading. The seventeenth is another short par four that goes from an elevated tee to a green roughly on the same level, with a fifty foot drop in between and a fairway that slopes from right to left. The beauty of the hole is that it provides the player limitless options on how to attack the hole. The key to the difficulty of the hole is that it often plays into the wind, which adds about twenty yards or more at times. The other key about the hole is that it transitions the player back out to the open area of the course. This presents another excellent skyline. The green slopes from back to front dramatically to receive many long approach shots into it. Those that put to much spin on the ball will into the fairway. There is a small knob behind the green, that when stood upon makes you feel as if you are standing on top of the world and can see for miles on a clear day. Ten feet below you is the primary tee for the eighteenth hole.

The finisher is from an elevated tee down to another low level fairway. Maxwell varied from his traditional uphill finisher and from the original layout, if legend is true. The original greensite was to be just short of the clubhouse on the far hill. Instead Maxwell constructed a dogleg that has one of the greatest bunker complexes in the world on the right hand side of the hole protecting the green and leaving a difficult entry into the putting surface. It is a fitting end to the course as the player would have a view of Lake Michigan in the distance as they walk off of the last green.

199

Crystal Downs has one of the most compelling routings in the world. The front nine makes use in imaginary ways of the deep valleys and the drastic rises. The lack of trees also makes the wind one of the major factors on play. A player may in one round encounter forty mile an hour breezes off of Lake Michigan and then almost a small warm zephyr blowing from Crystal Lake in the opposite direction. This can play havoc on the ball in the air and on the ground. Though somewhat short by today's standards, the course at Crystal Downs is one of a handful of near perfect courses in the world and is a true reason to love this game and want to study the career of Maxwell.

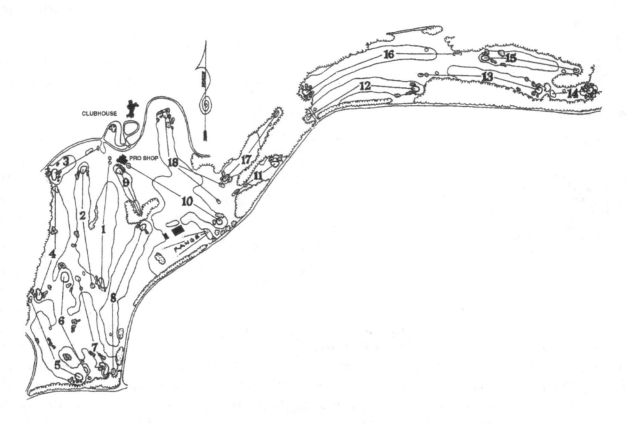

Routing of Crystal Downs (courtesy of Crystal Downs)

Southern Hills Country Club
(1935-1936) Tulsa, Oklahoma

Due to the intended nature of the course, to hold national championship, Southern Hills was intended to be much more difficult than most courses. Maxwell was intent on bringing local pride to Tulsa. The course at Southern Hills was also an example of excellent routing. The use of the natural hill on the southern edge of the site with the clubhouse sitting atop it is a great backdrop for several of the holes. This combined with much of the undulating terrain on the second nine holes of the course make an ideal location for a wonderful course. Add in some of the best green complexes in Maxwell's career and you have the makings of one of the top designs in American parkland golf.

Southern Hills has recently come under fire for not representing the true nature of the original design of Maxwell. This cannot be further from the truth. The course to this day retains most of the character that was put into it by the architect. The main reason for the criticism is the number of large and mature trees that now inhabit the site. For the most part, these trees do not affect the line of play, but do narrow the holes quite considerably from their original widths. But the course that Maxwell designed, with a couple of exceptions noted below, still exists near the original form. In the author's opinion this course truly represents the Oklahoma style of Maxwell better than any other work of his career and when taken in totality, the original design, compares favorably with any course in the country and is equal in stature to Crystal Downs and Prairie Dunes in the Maxwell portfolio.

Par Threes

As a whole, the one shot holes at Southern Hills are often overlooked, but they consist of a solid set that has great variety. There are two holes that on the longish side and require completely different shots. The other two are somewhat shorter and test the player by having them hit a more lofted club with different wind influences. As with many of Maxwell's courses, two of the holes are template holes from his personal inventory.

The first par three of the course is one that is heavily influenced by the wind and with club selection. It is also the shortest of the three pars and provides the most photogenic hole on the course. A creek on the left side of the green will penalize hooked tee shots, and out of bounds is close behind the green. The fast green is also heavily trapped in front. The ideal tee shot is short of the pin for an uphill putt. The front half of the green actually funnels balls to the middle while the back half pushes shots away. The back left is a devilish shelf that is often used in tournaments. This hole is picture perfect and really provides a contrast to what many would expect of the most underrated portion of the course at Southern Hills. The inspiration for this hole was also drawn from the early work of Maxwell as he used a similar formula on the second at Dornick Hills, although almost as a mirror image as everything is flipped from right to left.

The longest par three on the front nine is the eighth hole. This hole features the best green complex on the front side. The green has the back left portion hidden by the bunker tightly guarding that side of the green. The green has a ridge halfway through the green and begins to roll away from the player towards the back left corner. Two humps dominate the contours of the green on the right side of the putting surface. This hole is a similar concept as the original eighth at Dornick Hills, but with a much less pronounced Redan style of green. The hole has met its share of controversy. Gene Sarazen was quoted during the 1958 Open as saying, "That's the worst three-par hole I've ever played." Maxwell was quite of the opposite opinion as he described it, "It looks so simple from the tee that everyone will go for it, but if the ball isn't exactly on line, they'll take a five."[60] Which, of course, is what Sarazen did just prior to his outburst about the quality of the hole.

The next par three on the course, the eleventh, requires pinpoint accuracy. The combination of an elevated tee and the prevailing right-to-left wind will test the players' skills. The green is a frightening sight as you stare at bunkers that partially conceal the front of the green on this short hole. The length of the hole being a little longer than one would like for this shot makes it a little more difficult. The green is cut into the side of the hill that feeds down from the clubhouse. Short of the green is a ten-foot deep swale that will catch anything that hits into the false front of the hole. Beyond the hole is a chipping area for those running off the green due to the slope. This hole is a template hole that Maxwell used on many courses with the green being angled from the tee with the toughest shot being to the back left pin positions. The bunker layout was similar to many other courses that Maxwell designed. Maxwell placed five bunkers around the tilted green complex.

Aside from the final hole, this was the last hole that Maxwell would incorporate in the use of the large hill the clubhouse sits upon. In total, six holes on the course had their routing based solely on this one feature of the site. Maxwell often used dominant routing features, such as the large hill as the focus of the routing. Another example of Maxwell's routing skill can also be shown by the use of creeks and water on the course as exemplified by the next hole, which has received some recognition over the years since the holes inception.

The toughest par three on the course is a great and picturesque hole that has length, six bunkers and out-of-bounds on the left. It will require a wood or long iron firmly struck to negate the prevailing right-to-left wind. A three here will be well earned and could very well win the hole in a match play situation. The green is one of the best on the course as it features bold undulations. It also creates a peninsula affect in the back left portion of the green. The hole runs downhill and the green does as well and creates another green that slopes away from the player. The use of the green that sloped away from the player was a tactic that Maxwell seemed to employ in many instances. He also had taken notice of how many players had played his course, Twin Hills in the 1935 PGA Championship and thought that greens that sloped away from the player would be a greater challenge than the more common greens that sloped towards the play on the hole. Maxwell was aware that Southern Hills was intended to be a championship course and designed it to be one of the more difficult in the country.

The fourteenth is a majestic par four that is difficult for any player.
(courtesy of Southern Hills)

Par Fives

Southern Hills was one of the few courses that Maxwell laid out with three of the longer variety of holes. Most of his courses contain either four or two of the three-shotters. As with the short holes, Maxwell used a template style of design on the green complexes of all three of the par fives on the course. The first par five on the course is the characteristic long par five that Maxwell always seemed to use on many of his courses. The fifth is the hole on the course that has seen the most changes. The tee was moved back to 592 yards for the 1958 US Open and has been moved further back each time a major championship has been hosted at Southern Hills. This hole was lengthened again for the 2001 U.S. Open to 660 yards. The par five doglegs slightly to the left. It is the longest and one of the toughest holes on the course. Due to the fairway bunkers, a narrow landing area on the tee shot will cause problems, but the hole does present a birdie opportunity to the straight hitter. There are plenty of trees and heavy rough awaiting the errant shot. Many players will play a wood as the second shot and then a short or mid-iron third shot to the well-bunkered undulating green, which is split in half by a ridge from front to back. This ridge is the key to the strategy of the hole. Pin locations on the right hand side of the green are much tougher to approach than those on the left. The bunkers fronting the right side are what make this such an intimidating shot. The left side is protected by the ridge in the green, but is open to those who play up the left side of the fairway. The ridge also creates an almost impossible approach if the player is coming from the wrong side of the fairway.

The thirteenth green from above and behind during the 1958 United States Open
(courtesy of Southern Hills)

The greenside bunkering by Maxwell is a standard design by Perry on many of his three shot holes. He would often put tight bunkering on one side of the green with an opening to the front of the green on the same side. The other side of the green would be protected by a bunker cut close to the front side of the green. On the fifth at Southern Hills, Maxwell strung three bunkers on the left side of the green and put one directly in front of the right side of the green. A monster hole as Maxwell designed like this is a perfect example of why distances and equipment will soon make courses like Southern Hills seem obsolete to the golfing public. Courses by Maxwell and many other architects are getting stretched to their limits to be able to host tournaments such as the US Open and soon these historic courses will get thrown to the wayside because they no longer can withstand the assault of the modern day player. Instead of letting the courses rely upon their merits and make the players come up with strategic decisions on their shots instead of making the courses easier for them, by eliminating the thinking process.

The thirteenth is possibly the last good birdie opportunity on the course and will provide plenty of excitement. It requires a big drive on the slight dogleg left hole, which will leave an opportunity to reach the green in two, but not without risk. To reach the green in two the player must clear a small depression in the fairway that creates a blind shot to a small green well protected by sand and water. Water is omnipresent on the sides in the form of two small ponds, one on each side of the fairway, but allows for a running shot to reach the green, which is protected by numerous bunkers. With a tough finish ahead, the opportunity to make eagle or birdie might well be worth the risk, although laying up in front of the two small ponds will still provide a good chance for a birdie. For those laying up, the landing area is full of rolls and humps and will provide a testing pitch to the green that has one large hump in the middle that really plays havoc for shots coming into the putting surface. This hole derailed a comeback attempt by Tiger Woods in the 2001 US Open as his second shot found the water instead of the putting surface. Woods would go on to make a bogey on the hole instead of a much-needed eagle. The hole was altered to be a long par four of 470 yards in the 1958 US Open. It was the toughest hole in the 1958 championship and was described by many as unfair. Many players were presented with blind or semi-blind shots into the green protected by two water hazards. The hole remained as the most difficult par four in Open history until well into the 1980s when 490 yard par fours became commonplace.

The longest par four on the course for tournament action is the sixteenth. It requires both length and accuracy off the tee. It is a par five for the members, but is changed in an insane move to protect par during championships such as the US Open. The drive is to a rolling fairway and is downhill from the back tees where the elevation change in the fairway is most obvious. The flatter spots in the fairway are like islands as these are the only places that going for the green in two will be possible. Anything else will be suicide as a pond pinches in on the left of the fairway short of the hole. At about the 160-yard marker the fairway rolls gently down to the green location. The green is sloped towards the player and features three of the famous rolls. With the use of the "islands" in the fairway, it appears that Maxwell may have been trying to mimic the concept of the eighth hole at Crystal Downs on this three shot hole and instead of a deep hollow, the green is protected by a small pond. The other ground contour that Maxwell used in a similar fashion previously was the right to left slope feeding to the green.

Opening tee shot with the Tulsa skyline on the horizon

Par Fours

Regardless of what one may think of the one and three shot holes that Maxwell designed on the course, no one can argue about the two shot holes. They were one of the best complete sets in the country with variety and use of elevation throughout the course. Unfortunately, they are not in tact with the original design elements in place. The seventh has been altered in an extreme manner with the movement of the green and several other holes have been touched to some degree. The opening of the course is set up with four beautiful par fours that make excellent use of the sloping terrain with fairways that are canted away from the flight of the ball and thus making it tougher to stay within the confines of the fairway. The first hole has an inspiring tee shot that allows a view of the Tulsa skyline in the distance. It starts from an elevated tee of almost seventy feet to a slight dogleg left with the ideal tee shot position being in the left side of the fairway to avoid the fairway bunker on the right. This tee position will allow an open second shot with a medium-to-long-iron to a green, which slopes from front to back and is guarded by three traps. This is the best-known opening hole that Maxwell ever designed to much of the golfing public and among the best that he and Dean Woods ever constructed. The strategy is fairly simple from the tee and provides the player an opportunity to settle into their round, albeit on a long par four. From the tee the narrowness of the fairway is evident to the player and immediately shows how trees may be impinging on the true design intent of the course. As with most of Maxwell's superior opening holes, it was a strong introduction to what the player would encounter on the course.

The second, to the average golfer, is a nightmare from the tee. This is perhaps the most demanding driving hole on the golf course with a 225-yard carry over the bunkers and a winding creek that turns and parallels the fairway and it is tight with trees on the left. It is also the only forced carry off the tee if you want to make it to the green in two shots. Anything not in the second part of the fairway will require a pitch near the pin to make par. A long-iron second shot is required to reach this well-bunkered green. The green is a square shaped putting surface. The player will have a double breaking putt if they are more than fifteen feet short or behind the hole. The front half of the green slopes to the left and the back half slopes to the right providing some players with a putt that breaks in multiple directions.

This hole may have been the greatest hole on the course by Maxwell. The original design was based on the "bottle" hole concept by Charles Blair MacDonald. The creek ran through the fairway at a slight angle that created an

The world famous twelfth hole at Southern Hills

optional carry over it and two bunkers on the right side and the left side or short of the creek was accessible to the player from the tee. The carry was the key to the hole. Those that played to the left side and longer would be faced with a carry over a bunker on the front left of the green. The player that plays short of the creek has a long and difficult shot into the green.

The third hole appeals to the senses of the golfers as it is a hole that just is subtle. The hole starts out to the right but has a sharp dogleg left and requires a long tee shot. Bunkering and pin positions will demand skillful short-iron second shots on this very deceiving hole. A creek protects the left side of the fairway and is a must carry on the approach to a green surrounded by bunkers. The fairway runs slightly right to left and downhill so it plays shorter than it's yardage may indicate. The ideal area to attack the green from is determined by the flagstick. Depending on which side of the green the hole is cut that day, the opposite side will be the desired location in the fairway. The green runs from right to left with a spine dominating the back half of the green.

The picturesque short par four fourth features a rolling fairway leading to the heavily bunkered, elevated green. The absence of level lies makes for difficult second shots. The severe back-to-front sloping green will prevent many aggressive birdie putts. This is another hole that plays almost identical to a counterpart, in this case the eleventh hole at Maxwell's home course, Dornick Hills. Though this type of uphill par four was not one of the conceptual copies that Maxwell liked to employ, he seemed to have more than his share of uphill par fours that featured similar characteristics. This is also the only hole that Maxwell redesigned on the front part of the course in subsequent visits. The fairway runs down to a valley that creates an uphill shot to the green with no visibility of the putting surface. The green even creates more of this effect as it slopes from back to front. This caps off a very good opening stretch of holes that really test many aspects of the player's game to this point. Often lost to many players on the course is the amount of elevation change that exists on these particular holes. Television coverage of the many tournaments held at Southern Hills has often minimized the movement of the terrain through these holes.

The lost hole of the original design is Maxwell's original seventh. The green was moved to help with drainage on the course. The original layout worked from the same tee location and doglegged slightly to the left around the slight rise on that side of the hole. The landing zone was protected by a bunker on the left side of the hole and one to the right of the fairway. The drive needed to clear the ridge in the fairway. The fairway past the ridge then immediately rolled from left to right towards the creek far to the right. The green was then perched at the top of the hill along the left side and was well guarded. The longer drives would finish in the low area where the current green is now situated and provide a short shot up the rise to the green. The drainage in the depression was what prompted the construction of the new green by Floyd Farley in the 1960s.

The front nine closes with a dogleg right that features a fairway bunker guarding the corner that requires a well positioned tee shot. The prevailing wind and an elevated green make this hole play longer than its yardage. A severe slope from the back to the front of the green also makes this one of the most difficult greens to putt. The three rolls that Maxwell put into the green only add to the drama of any downhill putting. The key to the hole is avoiding the fairway bunker at the corner of the dogleg and setting up the approach into the green that is part of a slight dogleg back to the left. The fairway also slopes from right to left towards the creek, which only compounds the problem of getting the ball in the right location. This hole plays like the fourth hole at Crystal Downs in many ways. Maxwell also placed the green of the hole is close proximity to the eighteenth green. He did this on many of his courses in his career.

The tenth hole features trouble on the right of this dogleg right and will require a tee shot to the left side of the fairway. Most players will hit a drive from the tee in an attempt to fight the flow of the fairway and keep the ball out of the thick rough. The short approach shot to this elevated two-level green must be kept below the hole to have a reasonable birdie chance on one of the trickiest greens on the course. This is one of the finer short par fours that Maxwell ever designed. It was laid out at the base of the hill the clubhouse sits atop and around a nest of trees. The terrain of the land on the hole actually tilts from right to left and down the natural grade of the property, but the hole was routed to dogleg from left to right and force the player to deal with the terrain in executing their shot. The use of the terrain in this way, effectively, cuts the width of the fairway in half and makes the shot that much tougher. The green was cut into the side of the hill and an amazing hole was created. Protecting the front of the hole is a large swale and a large hump that plays tricks with the sight line of any ball on the far left side of the fairway or farther out. This is one of the last good scoring chances on the hole. The use of the swale in front of the green is a similar theme that was used extensively on the back nine on the course.

If any one hole would be used as an example of Maxwell's design it would probably be the twelfth at Southern Hills. It is a dogleg hole with a sloping fairway that flows away from the tee shot. Then it requires an exact shot to a green surrounded with small round bunkers that will only let the best survive. It has a subtle creek that seems to be an afterthought but it will catch any ball that is short or goes to the right of the green. This hole was singled out by Ben Hogan and Arnold Palmer as one of America's greatest par four holes. Golf Magazine also named it as one of the 18 greatest holes in the world in 2000. A truly beautiful hole that has stayed as Maxwell designed it except for the stonewalls of the bridge going over the stream. The hole though, may not have originally been planned to play as it currently does. As the story is told in the book, The Majors of Golf, according to Southern Hills lore the hole came about by accident. Maxwell had originally staked the green to the right of the stream. He was showing the course to founding member Don Bothwell, and Bothwell was trying to hit shots to the green and couldn't do it. He then turned and saw the shelf the green currently resides on and suggested, "Why not put the green there?" Maxwell replied, "Why didn't I see that before?" The green was definitely more reachable, but much more treacherous. The hole has been pivotal in past championships as well. Tommy Bolt played the hole with three birdies and a par in the 1958 US Open. In 1970 at the PGA, Palmer was making a late charge at Dave Stockton when his approach found the creek. He actually hit the ball from the creek, but found one of the bunkers and ended up with a double bogey on the hole.

The most unrecognized hole on the course is the fifteenth. The hole is a nice dogleg to the left with the most memorable aspect being the wonderful green. The complex is protected short by ripples in the fairway just in front of the green and deep bunker to the right side of the green with the undulation of the green running off of the ridge feeding from the bunker lip into the green. This hole also featured a wonderful bunker configuration that directly impacted the angle of approach into the green. Anything from the right side of the fairway was much more difficult than the shots that flirted with the long fairway hazard as all the undulations in the putting surface worked against anyone to full of cowardice to attempt the daring tee shot.

Originally, the seventeenth hole was designed with a tree at the corner of the dogleg. The tree was subsequently eliminated. A pushed tee shot into the trees that run along the creek will mean real trouble. Most players will endeavor to place the tee shot on the left side of the fairway with a wood or long iron. An accurate

Above: The approach to the final hole in the 1958 United States Open

Right: The approach over rolling terrain to the short two-shot seventeenth.

(courtesy of Southern Hills)

concept from CB MacDonald. In this case Maxwell wanted to make the player get into position to attack the hole. The play again is determined by the location of the pin on the hole. Anything on the right side can be approached from the left side of the fairway, as this is the widest portion of the green. Anything on the left side, should more than likely be aimed at from the right side of the fairway. This will allow the player to have the angle to go with the length of the green and use the slope of the green away from the player to roll the ball into the ideal location. When one looks at the contouring of the green, combined with the angle of the green it is easy to see why this is one of the premier short par four holes in all of golf and is prime example of how Maxwell could make any type of hole. The green was enlarged by Floyd Farley following the 1958 Open and is now one of the best on the course.

Aerial view of Southern Hills in mid 1950s
(courtesy of Southern Hills)

The eighteenth at Southern Hills is not only Maxwell's greatest finishing hole, but is one of the finest finishing holes in all of championship golf. The strategy from the tee gives the player the chance to either play with caution of with abandon. The cautious player can lay back and have a long shot into the green. The player who wants to risk tragedy can use the slope down to the creek to roll down to the level area just short of the creek for an uphill shot to the putting surface. Some players will be fooled by the bunkers visible from the tee, but they want to play wide of these or they will be blocked out by the trees on the right side of the hole. One of the differences between the current design and Maxwell's original plan involves these bunkers. They were much larger and had a turf island in the middle that struck the original members as rather odd. It was eliminated during the work by Robert Trent Jones, as was another large bunker up the hill and short of the green that tormented those that chose to lay up short on their second shots. A long-iron or fairway-wood second shot must carry to the green as anything short will roll back down the hill and leave an extremely testing pitch shot. The severely sloping green from back to front will cause many three-putts. The green was perhaps the most controversial part of the 2001 US Open as many claimed it was unfair. It is the most difficult par on the golf course. More than any other finishing hole, this is what many envision of Maxwell and his work in the Oklahoma area. The use of the large hill at one end of the site not only provides a natural amphitheater but it also creates the two things that Maxwell repeatedly searched for while creating his routings, elevated green sites and tees. That is why the first and last holes at Southern Hills are often seen as the prototype of Maxwell design. Southern Hills was one of the truly great parkland layouts of the "Golden Age." It also represents the best example of the simplified style of layout and design that Maxwell used almost exclusively in Oklahoma. This style was what made him so popular early in his career and would be the hallmark of the last few years in the profession as he would return to the same style and to Oklahoma and Texas after World War II for the brunt of his work.

Prairie Dunes Country Club
(1937) Hutchinson, Kansas

Without any argument, the course at Prairie Dunes was the most artistic in nature of Maxwell's designs. This course, perhaps more than any other reflected the thoughts and influence of Mackenzie on Perry's personal style. Perhaps that is why many feel similarities exist between this course and the layout at Crystal Downs where Mackenzie had such a hand in the final design. Due to the original course only being nine holes, a review of the course is done by hole order instead of par distinction.

At Prairie Dunes, the Scottish feeling of the course in enhanced as each hole is named, as with many of the old courses in Maxwell's ancestral home. Carey Lane is the name of the road that runs through the course and divides the front and back nines. It is also the name of the hole that opens the round. The hole is quite different from most opening holes done by Maxwell as the tee is not elevated well above the fairway. But it does provide an excellent introduction to the round as it captures the character of the course. The hole features an offset tee that provides the player the chance to hit their opening shot into the "gunsch" with plenty of room out to the right. The green is a fine introduction to perhaps the greatest green complexes in the country. The first green was one of only two that have been touched since the work done by Press Maxwell on the course. The green is triangular in shape and has several major undulations that affect play. It has slight false front with a large roll on the right side. The left side features a ridge leading in from the rough and the back has a large hump in the middle of it. The back right and

Aerial view of Prairie Dunes with current sixth hole running along the bottom left of the photo

left corners fall away from the player. All of this and the green features a three foot slope from back to front.

Willow, the second hole, is one of the finest par threes in the country. It was recognized as one of the top 100 holes in the world, but it isn't even the best on the course, at least in the mind of Perry Maxwell and a few others. It is a par three with a green that is on a plateau, angled away from the tee. The putting surface from the tee is obviously anything but flat. The bunkers short of the hole are deeper than they appear and are to be avoided at all costs, one even measures twelve feet below the putting surface. The only safe haven is long, but that's only if the player wants to hit from the plum brush. Like the first hole, the second also has had the green rebuilt and was part of the same project by Bill Coore and Ben Crenshaw, two noted modern golf course architects, but the greens were rebuilt to contain almost identical contouring to the originals putting surfaces.

The second green is a version of a template that Maxwell used on several other courses. It features a slight forward tilt while being divided into three distinct sections by two ridges. The far right section features a ridge running through it and the middle section has small humps while the far left runs away from the rest of the green. The angled green on this hole also creates an even more exciting shot the further the pin is to the left side, as it requires more carry from the tee. Some believe Maxwell may have been inspired by the twelfth hole at Augusta National during the construction of the hole. But a very similar hole was created by Maxwell earlier at Hillcrest in Bartlesville over ten years earlier and many other variations of this same putting surface can be found on his early works. As the study of his career has revealed, Maxwell designed various types of template holes that he used repetitively, and this is one.

Perry's third hole, Cedar, has an elevated tee behind the second green. A subtle dogleg is in full view with a somewhat flat fairway from the tee. One of the few fairway bunkers on the course protects the inside corner of the hole. There is also a bunker twenty yards short of the green providing a cross hazard for the player who hits into the rough on the tee shot. This type of cross bunker was seldom used by Maxwell over his career but provides a wonderful folly for the player to avoid on their second shot. The bunker has two purposes. It provides a deception tool as it tricks the player into thinking the green is directly behind the hazard, while also hiding the swale short of the green. The use of the deception to the player was not new for Maxwell, as can be seen with Southern Hills, but the fact that a bunker was the implement used was something that was a rarity for Maxwell. The green is not as elevated as the others have been thus far. But it contains the same style of rolls used previously. A distinct ridge divides the green into two halves. The front half features three small rolls while the back features a hump just left of center that creates a precarious pin location to the back left portion of the green.

Maxwell was not afraid to design a long par four and the next hole is evidence to that. South Wind is the name of the next hole. It is named for the prevailing gusts that arise in the Kansas sand hills from the south. Part of the

The famous second and the approach to the final hole
(courtesy of Peter Herreid)

genius Maxwell exhibited on his courses, was the way wind influenced play. The green features an open front, which encourages the a long iron or wood approach into the green. The sloping green goes from left to right and is much more complex than appears at first glance. For being one of the lesser known holes on the course it features one of the most notorious greens. The green appears to have some sort of false front from the fairway, but this is an illusion projected by a ridge that runs through the green about one-third of the way onto the surface. The left side features a roll feeding off of a slight hill. The back right portion features a massive hump that dramatically affects everything to this side of the green. The sides of the green also roll away from the heart of the putting surface. The bunkers short of the green originally did not pinch in as much as they do today. This was changed when the par on the hole was changed from a par four to a par five because the members felt the opening was too wide for such a risk-reward type shot. The tee location on this hole by Maxwell was originally directly behind the sixth green and that tee still exists as the forward tee. The movement of the tee added seventy yards to the 440-yard par four. Originally, trees were directly behind this tee and provided a block to the wind for the player. This forced the player to take note of the wind direction and speed while walking up the prior fairway so they would be able to hit their tee shot accordingly on this hole. With the movement of the tees back to their current location and the removal of the trees to block the wind, this aspect of the design has been lost.

215

The Dunes hole at Prairie Dunes is the best hole on the course. It has often been named the best eighth hole in America and with the possible exception of the twelfth at Southern Hills, the best-known hole Maxwell ever designed. The hole originally played from what are now the forward tees at a distance just under 400 yards. The prevailing wind creates a cross wind that will blow the ball towards the deep fescue and sand dunes that line the right side of the hole. If the player plays it conservatively, an incredibly long second into a tightly bunkered and extremely undulating green almost assures a bogey. The player that plays to the right of the fairway is left with a shorter shot, but must carry the dunes and the bunkers short of the green. Regardless of which way the player chooses the hole is difficult and requires exact shot making. This doesn't even take into account the wildly rolling terrain, including a small hill that conceals at least part of the green on all approaches exceeding 150 yards. The green on this hole is the best Maxwell built on the course, if not in his entire career. There is a four foot elevation change with a spine that runs through the middle of the green with a fall away to the right side. Players today still argue in the clubhouse about the best way to approach the hole. The difficulty of the green is in the way that the approach must come into it. The further up the fairway the player goes, the better angle they have in the approach to the green. But the lie becomes more difficult as the terrain becomes more undulating. Most just say, "Write a five on your card and move on. Because if you play it, you probably will get more than that." The hole is reminiscent in shot values to the famous Road Hole at the Old Course in St. Andrews. The layout of the green of the Dunes hole is almost a mirror image of the hole with the four bunkers fronting the green serving as the road hole bunker. When the green was originally constructed the crew had to water the green for several hours at a time to keep it from drying out from exposure to the winds.

The front nine today concludes with Meadow Lark. It runs parallel to the Dunes hole, and is equally difficult. A sloping and rolling fairway that was constructed by hand and with mule-pulled fresnos is the primary defense of the hole. The fairway plays with the prevailing wind coming across the hole, which makes it extremely difficult to stay in play off the tee. When the wind is up, the player is often faced with factoring in both this and the uneven lie they have acquired in the fairway when deciding upon an approach to the green. The run-up to the green is quite open, but is filled with moguls, dips and ridges that throw the ball in different directions, just like the landing zone of the drive. The green is a slightly elevated push-up green and slopes dramatically from right to left and has some of the largest "rolls" on the course. Three mounds effectively cut the green into smaller sections for pin locations. If not preceded by such a superlative hole, this hole would be much more talked about. The only change to this hole over the years has been the addition of the back tee that exists today.

The best par three on the course is the Yucca hole, now the tenth. Named appropriately for the wild plant that grows around the course and is always among the nastiest hazards if you try to take it on too aggressively. The green is punishing and like the other par threes at Prairie Dunes, is surrounded by

216

trouble. It has a brush covered dune, a gaping bunker, steep drop-offs and the forced carry over the brush in front of the tee. The green slopes from back to front and also has a slight false front. A mound about ten paces behind the bunker in front makes for a sucker pin location while a ridge on the left side along with a hump in the middle back create dramatic roll off areas as well. The unique placement of this green was perhaps the most difficult to find of all the original nine holes. Maxwell even realized the jewel he had on this hole, "This is the most beautiful par three I have ever constructed. Cypress Point, St. Andrews, Pinehurst and Augusta National have nothing to compare with it."[61] Some of that talk may have been hyperbole, but it is definitely one of the best holes in the country.

The view back up the eighth fairway (courtesy of Peter Herreid)

Pleasant Hollow is perhaps the finest short par five in the United States. P. J. Boatwright unabashedly called it his favorite short par five in the world. The drive was very taxing as the player was confronted with a forced carry from the tee over about 150 yards of scruff. The tee was located almost directly behind the current tenth green. The slope of the fairway runs from left to right, as the player tries to stay in the right side of the fairway to have the best approach into the green. The landing area of the fairway again features some amazing detail work as the rolls in the fairway seem to be in the right spot, or wrong if you're the player with a seemingly side hill lie in the fairway. As tight as the drive is, the approach is even more challenging with an uneven lie. The question then becomes for the longer hitters, "Do I attempt to hit the green in two?" The younger more ambitious player often replies with a yes and then finds the trouble on the left or right side of the green as their shot is repelled by the rolls just short of the green. The player that lays back and hits a full wedge into the green has just as much of a chance at birdie, if not better than the more foolish and daring player. A deep hollow short of the green, steep drop-offs behind the green and moguls that make a snowboarder quake in his boots protect the smallest putting surface on the course. That says nothing of the uniquely shaped bunker to the left that has yucca and gorse running into it and making a save very difficult with the green running away from the player. The green has a ridge that runs through the middle, which effectively makes it two greens. A small shelf exists on the back left, but a slight error and the ball could roll all the way down to the hollow on the right side of the green. If the ball is on the wrong side a two-putt is unlikely. This hole was also the only one that Press touched when he came to Prairie Dunes from the original nine. He created a new back tee that eliminated the dogleg and shortened the hole to the current yardage. The movement of the tee shortened the hole by only ten yards but straightened it out and presented the opportunity for the player to try and reach the green in two.

The last hole at Prairie Dunes is Evening Shadow and is a medium length par four from the tee. The tee shot is very testing as the fairway runs from right to left for the player, in typical Maxwell fashion, and the landing area is squeezed by plum bushes on both sides as viewed from the tee. The tee is offset slightly to the right of the centerline of play. The farther out the fairway goes, it becomes narrower and more undulated. There is a depression at about 260 yards from the tee that provides a blind shot into the green for the unlucky player to stop there. Just beyond that is an amazingly flat spot that provides the perfect angle into the green. Without using water or sand, Maxwell was able to create a carry hazard from the tee that provided strategy to what many think of as a short and dull finishing hole. From the tee, the player will notice a large dune to the left of the fairway. That dune was put there as part of the renovation work done by Coore and Crenshaw. The slope of the fairway would often lead to heavy rains flooding the area after storms. The dune is used to conceal a natural low area that uses a pump to send water out to the pond by the eleventh tee. The beauty of the work done by Coore and Crenshaw on the entire course is that it blends in beautifully with the original work. The green looks like Maxwell cleared a patch of fescue and cut some bunkers out of the ground on the sides of the green. Many call the green the fiercest on the course. The slope of the green is from right to left, but a large hump on the right side creates havoc for anyone that must putt from the front to the back part of the green or vice versa.

The routing by Maxwell in this case did not have a large elevation factor to center itself around. So Perry must have felt that the routing at Prairie Dunes was much more of a blank canvas than many of his previous works as his only limitations were built into the design by him and his crew. The original nine holes at Prairie Dunes can be an excellent example of constructing the course from the best that the site gives you, as he didn't design the course with any of the usual common design traits that he used at sites like Twin Hills and Southern Hills. The rhythm of the round is also accented in that the string of par four holes in the middle of the original routing speak to how the land dictated the design. The original set of nine holes contained four world-class holes. While the remaining holes were arguably as strong. This was the best nine-hole course in the United States for the first twenty years of its existence. In 1955, Press Maxwell was hired to construct a second set of nine holes to complete the original dream of the Carey family to construct an 18-hole championship caliber course in the sand hills outside of Hutchinson.

The Missing Holes

There is some question as to the origin of the holes that Press added twenty years after the opening of the course. It has long been believed that he used the routing and layout of holes suggested by his father years before. But in an interview with Ron Whitten he would later say he could never find the original routing his father created. It is also believed that Everett Queen, the super at the course during Press' work, had a copy of the routing and showed that to Press. One is often caught up in the feeling of speculation as to what would the complete routing by Perry have looked like. Would he have routed the course so the seventh would finish the opening nine or would it be the current ninth hole? Was the eighteenth the intended finishing hole? It seems to go against the character of most of Maxwell's designs. Would Maxwell have started a second nine with the par three tenth? Beyond the speculation no one can be sure what the course by Maxwell would have looked like. The only holes that are believed to have been constructed from Perry's original routing by Press and then later changed was the superb stretch of holes from the third to the fifth.

Today holes three and four comprise what was to be the third hole in Perry's routing. The drive from the dune out to the slightly rolling fairway may not have been exhilarating, but the approach to the green would have been all-world. The green setting was angled away from the player with two deep bunkers guarding the right side unless the player carried the brush to the left side of the fairway below the elevated green. The difficulty of the hole and the use of the dunes would have been a work of genius.

Unfortunately, the third hole never really saw final construction as the routing of the fourth had drainage issues when Press began his work. It can also be guessed where the original fourth green by Perry was to be located based on the original plans for the third and fifth holes. The tee shot was to be played from the current fifth tee location in a drop shot fashion to a green located at the base of the dunes that run behind the current eighth hole. One wonders if today, with the advancements in construction, this hole could be constructed and eliminate the drainage issue that kept it from becoming a reality.

The fifth was originally planned to be different than the current version. An original sketch of this by Press in a local newspaper portrayed this hole as actually being a 480-yard par five. It would have started beyond the dune the current tee sits on and work along the base and up to where the current green sits. It is believed that Press had already constructed the hole as his father laid it out on paper and only moved the tees when the preceding two holes were altered. The bunkering of the fifth is very similar in nature to many of the elder Maxwell's par fives with bunkering on along the side of the green and one lone bunker directly in front of the opposite side of the green. The angle with the best approach into the green was from the more difficult side of the fairway to play from due to the slope of the terrain. The characteristic bunker short of the green is also a Maxwell trademark.

The tenth hole looking back at the tee (courtesy of Peter Herreid)

Similar speculation has occurred in regards to the back nine holes, but no real concrete resolution has been brought to light. The thoughts of members and
220

writers over the years have theorized about a monster par three in the dunes out near the twelfth hole. Or a Cape style hole around the pond used for the irrigation system. Or perhaps a back tee for the thirteenth on the dune that stands over the current twelfth green. But much of this is idle speculation that without the original routing of the course should perhaps stay that way as the course the course that Perry and Press combined to construct is one of the best in the world and without few peers.

The Old Town Club
(1939) Winston-Salem, North Carolina

When one takes a tour of the Old Town course many recurring themes appear. Proceeding backwards from green to tee you can easily see the strategic value that Maxwell placed on all of his holes at Old Town. The green complexes at Old Town are almost all situated on areas of the course that are elevated on little knolls. The greens themselves contain several undulations, bumps, swales and dips. This creates an interesting strategic issue of "greens within a green" and provides an additional challenge of hitting approach shots into the proper portion of the green. The green sites also have some amazing surrounds. Many of the greens at Old Town are protected by collection areas or depressions that are reminiscent of the type of areas found on the Old Course at St. Andrews and other Scottish links style courses. The greenside bunkering at Old Town was often wild, weathered, and natural looking, and in many cases was tight to the greens.

Approach shots to the greens are very difficult. The fairway bunkering was almost always in a location that would tempt the daring player to try the difficult shot for the best angle into the green. Add in the fact that most of the fairways at Old Town are undulated and maintain tremendous slopes with awkward lies and this only magnifies the challenge. Thus, there is a premium placed on approaching the green from the correct location in the fairway, which relates to where the tee shot is placed. Many of Maxwell's holes place enough value on the placement of the tee shot that fairway, or carry hazards, were not often implemented by Maxwell. But at Old Town, Maxwell used fairway bunkers to even add to this intensity from the tee. This was the essence of shotmaking, and the player being able to shape his shots accordingly, scored well on many Maxwell courses.

The course contains several of the notable Maxwell routing traits as well. Two returning loops of nine, with more than one stop near the clubhouse. Canted fairways, undulating greens, template holes and elevated tee shots are common around the course. Another key component was the return to the use of water as a parallel hazard on most holes, as opposed to a head on approach. This combined with the elevation changes on the site truly show that Old Town was one of the more complete Maxwell courses and worthy of examination. The routing was also an example of how Maxwell could route a magnificent course on difficult terrain complete with large elevation changes and a natural creek Maxwell. Perhaps the one negative that anyone could proclaim about the course is the lack of a signature hole as almost every hole is unique and provides a different challenge, but no one hole stands above the others.

Par Threes

Maxwell again did not disappoint the player on his short holes. All of them are original in design and fit the terrain in an exemplary manner. Two of the holes are also template hole designs. One of which was the second hole on the course. The second hole has one of the more interesting stories on the course. Originally in the marketing of the course, it was noted that one of the holes on the course would be based on a hole at Augusta National. The second is that hole. The green site is almost a replica of the green site of the seventh hole that Maxwell reconstructed at Augusta during his work there. The green itself is divided into distinct sections by two notable ridges rolling through it as it runs from back right down to front left. It is also the most heavily bunkered green on the course, originally with five bunkers and now with seven. It should be noted that instead of the holes it is often compared to, the second at Prairie Dunes is

Top: The sixth perched atop an isolated knoll (courtesy of Dunlop White III)
Bottom: Early photo of the fifteenth green (courtesy of Old Town Club)

223

actually closer in style and design to this hole.

The sixth hole is the next par three and is basically a long to mid iron to a push up green that is full of undulations and slopes dramatically from front to back. The significant drop-offs behind, left and right of the green make the tee shot visually deceptive and intimidating. This would be accentuated if three trees directly behind the green were removed and provided no framing to the hole as Maxwell designed it in 1939. The push up green used by Maxwell here contains some of the most severe "rolls" on the course and is one that many point to as being a caricature of the true design of many Maxwell greens. The front section of the green creates perhaps the most challenging pin position on the course. When the hole is located here, it is comparable to "trying to land a golf ball on the hood of a car." Also a ridge along the left side effectively creates a separate green that will provide a three putt for anyone coming into it from another section of the putting surface. The excellent green contouring on holes five and six can be held up as an example of how great Maxwell's "rolls" were at the height of his powers.

The next par three on the course is the eleventh. It is a tight target that is guarded on the left by a large bunker and protected on the right by the creek that runs the length of the hole. The creek is a dominant feature that affects the player mentally as it engulfs the right side of the green. But anyone that ends up on the left side of the hole will be left with a fast downhill putt towards the cup. Not only is the left side protected by the slope but also by one of the famous "rolls" on the green.

The longest par three of 215 yards is a Redan style green that gradually slopes from front right to back left on the fifteenth hole. A creek runs the entire length of the left side of the hole. The original construction by Maxwell of the hole actually had a small pond that Maxwell created to add to the psychological trauma on the tee. The pond was later filled in and the creek is now back to its original path. The original size of the green was much larger than the current green. The left side of the green is protected by two bunkers today. The inspiration for the hole is clearly from his previous work at Dornick Hills and also bears a strong resemblance to the version of the hole at Southern Hills. Many have attributed the design of this hole to his association with Mackenzie but Perry had designed this type of hole on several courses dating back to the design of Dornick Hills.

Par Fives

Maxwell, as with most of his designs, only laid out two par fives on this design. Both in this case were exceptionally long and will force almost all players to hit a short shot into the green as their approach. The fourth is the prior of the two holes and is perhaps the only hole on the course that someone could find a glaring problem with in the design. The drive is to an elevated fairway, but the problem is with the second shot. Unless one can clear the top of the rise and get a wonderful roll to the bottom of the hill, the player is left with only one shot on their second, a layup to the left side of the fairway at the base of the hill. The approach though is enticing to a beautifully bunkered green that contains many of the typical Maxwell fare.

The seventeenth is a typical Maxwell long par five of almost 600 yards. The landing area for the drive is ample, but was pinched somewhat by the dammed portion of the creek. The second was often up over the crest of a hill to either the flat plateau at the top, or for the longer players the downslope leading down to the creek. The player is faced with a downhill approach to the near side of a double green. The double green, if rumor holds true, was suggested by Clifford Roberts as he was touring the course with Maxwell and Babcock prior to when the final touches were added. He suggested they make a double green, if for no other reason than to promote discussion in the clubhouse. It also provided a direct link to St. Andrews, which Maxwell was so fond of.

Famous double green of the eighth and seventeenth holes
(courtesy of Dunlop White III)

As mentioned with the second hole, the course marketed a hole being similar in nature to the famous course at St. Andrews. The double green was perhaps what was referred to. The beauty of the double green is that it actually provides enough putting surface for both holes as they both usually require wedges or nine irons into the green. The other thing of note is the separation that exists between the two due to the large ridges and swale in the middle of the complex.

Par Fours

In what seems to be an all too familiar refrain the par fours at Old Town are various in nature and truly unique in form. Maxwell drew from his past experience on this design and the details in all the holes really give a true feeling of this being an inland links as the nature of the land was the primary contributor the layout of the holes. The first hole, as with almost all of Maxwell courses, starts out close to the clubhouse and has a downhill shot to the fairway. The difficulty from the opening tee is that the line of play is unclear as the player is led to hitting the ball toward the green when the correct shot is to the right side of the fairway in line with the bunker on the opposite side of the creek bed. The approach then goes up the hill to the green. The somewhat blind shot must hit on the correct part of the green as well. The green drifts from right to left and has a large knoll in it that divides the green in half. As with every other great course that Maxwell constructed, he opens the round with a par four that allows the player to get acquainted to the course and acquire a feel for what the entire round will be like. The use of deception from the tee is a technique that Maxwell picked up from his time with Mackenzie and it would only be fitting that he would use it on a course with a similar theme as what his late friend featured on Augusta National.

After the opening two holes the player is faced with a daunting shot to the uphill third fairway that also runs significantly from right to left and back towards the depression in the first fairway. The second shot will be a difficult one with the hanging lie into the green with a bunker directly in front of the green. The green itself also requires the player be on the correct portion to have any shot of recording a birdie.

The fifth is a dogleg left that was designed with a large and deep bunker protecting the corner. The more the player tries to cut the hole, the closer they would have to get to the bunker. The better the tee shot, the safer the approach will be into the incredible green. The fairway for the hole is very much a hogs back by nature. The tee shots that land left of the ridge will roll closer to the green. Those that hit to the right of the ridge create a much longer and more difficult approach into the elevated green. It is a large green, which flows from left to right and has bold ridges and swales, which create several greens within the green. Some players will also play a running shot along the left of the hole that will roll down onto the green. The green itself on this hole merits an architectural study as the pin position determines how to play this hole from the fairway. The use of the rolls in the green effectively splits the green into smaller zones while also subtly providing a punchbowl effect. The simple use of the dogleg and the fairway bunker helps to create a strategic aspect to the hole, that causes the player to think from the tee not only about the angle of approach to the green, but whether they can risk the daring shot over the bunkers from the tee.

In the opinion of the author there is no greater hole at Old Town than the seventh hole and it elegantly caps off an excellent three hole stretch. The original hole contained one of the few forced carries that Maxwell designed on the course. A creek ran in front of the tee and for the optimum position in the fairway, the player must hit a 200-yard drive over three cross bunkers. This part of the hole is the same, what has changed over the years is that the fairway has been narrowed, eliminating the chance for the shorter player to play along the right side and a bunker that protected this route. Also eliminated over the years was the signature tree that was just to the right of the cross bunkers, thus dividing the hole between right and left. Once the decision was made at the tee, the approach would preferably come from the left side of the sloping fairway. The green slopes away to the right and has a mound that divides the green, while sloping from back to front. Two bunkers on both sides and another of the depressions short of the green, make it a very difficult green complex and perhaps one of the best of Maxwell's career. The seventh was expanded to it's original widths and merges with the fairway of the seventeenth hole. It should be noted that the merged fairways that Maxwell used at Old Town were probably done in recognition of his newly found love of Augusta, but also as a measure of respect for the Old Course. These merged fairways though were not a new concept as Maxwell had used them previously at Dornick Hills, his very first design.

The player is finally given one of Maxwell's template holes in the form of the eighth as it starts with a crowned landing area that precedes a steep slope down to a creek fronting the green. In most cases, the player would just bomb away down the hill, to only realize that the preferred spot to hit from is at the top of the hill, as the lie is much more level. This common technique is a Maxwell trademark. This hole has been designed on several of his works in many forms. The approach to the green from the elevated landing zone in the fairway is made much more difficult by the creek fronting the green and the false front that adds to the protection. The green itself is one of the more subtle thus far but is part of the most famous feature at Old Town, the double green. The right side of the double green serves as the putting surface on the seventeenth hole. The side of the green that is used by the eighth hole also slopes towards the player as it moves from right to left and towards the creek, thus creating a real problem in keeping the ball on the putting surface from the approach if too much spin is applied by the player. The eighth and seventeenth also feature a merged fairway that ran side-by-side in the original design. The only thing separating them today is a lone bunker.

The ninth is a long par four that goes through hilly terrain and goes back up to the clubhouse. The routing of the hole goes directly into the hillside that gives the dogleg right another tilting fairway that Maxwell was famous for. Maxwell then used the slope of the terrain as a defense and placed a green on the other side of a deep wash area that runs along the right side of the fairway and

Fifth at Old Town (courtesy of Dunlop White III)

cuts back in front of the green making the approach seem almost downhill in nature. The green itself is somewhat calm, while sloping from right to left, but is protected by three bunkers, one front left and two back right. Above the green to the right is the eighteenth green, which is only raised higher and separated by the two bunkers between the two greens. This hole originally featured a merged fairway with the eighteenth hole as they both turned around a grouping of trees in the middle. The front side of the course features some excellent holes and often points out the splendid nature of the site and the design. Aside from the double green, most people are left with no single hole being above the others, unless it is the seventh.

Original design of the seventh circa 1939 (courtesy of Old Town Club)

After a quick break in the clubhouse, the player begins the second nine holes within feet of the clubhouse with a crowned fairway greeting the player. As with most of the holes the drive leaves the player with a hanging lie and an approach that requires being on the correct side of the green or bogey is almost a definite outcome. The twelfth is a long par four with a sloping fairway from left to right. The fairway is also the widest on the course in the landing zone, providing

228

the player a chance to play from just about any angle into the green. Again, even though the hole is blind from the tee, the player can check out the pin location while playing the seventh and eighth holes on the other side of the creek. The real problem though lies in the fact that the approach is blind to the largest green on the course. A creek, fifteen yards short of the green, usually finds any mishit shots. Maxwell designed a feature into the green, called a kick-up, which could be used as a backboard. A player would hit shots that could carry through the green and would stop at the kick-up and roll back down onto the playing surface. Unfortunately, due to the redesign of the greens by Bob Cupp this feature was altered, and does not serve the same function as it was intended.

The most difficult hole on the course and one of the longer par fours is the thirteenth and it again uses the same formula as many of the other holes on the course. But it is a nice change of pace when one is faced with the next hole. The fourteenth is the shortest par four on the course. A creek travels along side the entire left side of the hole as the approach goes slightly uphill to the green while the terrain all slopes down to the creek. The green gets back to the theme of divided greens. The fourteenth is an excellent study in the use of the ridges and humps that Maxwell used consistently at Old Town. The bunkering at the back of the fourteenth hole originally was an excellent example of what type of bunker work Maxwell and Woods implemented with their designs during the period. The bunkering was very artistic and freeform in shape. Maxwell also wanted to use a prairie style look as blue stem was allowed to grow around the edges of the bunkers and in some cases within the bunkers to provide a raw and natural appearance.

The sixteenth hole is an example of the extreme contouring on the course at Old Town. It is a mid-length par four that slopes drastically from left to right with an approach to a small green on a knoll. Maxwell laid out two bunkers diagonally situated so that they could provide visual cues to the player on how to shape their shot. The bunker short was the line for those who hit draws off the tee. Those that preferred to fade the ball wanted to start out at the deep bunker on the left side. At the crest of the hill, the terrain flattened in comparison to the rest of the hole and provided a tough shot into the putting surface. The green is again divided into sections that create the added incentive for a solid shot to the correct portion of the green, or a three putt is likely to follow. The green features a tier on the left with a steep slope running to the right side. Even on an extreme site like the one at Old Town, Maxwell was consistent in trying to provide the player with as many elevated tee shots and green complexes as possible. The steep slope of the sixteenth hole would not be used in many modern designs and would be passed over, but without this connection, the seventeenth hole would not have been a possibility.

In the form of the eighteenth the player is confronted with a typical difficult finishing hole for Maxwell as it runs up the hill to the clubhouse. The tee shot is defended by four fairway bunkers to the left, as the fairway slopes toward the right side. The approach is often a mid-iron from the uphill and sidehill lie to the

229

elevated green with severe undulations and rolls. The back nine at Old Town is much more difficult than the opening sequence but you find a consistent theme and use of the land that creates a sort of magic when a course is designed thoughtfully and routed well within the natural movement of the terrain.

Aerial view of Old Town after construction (courtesy of Old Town Club)

Colonial Country Club
(1934, 1940-41) Fort Worth, Texas

Though the routing of the course is similar in nature to the original design, the components of the course have drastically changed. Many references to the holes in the 1941 United States Open Championship program note the "narrow" fifty-yard wide fairways. This so-called narrowness has been one of the major changes since the peak of the design, as it was in 1941. The actual green designs also appear to have been drastically altered over the years. Many of the greens featured large undulations and slopes, where today, the only dramatic nature to the greens is the speed at which they are maintained. The bunkering style of the course has also been changed significantly. The original bunkering scheme was very reminiscent to other Maxwell courses. Flat-bottomed bunkers with roughed out edges that had a very natural look were abundant on the course. Some of the bunkers even featured the turf islands that Perry used often during this period of his career. The numerous doglegs on the design warranted the comment from the club's most famous member, Ben Hogan, "A straight ball will get you in more trouble at Colonial than any course I know."

The course has become a favorite of many of the touring professionals due to the old-style design of the course and it is rightly treated as one of the crown jewels of golf course architecture on the modern-day tour, ranking alongside courses like Riviera and Westchester. But as much credit as Maxwell gets for this course, that should be shared with Dean Woods in this effort as his repoir with Leonard in the early construction phases assured Maxwell being the man that was called back in to create the world-class design that would become famous over the next several years. Due to the course beginning in an untraditional manner, with a three shot hole, the narrative below will as well.

Par Fives

The opening hole to the course was a long par five that snaked around the treeline with Country Club Circle along the right side of the hole. The fairway was very wide, with only the long player possibly being affected off the tee by the bunker on the left and the trees that were tight on the right. The longer player was also challenged on the second as the landing zone for the second shot was protected by a group of bunkers. The green was designed with a large slope from back right to front left and also featured two large Maxwell rolls on the sides of the green. The bunkering around the green was difficult to get down from as the green sloped away from all angles. The telltale bunker on the hole was the one directly behind the green that featured a turf island. The hole also featured Maxwell's typical bunkering on one side of the green and one bunker fronting the opposite side, as he did on many other long par fives.

The other long hole on the course was the eleventh and it was mostly a hole where avoiding trouble was the primary concern until the approach to the green was to be struck. On the tee shot water and trees were on the right side and then on the second the hazards were on the opposite side. Other than those water and the trees, the other defense was the immense length. But the green was well protected as bunkers pinched the area short and more sand was tightly place on both sides and behind the putting surface.

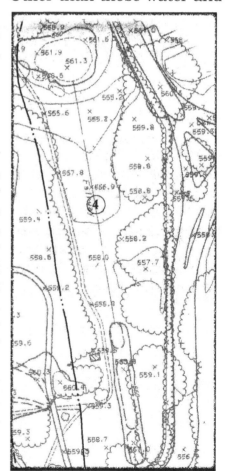

Par Threes

Colonial featured, four exciting holes of the par three type. The first of these to be encountered was the fourth, but it will be discussed in a section later about the most famous part of the course, the Horrible Horseshoe. The best par three on the course though was the impressive eighth. The par three eighth was an excellent hole as well that Maxwell and Woods rebunkered for the 1941 event and was a hole that they routed for the original course. The hole curved around the banks of the Trinity River to a well-placed green, using the water as a diagonal hazard. The layout of the hole was exactly like many other Maxwell designs of the same style of hole. A difficult carry directly to the green was required for the more skilled player and an alternative routing to the left for the lesser player was also accessible and provided a much easier way onto the green and still a chance to save par. The hole was laid out directly into the wind, to provide even more of a challenge in carrying the Trinity. The green was described as sharply rolling and offering many varieties of "breaks" on the putting surface. The carry on the hole was eliminated in 1968 when work was completed to reroute the Trinity for flood considerations. Byron Nelson referred to the hole as "the toughest par three I ever saw."

The thirteenth hole is another excellent par three on the course and

provides a similar challenge as the eighth with a dramatic carry of the Clear Fork off of the Trinity River. The exposed sand bar at the time of the design of the course added a dramatic flair to the hole. As with most Maxwell designs, the wind plays differently into all the par threes. On this hole it plays into a quartering wind that helps balls drift toward the water. The smallest green on the course was also one of the more undulating. A similar design was originally done by Maxwell on the second at Prairie Dunes a few years earlier with the hole traversing a depression between two dunes as opposed to the riverbed used at Colonial. The thirteenth was the first par three aced during competitive golf on the course. It took almost thirty years and was done in 1961 by Kel Nagle. Nagle was playing with Ben Hogan, famous for his concentration during his round, when Hogan replied simply, "Nice shot."

The most underappreciated of the quartet was the spectacular sixteenth. This hole was unique in that it featured a creek that ran back into play and bulged into the form of a small lake and was between the player and the green. The long-iron shot was one of the best final tests on the course as the player had to hit their approach on the correct level of the green or face the distinct possibility of three-putting and making a fatal bogey late in the round. The natural slope of the terrain from right to left was perfectly used in orientating the green to use that same flow. The bunkers also were cut into the hillside on the right and created an uneven lie for any that pushed their shots.

Par Fours

The par fours on the course were perhaps the least dramatic that Maxwell ever designed when one sees the natural terrain. Colonial is one of the flattest plots that Maxwell ever saw. To make up for the lack of elevation change throughout the site, he implemented the use of several bunkers on the redesign for the 1941 U.S. Open. The second hole is a prime example of this technique. The original hole consisted of a bunker at the corner of the dogleg and then one protecting the left side of the green. Dean Woods and Perry Maxwell inserted four more of the hazards around the putting surface, including one on the left that had a characteristic Maxwell turf island in it. Following the second was the sequence known as the Horrible Horseshoe and, as mentioned earlier these will be discussed separately.

The sixth hole was originally laid out to play as a traditional dogleg, again with a bunker protecting the corner. The final results created a hole that almost played as a reverse-dogleg and presented the best angle of attack to come from the outside of the fairway. That necessitated the addition of two bunkers on the left side of the landing zone. The bunkers at the green were increased in size by Maxwell. This was followed by a hole where the player had to hit it straight as it bottlenecked closer to the green due to trees pinching in the fairway. It is believed that Maxwell did not touch this hole in his renovation except in rebuilding the bunkers.

The ninth hole was almost a mirror image of the tenth hole at Muskogee. The hole was designed with the optimum angle to approach the green being from the side with the bunkers. This side also had to attempt the shot over the most water. Those that played from the outside of the dogleg had to clear less water, but were going into the putting surface with the narrowest target. The slope of the green was also a very characteristic of Maxwell greens; with subtle rolls that made every putt an adventure. By this time through the round it is obvious that Maxwell saw a similar piece of land to what he encountered at Muskogee with natural swales and a slight rise up to the area where the clubhouse resides. The ninth is a perfect hole to demonstrate this thought as it bears such a strong resemblance to the tenth hole at Muskogee. The hole today is one of the more photographed on the course as the pond fronting the green has been expanded and augmented with brick walls for aesthetic purposes with much of this work coming when the Trinity River and Clear Fork were rerouted to eliminate flooding problems the course has had over the years.

The back nine of the course commenced with a straight par four with a tee hard against water, but straight out was a wide fairway. The left side was the preferred side as the right side was protected by trees that lined a narrow wash

The eighteenth green as it appeared in 1941 for the United States Open

area fifty yards short of the green. The use of wash areas was a familiar design trait to Maxwell as well as many other designers during the era as it helped with drainage in the plains and Southwest. One of the bunkers protecting the green featured the familiar turf islands, which no longer exist on the course. The twelfth was one of the more heavily bunkered holes on the course and was a dogleg left, the first of the round.

As difficult as the stretch in the middle of the front nine was, perhaps the next three holes were an equal. The fourteenth was a long par four with trees on the left side that forced the player to take a line that added yardage to the hole, unless the could hit a controlled sweeping hook on their second into the deeply bunkered green. The other factor that added to the difficulty was the prevailing Texas wind blowing into the face of the player. The fifteenth was routed around a mound on the right side with beautiful bunkering in the face of the hill. The outside of the dogleg was also protected by a deep bunker that saw action often due to the wind pushing shots into its clutches. The subtle movement of the terrain also forced balls this way. But the left side was where the player wanted to be to hit into the green. Hazards were prolific on the hole as short and right was a notorious bunker and another was on the left side of the green. And for the badly

235

pulled shot was a creek that ran into the pathway of the sixteenth, which followed. The sixteenth then completed this difficult stretch.

The finishing duo of holes was not a walk in the park either. The seventeenth was a difficult drive. From the only truly elevated tee on the course, the player must account for the wind and avoid the right side of the hole on one of the few true birdie opportunities on the course. A creek runs the entire length of the hole and anything to the right side that stays in the fairway is blocked by the famous tree, "Big Annie". The green was also protected by a deep gulley short, a former creek bed, and two tight bunkers on either side.

The final hole is one of the finest finishing holes on the PGA Tour. The left side is protected by a row of trees up to 100 yards from the green where a pond picks up and runs just off the putting surface. The fairway in the landing zone features many of the famous Maxwell rolls in the fairway, much like Maxwell used on many of his courses. Thus creating an uneven lie on one of the more demanding approaches on the course, to a green set hard into the hillside that slopes sharply from right to left. The right side of the green was protected by three bunkers that made any save impossible with the green sloping towards the water and saw more than one victim hit their shot into a wet demise. The lake alongside the hole has been referred to as Crampton's Lake since 1965. In the 1962 tournament Crampton pulled his approach to the green into the water. He also did the same thing the round previously. He lost the tournament by one stroke to Arnold Palmer. A few years later he was in the same situation but instead placed the ball in the middle of the green, putted out for par and won the tournament by three strokes. A plaque was erected before the 1968 tournament honoring Crampton on the hole. Just a few days later he lost the tournament with a six on the hole due to trouble. He only needed a bogey to force a playoff with Tom Weiskopf.

The Horrible Horseshoe

One of the greatest and best-known portions of Maxwell's career was his work on the famed, Horrible Horseshoe at Colonial. This work, with good cause, overshadowed the rest of his work on the course. The fame associated with these holes and Colonial helped to cap the most spectacular and varied portion of Maxwell's career. Apart from his work at Augusta, it is possible no other work has been more noted from all of his efforts.

The beginning of the most famous stretch of holes west of the Mississippi was with the third hole. It is a long par four and the second toughest hole on the front nine, behind only the infamous fifth. It measured around 470 yards at the time of construction and was one of the early "Super Par Fours" designed in golf to combat the length the top players were achieving even during this period. The hole provided a short cut along the left side of the fairway as a carry of 230 yards was necessary to clear the nasty waste bunker on the left side. The player who played out to the right, had to deal with another bunker short of the green and lacked the proper angle into the severely sloping green. The original green location was just past the short bunker on the right hand side of the fairway. Maxwell's reposition of the green was perhaps the precursor to the strategy employed by the USGA in course setup for many years to come.

The fifth hole during the 1941 Open (courtesy of Colonial Country Club)

The fourth hole is one of the longest par threes on the professional tour at almost 250 yards. This hole is the middle of the "Horrible Horseshoe." It has a severe green that requires a purely struck wood to get on the elevated green and have any shot at birdie. The somewhat false front was the only real protection, aside from length, on this bunkerless par three. The green was the largest on the course and did feature some unique undulations on the left side that almost created a gulley in the middle of the putting surface. In the complete history of the Colonial tournament the hole has never been aced. It is the only par three on the course able to make that claim. Two bunkers have been added to the front and left of the green since the Maxwell construction.

The par four fifth hole has become known throughout golf as "Death Valley." It is a gargantuan par four that doglegs along the edges of the Trinity River and is often regarded as one of the great holes in golf. At 470 yards it is no small feat to reach the green with today's equipment, but in 1941 it was a true monster of a hole. The original hole was a much sharper dogleg around a small hill and had a green site in a similar position to the current version. Maxwell graded the hill slightly and placed this hole along the edge of the Trinity River. At the time of Maxwell's work many of the trees along the right side had not been planted. So it was a distinct possibility of putting your tee shot in the river. One pro who feared the hole so much commented on his pre-shot ritual at this hole, "I take two balls and throw them in the river, then I puke into the river, then I hit my tee shot into the river and play my third onto the green." The original design of the hole, like the fourth was bunkerless and relied simply on the contour of the land as a defense. The driving zone was tight and the fairway tightened even more up by the green, which was described in the 1941 program as "waving" in nature. The hole that Maxwell replaced was a 370-yard dogleg that played along the edge of the trees that were cleared to make room for the new holes.

237

Though not every hole was originally designed by Maxwell, by examining the characteristics of each hole it is easy to pick out some of the designs that were originally contributed in his submitted routings to Marvin Leonard. The original design of the course was a true collaboration with Leonard and Bredemus, but the final product for the 1941 US Open was significantly in the form of a true Maxwell and Woods design and due to that amount of influence should be characterized as one of their masterpiece layouts.

Oak Cliff Country Club
(1951-1953) Dallas, Texas

Maxwell's penchant for template holes was on display at the last design of his career. Over half of his final routing contained some of Perry's favorite hole layouts. The course in many respects created the opportunity for Maxwell to use similar techniques to what he had pulled off at several of his best designs, including placing the clubhouse on the highest point of the property. The wandering stream cutting through the course created a dramatic valley below that would provide many opportunities for exciting holes to be built into the terrain. Due to this being Maxwell's last effort, Oak Cliffs deserves to have the reader go through the routing as they would encounter the holes on the course to get a better sense of the great layout that Perry designed.

The design began with the typical Maxwell opening hole, a somewhat long downhill par four with a drop of twenty-five feet to the green below. This was followed by the excellent second that was a

The second and third holes at Oak Cliff
(courtesy of Eric Dorsey)

239

risk-reward par five with a deep chasm short of the green. The decision to play for the green was tempting as the player would have a downhill approach to the putting surface and be able to see the ball in flight all the way down to the green. The player could also get a little more run by playing off of the ridge that fed into the right side of the fairway if they played a running draw and perhaps have an ever shorter approach into the green.

The photogenic third hole was a wonderful par three that played directly across the stream. After this came three par fours that offered different challenges. The fourth was an uphill hole that climbed straight up from the tee in front of the player. The fifth featured a semi-blind drive to a fairway that doglegged to the left and ran away from the player creating a slightly hanging lie to the green perched on top of a precipice with a steep fall off to the right and into the creek. The sixth hole was an excellent version of the Bottle hole with a steep drop off to the creek and a depression feeding into the fairway from the cliff area on the left and providing an excellent carry hazard to get into proper position to attack the pin. The fairway was originally the widest on the course and invited the player to attempt the risky shot. Today the left side if filled with rough and trees and takes away this temptation.

The fifth and tenth holes at Oak Cliff
(courtesy of Eric Dorsey)

Maxwell then routed the course to go back across the creek with another one shot hole. The hole was originally designed to be about 180 yards and ran uphill to a green that sloped towards the player and to the left. It was the most difficult par three on the course and was quite intimidating with the creek just in front of the tee to accompany the dramatic rise in the terrain.

Following the difficult seventh, the eighth was essentially routed to get to the ninth and take the player back up the hill and to the clubhouse to complete the opening circuit of nine holes. This then led to the back nine and the tenth hole. Again Maxwell used his favorite methodology in laying out a course with opening holes having elevated tee shots and the returning holes being difficult uphill test on each set of nine.

The dramatic tenth was the best hole on the course. It was the best version of a Cape hole that Maxwell ever designed. The hole had a challenging diagonal carry over a creek from the elevated tee with the longer carry cutting off significant distance on the approach. The green also had the traditional Cape concept as it was surrounded by steep drop-offs on two sides with the back right portion of the green jutting out slightly and seemingly hanging over the edge of the hazard. It is possible that this hole was the best laid out by Maxwell after World War II.

The eleventh was also a template hole that Maxwell would use repeatedly over his career. This time it was the hole that he laid out more than any other. The tee shot went out to the sloping fairway and gave an elevated approach to the green on the other side of the creek on the mid-length par four. Today's player may even think about carrying the hazard from the tee as the carry is just at 300 yards in length. The twelfth was an excellent version of the fallaway green design with the creek directly behind the green. This was followed by Maxwell long version of a Redan that came in at 180 yards in length but has been extended to almost 230 yards today.

The lone par five on the back side of the course runs up hill all the way to the green at almost 550 yards in length. This is followed by the dramatically downhill dogleg left fifteenth. The drive goes downhill forty feet from tee to the eventual landing zone as the fairway runs away from the player. The terrain of the hole was similar to what Maxwell had encountered at Augusta when he remodeled the famous tenth hole at that course.

The sixteenth was a fine version of the Knoll hole and was originally around 300 yards in length. The hole used the right to left slope of the terrain as a defense in one of the few times that Maxwell went across the elevation change of the course. The green was benched hard into the hillside and protected by two bunkers in a similar fashion to his other Knoll holes in his career. With the last two holes Maxwell ran them uphill. The par three 17th presented a skyline green with a runoff on the right side of the green and a bump on the left provide a dramatic roll on that side of the putting surface. The last hole was again a typical Maxwell finisher as it was a difficult uphill dogleg hole to a green with the clubhouse in the background with the landing zone being canted from right to left and repelling most shots away from the direct line to the green.

Perry Maxwell only saw this course in the initial routing stages, which is a true injustice. Press Maxwell though constructed the course per the routing that his father left. The course was obviously deemed difficult enough to challenge the best players as it quickly was awarded the Dallas PGA Tour event, the Byron Nelson Classic. The course was one of a unique stature in the Maxwell portfolio and really took his career full circle. The course contained eleven different template holes from his career. The largest number since his work at Dornick Hills, his very first course and directly inspired from the National Golf Links. It was almost as if this was a return to his original style that had only appeared on one other course, but in bits and pieces throughout his career.

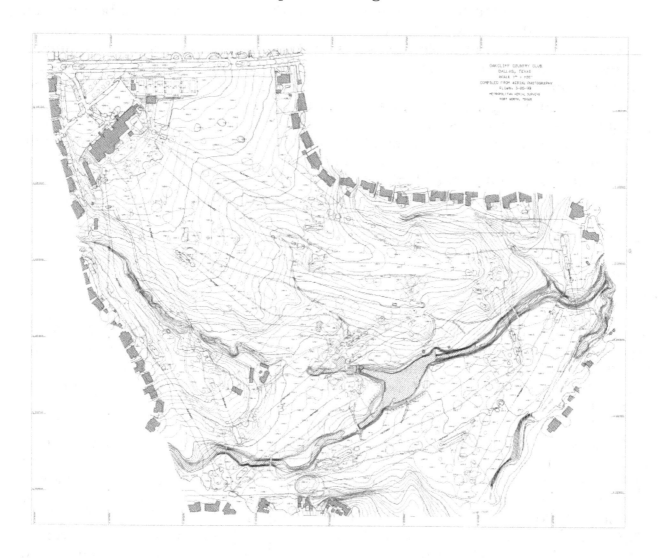

Topographic Map of Oak Cliff (courtesy of Jeffrey Brauer)

Appendices

The Collaborators

As with anyone of great success, Maxwell owed a great amount to those who directly impacted his career. Brief biographies of the four main influences on his career follow and provide some insight on them and how they impacted the career of Perry. They are presented in the chronological order that they impacted Perry's career from getting him started and providing the initial inspiration in his career through the passing of the family business to his son.

Charles Blair Macdonald, The Evangelist (1855-1939)

Macdonald was the first architect to promote the design of strategic golf courses in the United States. His greatest design, the National Golf Links, was inspired by a group of conceptual copies of the greatest holes in Great Britain. The course was brought to national attention in an article in Scribners Magazine in 1909 and was the first thing that sparked the interest of Maxwell in golf. During a tour of the great courses of America years later, Maxwell would make the acquaintance of Macdonald and those discussions, along with visits to St. Andrews, would be the formulation of the early strategy that Maxwell developed in his own course designs.

Macdonald in 1894 (courtesy of George Bahto)

As can be noted from a study of the first course by Maxwell, he was a devoted follower of the "National School of Design," as his course contained many of these same conceptual copies that Macdonald used on his famous works. Maxwell would continue to use these conceptual copies (Capes, Redans and other) over the years, but more sparingly, perhaps only one or two per course. But he would use the concepts throughout his design work. What Maxwell would do was to develop his own templates to use repeatedly in his designs over the years.

Another way that Macdonald also influenced Maxwell was in the way his practice was organized. Once Maxwell was aware that he would need continued assistance he modeled his "crew" after his teacher and started to work with an engineer, his brother-in-law Dean Woods. The two of them formed a team that would be involved with every major work done by Maxwell from the early 1920s until they split some twenty years later due to Dean's health problems.

One of the great achievements and compliments to Maxwell was his opportunity to work on the course that originally peaked his interest in golf in the mid-1930s with the oversight of Macdonald. Macdonald was impressed with his work as he referred him directly to the Maidstone Club and another Macdonald design, the Links Golf Club. Ironically, this much-publicized accomplishment by Maxwell has little or no documentation in the annals of the National's history and is only alluded to in other articles from the period.

Dean Woods, the Forgotten Man (1880-1950)

Photo of Dean Woods

Shortly after the urging by Ray Woods to build a golf course, Perry Maxwell went around the country to visit the greatest golf courses in the United States. One of those was the National Golf Links of America on Long Island. During his visit, Maxwell did talk with Charles Blair Macdonald about the course and golf course design. One of the topics most assuredly was the necessity to have a second man. In Macdonald's case it was Seth Raynor who could oversee the construction of the courses. Raynor was an engineer by trade so he was able to plan and oversee the construction of the courses in a way that best presented the artistic nature that Macdonald wanted on his courses, especially the National. As luck would have it, Maxwell had a family member who was a civil engineer as well, his brother-in-law, Dean Woods.

Dean Woods did electrical work in the Arizona copper mines for many years before moving to Oklahoma City after Oklahoma became a state. His sister, Ray, and Perry had recently moved down from Kentucky to the Ardmore area and the remainder of the Woods family also soon came to the state. Once in the Oklahoma City area Dean continued working in the engineering field, but also played semi-pro baseball. It is not known how good he was at the game, just that he played catcher. In 1923 or 1924, he was asked by Perry Maxwell if he would be willing to help him build golf courses. Dean bought a house in the area and began working with Perry for what would end up being a 30-year working relationship.

From that point on the rest was history, as they say. The two of them worked very closely in the design and construction of several golf courses including most of the notable designs by Perry Maxwell. Dean and his wife, Sarah, would often go to the town the course was located in and rent an apartment until the completion of the job. The list includes such courses as Oklahoma City, Southern Hills, Prairie Dunes, Crystal Downs, University of Michigan and Iowa State. Dean even helped with the best-known renovations by Maxwell at Augusta National, Pine Valley and Colonial.

The involvement at Colonial by Dean was of special significance. He stayed on with the club after the original layout was decided upon and actually helped with the construction of the course and oversaw all of the construction of the 1940 changes by he and Maxwell. He was also in charge of the course setup for the 1941 U. S. Open and was given the honor of being on the tournament committee. At Colonial, they awarded Dean a medal to help compensate for the out of pocket costs that he and Perry incurred on the job that went over budget.

Maxwell was so trusting of Dean's skill that he would leave him to solely oversee the construction of entire courses. A prime example of this is the Princeton Country Club. Why is Dean Woods the forgotten man? Mostly, because the second fiddle hardly ever gets the credit deserved but also because of a story about the work that Maxwell did at Pine Valley.

While working on Pine Valley, Perry would often go out each day and tell everyone what was to be accomplished on that day. Usually, he would then leave the crews to go out and do what needed to be done. Sometimes Maxwell would go into Philadelphia for the day and attend the symphony or visit some museum or some other cultural event. While he was gone people would try to find answers to some questions and the only person they could turn to was this gentleman who no one knew the name of. He was the forgotten man. That was Dean Woods.

Dean was the lead construction manager on almost all of Perry's projects until after World War II when Press Maxwell returned. Dean continued to work with Perry but he would retire, soon after Press' return, to California. He retired there with his wife, his tools and his Model A Roadster. Dean suffered a fatal heart attack in 1950.

Not only was Dean's skill at constructing the courses invaluable, but also his role as a manager of the labor was just as instrumental. Many of the courses that Maxwell designed were constructed using WPA labor. So many of the people had never set foot on a golf course before, let alone built one. Dean would have to instruct them on how to do things such as smooth a green, plant Bermuda in the fairway, pull a Fresno, or just dig out an area for a bunker. To say the least the labor was "unskilled." His ability to do this and take what Perry gave him and make a work of art was an extremely wonderful gift. Without him, the career of Perry Maxwell would possibly have been just a footnote in the annals of golfdom somewhere.

Alister Mackenzie, the Good Doctor (1870-1934)

Alister Mackenzie is recognized by many as the greatest golf course architect in history. Others don't have him very far down the list. Mackenzie was the first globetrotting designer the world had ever seen. He originally designed courses in

Portrait of Alistair Mackenzie
(courtesy of Raymond Haddock)

his homeland of England, including Alwoodley and Moortown in his hometown of Leeds. It was during this time that he made the acquaintance of Harry S. Colt and would ultimately join in a partnership with Colt and Charles Hugh Alison. The three of them made possibly the greatest group of raw talent in the history of the industry. They were an international firm that set the standard for other partnerships later on. Mackenzie and Colt soon parted ways as Mackenzie deemed he had greener pastures to explore. This timing also coincided with the divorce from his first wife and his almost banishment from his hometown. He quickly took to traveling to America to see what he could do there. He made an immediate connection with Marion Hollins and Robert Hunter and was given a great opportunity to design many courses in the United States. These courses included Cypress Point, The Valley Club and Pasatiempo. Mackenzie was also the consulting architect for the Royal & Ancient Golf in St. Andrews, Scotland. Through this association he was engaged to travel to Australia to help with the development of a new course for the Royal Melbourne Golf Club. He also did work at other golf clubs, including Kingston Heath, New South Wales and Royal Adelaide. He also traveled to South America and worked for two clubs, The Country Club of Uruguay and the Jockey Club in Buenos Aries. During this trip he created perhaps the finest golf courses on the continent to date. Upon returning to America he began a partnership with Perry Maxwell.

Mackenzie's life outside of golf was far from dull. Alister's father was a surgeon and he followed suit, as that was the thing to do. But medicine was not the calling for Alister. He became an expert on camouflage during his time in the Boer Wars and was often critical of the way the English Army prepared for the conflict. He gave numerous speeches on the topic and even tried to advise the United States President on the matter at one time. This expertise though would lead to one of the incredible traits that Mackenzie thought was essential to a good golf course. It taught him how to blend in features of the golf course with the surrounding terrain. One of the ideal characteristics of a true Mackenzie design would be hazards visible to the player that was playing the shot, but would disappear if you were standing on the green. Other new ideas that Mackenzie brought to the American landscape of golf architecture were freeform bunkers, as

247

opposed to geometric shapes and smooth edges, undulating greens that required imagination when striking putts as opposed to flat pancake type putting surfaces, and strategic design.

Mackenzie was also a wonderful writer, with an amazing wit and ability to tell a story. He wrote one of the lynchpins of golf course architecture literature. His little green book, "Golf Architecture" was published in 1920. Based on a series of lectures that Mackenzie gave, the most important component of the book were a series of 13 points that Mackenzie codified and documented for other designers to see. The 13 points have been published in many forms, but they focused on enjoyment of the game and making the golfer want more. He would also write a series of memoirs that further explained the 13 points and went into other areas of Mackenzie's thoughts on design, this book was title The Spirit of St. Andrews and was lost until the mid-1990's and was published after it was found by a relative.

For all the success that Mackenzie had, his life ended in great poverty. He lived in the fast lane but had large debts due to his way of living and from lack of payment from several clients, including Augusta National. When the Great Depression arrived, it almost destroyed Mackenzie's career, as with most architects during that period. He was so poor that he was not even able to attend the opening of his trademark work at Augusta, as he couldn't afford the cost of the flight from California. Even after his death this debt load affected him, as his wish to be buried with his parents could not be fulfilled, so his ashes were dropped from an airplane over the Pasatiempo course where he lived just off the 6th fairway for the latter years of his life with his second wife.

After his association with Mackenzie ended, Maxwell's designs seemed to change subtly, until his work at Prairie Dunes where it is quite apparent of the influence Mackenzie had on him as some of the bunkering is very reminiscent of the work done at Crystal Downs, where Maxwell and Mackenzie first really worked together. The two of them were without a doubt an unlikely duo, but the work that came from their partnership is still some of the best to have ever graced the golfing world.

Press Maxwell, The Son (1916-1999)

Press was born in 1916 to Ray Woods and Perry Maxwell in Ardmore, Oklahoma. The state was four years old at the time and Press would be one of the group of first generation Oklahomans that would conquer the world. The world was perhaps a simpler place even back when he was born. The US was about to join into "The War to end all wars." But something else was going on that greatly influenced the life of Press more than anything else in his life. Golf was beginning to spread like wildfire across the country. By this time his father had designed the first 9 holes at Dornick Hills. He was already contemplating retirement from the banking industry and beginning to think about golf course architecture as a new career.

248

Press Maxwell
(courtesy of Dora Horn)

Unfortunately, when Press was two his mother passed away from appendicitis. Press hardly knew his mother and would only hear stories of her from his sisters. Essentially though, Press grew up without a mother figure in his life, but to hear his wife Hodie discuss him, it was as if he was still the kindest man she had met in her life, except for maybe his father. Quite a refreshing story from the tales told today of children being raised in broken or unconventional homes that too often end with a story about drugs, crime or violence. Soon after this Perry Maxwell retired and decided to take a trip to Scotland to gain a fundamental understanding of how golf courses in Scotland were designed and incorporated the landscape in creating the greatest golf courses in the world. Press and his sister stayed behind with family friends and relatives until their father returned. Upon his father's return, Press started getting involved with the work his father was doing. He would go clear rocks from the ground; shovel dirt and sand, anything to help his father finish that next course. It was soon after this that Press decided this was what he was meant to do and what he wanted to be "when he grew up."

Thursday, October 29th, 1929 was perhaps the beginning of the worst period in the history of the United States and possibly the world from an economic standpoint. People lost their life savings, they began to jump out of windows, they lost their jobs in droves and there was nothing anyone could do to help. Ironically, this was the time period where Perry Maxwell's career seemed to take off. During this time period, Press not only got to work directly with his father on projects like Southern Hills and Prairie Dunes, but he also worked on courses such as Pine Valley and Augusta National. Press was able to absorb the knowledge of people such as Donald Ross, Alister Mackenzie and C. B. Macdonald while also working with his father. Quite an impressive way to get your education as a golf course architect.

It was also during this time that he would also meet his future wife, Hodie. They would fall in love and the courtship would last until the start of World War II. That's when Press asked for Hodie's hand in marriage. She unexpectedly declined and said that if he wanted to marry her, he would have to come back from the war alive. There is no incentive like true love to make a man come home from the incredible conflict of war. Press went to Europe and served most of his time in the war as a bomber pilot based in Italy. The story of Press' tour of duty was relayed in the history of Prairie Dunes by Mal Elliot, Perry Maxwell's Prairie Dunes.

Press came home in 1945, and after about 6 months of trying to get a clean break from the US Air Force and several trips across the country from Colorado Springs to the East Coast he decided to join his father in the golf course business. In October of that same year, he was wed to Hodie and they began their lives together. They got married in Lawrence, Kansas on a day off work from the course that Press and Perry were working on at the time, Excelsior Springs. After this Press became the construction foreman on all of his father's projects and is even credited with the co-design on a couple of assignments that they received at some old Air Force bases. Perry would begin to rely on Press even more in the business due to a leg amputation. Perry would still continue designing courses and would make some walks around the grounds, but most of this was left to Press and to him interpreting his father's message on the courses they did together. In 1952, Perry passed away after battling cancer that arose from the same affliction that cost him his leg. But Press was ready professionally to continue the family business.

Press continued the family business in a spectacular way. Unfortunately, the period after World War II and prior to 1965 is almost seen as a dead time in the terms of golf course architecture. The only person who was credited with making any type of significant contribution was Robert Trent Jones. Though he continued to design with the same simple style, his projects and most others were deemed by an unknowing populace as ineffective designs versus the much-ballyhooed designs of Jones at this time. Thus these projects were not often given their proper due. Press was recognized among his peers as he was elected to one of the more prestigious positions in the industry. He was elected President of the American Society of Golf Course Architects, the same organization his father was a founding member of, in 1960. Press would work on over 40 courses in his career.

Press also continued his flying ways after he came home from the war. He originally purchased an airplane from a used car dealer. Over the years he would trade up until he had adequate equipment to fly himself and his wife around the country to his jobsites. Golf course design may have been his love as a career, but flying was perhaps his favorite activity. He and Hodie eventually retired in the early 70's to Colorado, where they took up many hobbies including skiing, camping and fishing to the delight of both until Press passed away. The top courses during his career would include Hiwan Golf Club and renovation work at Cherry Hills outside of Denver. Other notable designs would be the Huntington Sea Cliff Golf Club, with scenic views of the ocean, Pinehurst Country Club in Denver and two resort courses in Aspen and Vail. His most famous work, though, was the completion of the course at Prairie Dunes, which his father had started. The original holes were basically intact when he came back to Hutchinson in 1956. He used his father's notes and implemented some of his own ideas while designing the remaining 9 holes of the circuit. The added nine holes would include the current 3rd, 4th and 5th holes on the front side. While on the back nine he created holes 11 through 16. The character of these holes is very much in line with what his father had imagined, but make use of the cottonwood trees that populate one side of the course to a great extent. This completed perhaps the finest work of Perry Maxwell and how fitting that it was completed by his son. The course at Pecan Valley Country Club would be Press' most recognized solo work as it has hosted numerous national and major championships. It has often been noted as bearing a strong resemblance to his father's work and has been called by some in error a Perry Maxwell design. The course uses a creek on eight holes and has many undulating greens much like his father's work from the years before. In a letter written by Press years later to a relative he commented that his work lacked the genius of his father's designs, but at Pecan Valley he captured some of that genius for a brief moment in time.

Perry Maxwell's Career

Perry Maxwell was quoted in an article late in his life as saying that he believed he was involved with the original or complete redesign of roughly 70 courses and did some other work on almost 50 courses and did work in 21 states. To help with the timeline of his work he also was quoted in a 1945 article that the Lakewood Country Club was his 44th original course design. Currently only 52 of his original designs can be documented and only 27 of his renovations in only 20 states. There have been many courses linked to Maxwell incorrectly over the years. But the list below is the most comprehensive to date. Currently, there are five courses prior to the Lakewood construction and eleven courses after the Lakewood construction that need to be identified to meet the Maxwell number. One of the largest possibilities is the window of time between 1926 and 1933 in the Philadelphia area, as Maxwell had an active office in the area, but no documented work during that period of time. Another is post World War II in Texas along what is now the I-35 corridor as he took several jobs during this period in this area and only a few are documented. The likelihood also exists that several courses from the early days of his career in Oklahoma are not identified as they fell under during the Depression or during World War II. It is known that he also did work on a course in Connecticut but no members of the Maxwell family know the details of the work as Perry only mentioned it as some additional work that he took on during his career. Using these as the basis for further investigation it is hopeful that one day a complete list of his work can be identified.

Solo Designs by Perry Maxwell

Dornick Hills Golf & Country Club	Ardmore, Oklahoma	1913-1923
Twin Hills Golf & Country Club	Oklahoma City	1920-1923
Duncan Golf & Country Club	Duncan, Oklahoma	1921
Bristow Golf Club	Bristow, Oklahoma	1923
Shawnee Country Club	Shawnee, Oklahoma	1923
Indian Hills Country Club	Catoosa, Oklahoma	1924
Muskogee Country Club (redesign)	Muskogee, Oklahoma	1924
Pennsylvania Golf Club (NLE)	Llarnech, Pennsylvania	1924
Kennedy Golf Course (NLE)	Tulsa, Oklahoma	1925

Highland Park Golf Course (NLE)	Tulsa, Oklahoma	1925
Hillcrest Country Club	Bartlesville, Oklahoma	1926
Hardscrabble Country Club	Fort Smith, Arkansas	1926

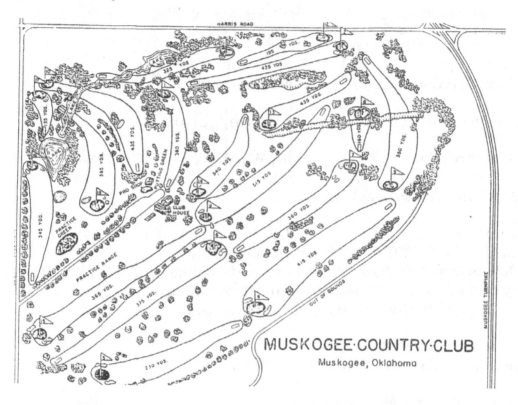

Original layout of Muskogee (courtesy of Muskogee Country Club)

Cushing Country Club	Cushing, Oklahoma	1929
Ponca City Country Club (redesign)	Ponca City, Oklahoma	1929
Rochelle Country Club	Rochelle, Illinois	1929
Princeton Country Club	Princeton, Kentucky	1931
Hillcrest Golf Course	Coffeyville, Kansas	1932
Iowa State University Golf Course	Ames, Iowa	1934-1937
Oak Hills Golf & Country Club	Ada, Oklahoma	1935
Southern Hills Country Club	Tulsa, Oklahoma	1935-1936
Arkansas City Country Club	Arkansas City, Kansas	1937
McPherson Country Club	McPherson, Kansas	1937
Topeka Country Club (redesign)	Topeka, Kansas	1938
Blackwell Municipal Golf Course	Blackwell, Oklahoma	1939
Mount Pleasant Country Club	Mount Pleasant, Texas	1939
The Old Town Club	Winston-Salem, NC	1939
Reynolds Park Golf Course	Winston-Salem, NC	1940

Walnut Hills Golf Club (NLE)	Dallas, Texas	1940
Duke University (Never constructed)	Durham, NC	1940
Gillespie Golf Club	Greensboro, NC	1941
Lawton Country Club	Lawton, Oklahoma	1948

Co-Designed with Art Jackson

Lincoln Park Golf Course (2nd)	Oklahoma City	1926

Co-Designed with John Bredemus and Marvin Leonard

Colonial Country Club	Fort Worth, Texas	1934

Co-Designed with Alister Mackenzie

Melrose Country Club	Cheltenham, PA	1924-1926
Oklahoma City Golf & CC*	Oklahoma City	1927
Crystal Downs Country Club	Frankfort, Michigan	1928-1931
University of Michigan Golf Course	Ann Arbor, Michigan	1931
Ohio State University Golf Course **	Columbus, Ohio	1935

*co-design in contract only
**construction by Maxwell, design by Mackenzie

Co-Designed with Press Maxwell

Prairie Dunes Country Club	Hutchinson, Kansas	1937, 1957
Lakewood Country Club	Point Clear, Alabama	1944-1947
Austin Country Club	Austin, Texas	1946-1948
Excelsior Springs Golf Course (NLE)	Excelsior Springs, MO	1947
Grandview Municipal Golf Course	Springfield, Missouri	1947
Oakwood Country Club	Enid, Oklahoma	1947-1948
Kentucky Dam Village	KDV, Kentucky	1948
Camp Hood Golf Course (NLE)	Camp Hood, Texas	1948
Randolph Oaks Golf Course	Randolph AFB, Texas	1948
F.E. Warren AFB Golf Course	Cheyenne, Wyoming	1948
Bayou DeSiard Country Club	Monroe, Louisiana	1949
Palmetto Country Club	Benton, Louisiana	1950
U of Oklahoma Golf Course	Norman, Oklahoma	1950
Oak Cliffs Country Club	Dallas, Texas	1951
River Hills Golf Club (NLE)	Irving, Texas	1951
Lake Hefner Golf Course	Oklahoma City	1951

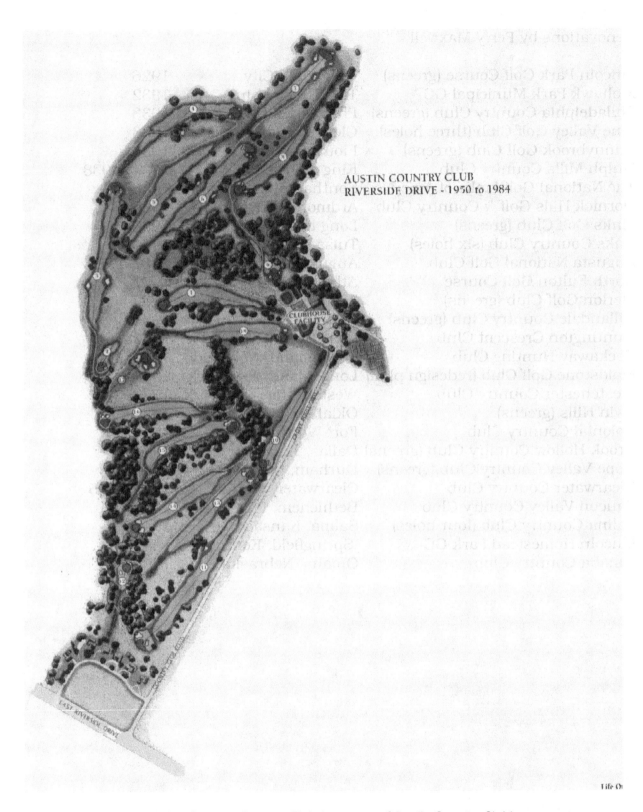

Routing of Austin Country Club (courtesy of Austin Country Club)

Renovations by Perry Maxwell

Lincoln Park Golf Course (greens)	Oklahoma City	1926
Mohawk Park Municipal GC	Tulsa, Oklahoma	1932
Philadelphia Country Club (greens)	Philadelphia	1933
Pine Valley Golf Club (three holes)	Clementon, New Jersey	1933
Sunnybrook Golf Club (greens)	Flourtown, PA	1934
Gulph Mills Country Club	King of Prussia, Pa	1934-1938
The National Golf Links of America	Southampton, NY	1935
Dornick Hills Golf & Country Club	Ardmore, Oklahoma	1936
Links Golf Club (greens)	Long Island, New York	1936
Oaks Country Club (six holes)	Tulsa, Oklahoma	1936
Augusta National Golf Club	Augusta, Georgia	1937-1938
North Fulton Golf Course	Atlanta, Georgia	1937
Merion Golf Club (greens)	Ardmore, Pennsylvania	1938
Hillandale Country Club (greens)	Hillandale, NC	1938
Huntington Crescent Club	Long Island, New York	1939
Rockaway Hunting Club	Long Island, New York	1939
Maidstone Golf Club (redesign plan)	Long Island, New York	1939
Westchester Country Club	Westchester, New York	1939
Twin Hills (greens)	Oklahoma City	1939
Colonial Country Club	Fort Worth, Texas	1940
Brook Hollow Country Club (greens)	Dallas, Texas	1940
Hope Valley Country Club (greens)	Durham, NC	1940
Clearwater Country Club	Clearwater, Florida	1940-1945
Saucon Valley Country Club	Bethlehem, PA	1944
Salina Country Club (four holes)	Salina, Kansas	1945
Lincoln Homestead Park GC	Springfield, Kentucky	1948
Omaha Country Club	Omaha, Nebraska	1951

The Best of Perry Maxwell

The *en vogue* thing in golf, and in life is to create lists of favorites. You see this in everything from the simple grocery list to tasks as difficult as the determining of the 100 most influential books in the history of man. When compiling a list of Maxwell courses that is easy, as you have a clear basis for inclusion on the list. When compiling a list of his best courses that is somewhat more difficult, but is still fairly easy to form a consensus upon the better courses in his career. But compiling a list of individual holes that appear to be superior to others suddenly creates a whole new level of difficulty. The list below was very difficult to arrive at and had many changes in the process. The larger problem is that Maxwell did such a wonderful job of designing his courses that on most of them, one hole is not noticeably superior to the others. The Old Town Club is a perfect example of this. No one can really find one or two holes that stand out, but that is because they are each of equal merit and are designed so well that they just blend together and form a sum that is greater than the individual components. Another factor in the difficulty is that Maxwell had no set regimen in how he designed courses. He didn't favor any particular type of hole, such as a Redan or Eden style of hole. This is not to say he didn't use particular lengths of holes or prototypes throughout his designs. Almost all of his courses have one of these holes. The keys in developing this list were to identify holes that best exemplified the traits of what Maxwell tried to do in his designs, identify superior holes that fell under the consistent type of holes he used, identify any odd style of holes that really stand out in his work, and to also spread the wealth among several of his designs if possible.

The final result of that list appears below with the original yardage of the hole included. The majority of his courses seem to end up with an exemplary blend of par fours, so that is where the strength of this list dwells. There were a couple of design quirks that produced some excellent holes and those have been included as well. Simply stated, this is a list of holes that anyone wanting to study Maxwell should be familiar with.

Par Threes

Prairie Dunes #10 – 160 yards - A mid length par three with dunes and deep grass between the tee and the green and runs slightly uphill. Maxwell considered this hole his greatest par three design. Who is to argue? This hole was voted as one of the top 100 holes in the United States by Golf Digest. The natural location of the green and the elevated nature of the hole create one of the most unique par threes in the world.

Old Town #6 – 180 yards – A downhill par three that has one of the most wicked green sites ever created by Maxwell. It has been described as trying to land the ball on the hood of a car and keeping it there. Extreme rolls create many small interior putting surfaces and steep run offs create the need to make sure the ball stays on the green. Even keeping the ball on the putting surface doesn't guarantee a par.

Dornick Hills #8 – 225 yards – The first version of Maxwell's concept of the Redan was also his best. The hole featured a carry hazard that ran at an angle from the tee. The longest carry was to the ideal landing spot to roll the ball the length of the green and reach back right hole locations that were protected by a bunker on the right side of the green. The slope of the green was too difficult to maintain and was eliminated in the 1960s and the cross hazard was eliminated in a later renovation of the course.

Colonial #8 – 198 yards – This hole is a version of one of the famous template holes by Maxwell. The Clear Fork intruded into the line of flight to the green that was surrounded by bunkers. The player could choose to play away from the green and not even have to carry the hazard and then be faced with a chip to a green that sloped slightly away from them towards the water. This hole was described by some players, at the 1941 US Open, as the hardest par three they had ever played.

Par Fives

Dornick Hills #16 – 535 yards - As with the short par fives, Maxwell used natural hazards to determine where he would place the greens on this length of hole. The best example is perhaps the most famous hole on Maxwell's first course. Referred to as "Old Stone Face" by the members, due to the forty-foot sheer rock face that goes from the fairway up to the green. Few players make it on the green in two. Another testament of Maxwell's ability to make a great hole out of what naturally existed on the site. But the fun isn't over once you reach the green. The three rolls and the deep drop off behind the green make it the most feared approach on the course also.

Crystal Downs #8 – 580 yards – This co-design with Alister Mackenzie is perhaps the finest par five either was involved with. The layout of the hole not only uses terrain to provide dramatic contrasts and hole strategy, but the added impact of the subtle contouring in the fairway that was done by hand with manual labor and horse-pulled machinery make the wave like motion of the fairway and amazing combination of man and nature creating a beautiful hole.

Par Fours

Oak Cliff #10 – 370 yards – On his final design Maxwell implemented a large number of template holes. The best of these was his final version of the "Cape" concept that he borrowed from Macdonald. The landing zone and the green were precariously close to one of the deep ravines that dominate the terrain of this Dallas course.

Hillcrest #11 – 355 yards – From an elevated tee, the player is shown a plateaued fairway with a slight slope feeding from left to right off of the ridge to the left of the hole. The drop is accentuated by the lowest spot on the hole being short of the green in the form of a natural creek bed. The green is then perched into the side of a hill with a bunker protecting the front left. The serenity and the view of the hole are a picture of the simple nature that Maxwell used on his best holes.

Old Town #7 – 375 yards – This hole completes the best three hole stretch on the course and is a real strategic joy to play. The player can either try to carry the bunkers on the left or leave the ball out to the right and have to clear the defenses of the green from the wrong angle. The player must pick their poison from the tee. As a subtle joke, Maxwell also included a tree dead in the middle of the hole to provide even more anguish for those that couldn't make up their mind.

Prairie Dunes #8 – 395 yards - The fifth hole of the original nine at Prairie Dunes is perhaps the best of the bunch. Named as the best 8th hole in the United States by Golf Illustrated and on many eclectic lists, its virtues go without saying. But for those unknowing of them, the hole is lined with dunes all along the left side and an approach from the fairway must dare with the dunes and the bunkers that protect the green if a par is to be had. This hole features everything that Maxwell loved. Undulating terrain, a rolling green and the fact that it was a modification on the Road Hole concept was an added bonus. From tee to green it is the best example of what Maxwell's design tenants were founded on.

Crystal Downs #13 – 442 yards - Often overlooked due the dramatic and splendid nature of the front nine and the finishing holes, the lakeshore contains a wonderful group of holes as well. None better than the 13th. An incredible sloping fairway from left to right creates a naturally appealing shot line that feeds down to a green with a false front and a canter from front to back. The green is protected by some deep bunkers but is an excellent example again of Maxwell's ability to make a hole look natural.

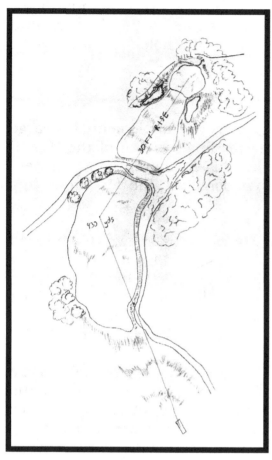

Drawing of Melrose's best hole

Oakwood #10 – 420 yards – The opening hole of the second nine at Oakwood is routed from an elevated tee through a series of three hills with the green cut hard into the last of the group. The fairway snakes around the other two rises and provides the player multiple options in attacking the hole. The preferred play is along the right side so a clear view of the green is accessible. Possibly this is the best hole designed by Maxwell after World War II.

Twin Hills #8 – 440 yards – The original version of the hole featured what would create the name for the course. Two hills dominated the hole as they even added to the downhill nature of the hole as the slope down the fairway was more extreme, but the fairway was blind from the tee. The green has also been rebuilt at least two times since the original version of the hole.

Melrose #13 – 435 yards – The elevated tee provided an excellent view of the wide fairway and allowed the player full view of their options. They could hug the creek and try to create as short an approach as they would like or play out to the safe left side of the fairway and have a much more difficult approach up the hill to the plateau green. The routing of the hole to traverse the valley that contained the creek was a brilliant move and to include the creek as a natural hazard as well was genius.

Oklahoma City #2 – 455 yards – The best hole on the golf course uses some of the best topography on the course as well. The green is situated at the base of a hill with a definite cant from the ridge running down to the green location. The player who doesn't want to get the ball in the Oklahoma breeze can definitely use the ground to his advantage on this hole. The slope of the green was described by Floyd Farley as "10 feet from front to back." That may be a slight exaggeration, but the definite reverse cant of the green makes any approach into it a measure of the players skill.

Oklahoma City #9 – 465 yards – Along with the second, this hole is one of the feature designs of the first set of holes at Oklahoma City. The tee shot ascends up what seems to be a massive hill on this relatively flat site and comes to rest at the highest point of the hole and provides a wonderful view into the angled green. The bunker on the left side sees many players as the lie dictates a draw and many just come up one club short on their approach. The steep green also provides some wonderful adventures with the flat stick.

Southern Hills #12 – 445 yards - Named by Golf Magazine as one of the top 18 holes in the world guarantees this hole's inclusion in this list. Though not the most difficult, it is the hole that best exemplifies the core strategy of Maxwell at Southern Hills. Sloped fairways, greens pinched by hazards, ability to shape the shot using the ground and the wind and using the natural terrain as it was before the hole was started help make this one of the truly special holes in the world.

Southern Hills #18 – 430 yards - One of the toughest finishing holes in golf, as shown in the 2001 US Open. An uphill approach, after a difficult drive, to a green with some of the fiercest slopes on the course. The hole plays almost as Maxwell designed it from inception. The most difficult hole at Southern Hills in the opinion of many is also the classic challenging par four to end the round. The view from the tee with the clubhouse up the hill is one of the best in golf. This became the style of finishing hole that Maxwell was most associated with around the country.

261

Acknowledgments

Many people have asked me since this project started what was the reason I became interested in the career of Perry Maxwell. At times, I have often wondered what it was also. It probably all started the first time that I went the course at Crystal Downs in Frankfort, Michigan. The beauty of the course was completely different than anything I had seen in central Indiana. Later that summer I also took in three other courses that were touched by Perry Maxwell and decided to start researching what other courses he had designed. I was aware of the courses at Prairie Dunes and Southern Hills but beyond that I was ignorant about his career. Upon an initial search of the internet, thirty or so courses were found and many of those were actually just renovation work. I wrote many letters to try and attain some information about the courses and received several phone calls and letters in response. I soon after this determined that I should contact some of the family members to see if I could find out anything else about Perry as a person. Before I knew it I had an accordion folder full of information. I was aware that there wasn't really anything documented about the career of Maxwell, so I decided to make use of what everyone had given me to write a book.

I must first thank God for giving me the opportunity to meet all of the people involved with this investment of time and energy. It has helped me to develop friendships that will last the remainder of my days. And without Him, I doubt this would have been a possibility. Second, I would like to thank my wife and her constant enthusiasm about my work on this project. She was always willing to set aside time for me to work solely on the book and take on much more than she should have around the house with our two little children. The next few months will consist of many nights of washing dishes and folding laundry.

Obviously, a work of this magnitude could not be completed single-handedly. The primary source of personal information and a great deal of information about the golf design career of Perry was provided by family members. Perry Maxwell's lone surviving child, Dora Harrison, was a fountain of information about Maxwell. The family archivist, Dora Horn, was an extreme assistance in many ways to this project. She was constantly sending me copies of anything she had about her grandfather. Hodie Maxwell, the wife of Press Maxwell also was willing to provide any information she could about her husband and father-in-law. She was extremely knowledgeable about the career of both as she accompanied them on many of their travels around the country from course to course. Jerome "Bruzzy" Westheimer, Jr. provided some excellent information about Ardmore and the Dornick Hills area as well as information about his grandfather, Dean Woods. Morton Woods, Jr. also was an excellent host and was extremely helpful with information of the workings of the dairy farm on the Primrose Hill area that was run by his father. He also provided general information about the summer he spent with his uncle on the road from course to course.

Two others of significant help were Del Lemon and Mal Elliott. Del was extremely helpful in regards to the history of many of the happenings in the state of Oklahoma and in Texas as well. His excellent work, The Story of Golf in Oklahoma, was an amazing source of information and provided much insight to the competitive aspects of many of the courses of Perry Maxwell. Mal Elliott also was an inspiration. His recently released history of the Prairie Dunes Country Club is an amazing resource for anyone wanting to learn more about the course and Maxwell. Mal also wrote a history of golf in Kansas that contained some wonderful information about many other courses in Kansas. He also was extremely knowledgeable about other Maxwell works. Without the assistance of these two this work would not have been completed.

I would also like to thank Paul Daley. His help through the entire process has been invaluable. Without his guidance what you hold right now would not be nearly as well put together. I would also like to thank Mike DeVries for the wonderful foreword to the book. Mike was a pleasure to talk with. And was an exceptional host at Kingsley.

One other person that provided some wonderful information about the banking career of Maxwell was Harold Pittman who grew up in the town of Ardmore and has researched the history of banks in Carter County in Oklahoma. Butch Bridges provided some wonderful general historical information about the Ardmore area as well. Several others have provided assistance and guidance in the writing and research of this work. The USGA was of immense help in providing old programs and photos of Southern Hills, Colonial and Prairie Dunes. Patty Moran and Maxine Vigliotta are without peer in my mind. Julie Ware at Golf Digest was also an extreme boon to the research process. The list also includes Geoff Shackelford, Daniel Wexler, George Bahto, Ron Whitten, Brad Klein, Tommy Nacaratto, Irwin Smallwood and John Holt. Providing an excellent view in regards to the architectural perspective were Bill Coore, Keith Foster, Jerry Slack and Kelly Blake Moran. Also thanks must go out to Floyd Farley for putting up with the bad connection we suffered through during our conversation. Others that provided wonderful insight about the playing of the excellent golf courses by Maxwell were Bob Crosby, Brad Miller and Ran Morrisett. Unfortunately, I can't help but feel that I have missed someone in this list.

I would also like to thank those that were proofreaders of sections of the book. Dunlop White III was helpful with some items on Old Town. Mark Guiniven gave an excellent view from another follower of golf course architecture. Dora Horn was instrumental in providing clarification on historical issues. Also my parents helped out in providing a perspective from someone that has a casual interest in the field of golf course architecture. All of them have helped me in many ways with this book. Also the people that helped with photographs that are seen through the book; Craig Edgmand, Matt Cohn, David Wigler and Lynn Shackelford.

The research though was not without some times of tribulation. Strangely enough the career of Maxwell and many of his courses have been touched by fire. In the research conducted, it was found that almost ten courses had lost their original clubhouse due to fires. Ironically, much of the information retained from the careers of Perry and Press Maxwell were destroyed in a fire late in the life of Press Maxwell. It is believed that a large amount of the records and drawings by Maxwell were destroyed this way. It goes without saying that there were probably several people that through the process I have either missed or forgotten, please know that I am thankful for your help and that without you this was not possible.

Bibliography

_____. Prairie Dunes: The First Fifty Years, 1937-1987. Hutchinson, Kansas: Prairie Dunes Country Club, 1987.

Bahto, George. The Evangelist of Golf: The Life of Charles Blair Macdonald. Chelsea, Michigan: Clock Tower Press, 2002.

Barclay, James A. The Toronto Terror: The Life and Works of Stanley Thompson, Golf Course Architect. Chelsea, Michigan: Sleeping Bear Press, 2000.

Christian, Frank, with Cal Brown. Augusta National and The Masters. Chelsea, Michigan: Sleeping Bear Press, 1996.

Colt, H.S. and C.H. Alison. Some Essays on Golf Course Architecture. Worcestershire: Grant Book, 1993 (Facsimile of 1920 edition).

Cornish, Geoffrey and Ronald Whitten. The Architects of Golf. New York: HarperCollins Publishers, 1993.

Darwin, Bernard. The Golf Courses of the British Isles. London: Duckworth and Co., 1910.

Doak, Tom. The Anatomy of a Golf Course. New York: Lyons and Burford, 1992.

Doak, Tom. The Confidential Guide to Golf Courses. Chelsea, Michigan: Sleeping Bear Press, 1996.

Doak, Tom and Dr. James S. Scott and Raymond M. Haddock. The Life and Work of Dr. Alister Mackenzie. Chelsea, Michigan: Sleeping Bear Press, 2001.

Dye, Pete, with Mark Shaw. Bury Me in a Pot Bunker. Reading, Massachusetts: Addison Wesley Publishing Company, 1994.

Elliott, Mal. 100 Years of Kansas Golf. Wichita, Kansas: Mennonite Press, 1996.

Elliott, Mal. Perry Maxwell's Prairie Dunes. Chelsea, Michigan: Sleeping Bear Press, 2002.

Gordon, John. The Great Golf Courses of America. Buffalo, New York: Firefly Books, 1997.

Hunter, Robert. The Links. New York: Charles Scribner's Sons, 1926. (Facsimile of 1927 edition by the United States Golf Association, 1994).

Jett, C. Kevin. History of the Muskogee Country Club: First Established Club in Oklahoma. Muskogee, Oklahoma: Jett Publications, 1991.

Jones, Robert Trent, with Larry Dennis. Golf's Magnificent Challenge. New York: McGraw-Hill and Sammis Publication, 1989.

Jones, Robert Trent, Jr. Golf by Design. New York: Little, Brown and Company, 1993.
Klein, Bradley S. Discovering Donald Ross: The Architect and His Golf Courses. Chelsea, Michigan: Sleeping Bear Press, 2001.

Labbance, Bob. The Old Man: The Biography of Walter J. Travis. Chelsea, Michigan: Sleeping Bear Press, 2000.

Lemon, Del. The Story of Golf in Oklahoma. Norman, Oklahoma: University of Oklahoma Press, 2001.

Macdonald, Charles Blair. Scotland's Gift – Golf. New York: Charles Scribner's Sons, 1928.

Mackenzie, Alister. Golf Architecture. London: Simpson, Marshall, Hamilton, Kent, and Co., 1920.

Mackenzie, Alister. The Spirit of St. Andrews. Chelsea, Michigan: Sleeping Bear Press, 1995.

Miller, Michael G. and Geoff Shackelford. The Art of Golf Design. Chelsea, Michigan: Sleeping Bear Press, 2001.

Paul, Thomas and Charles Lighthall. Gulph Mills Golf Club: Design Evolution 1916-1999. King of Prussia, Pennsylvania: Gulph Mills Golf Club, 1999.

Pedley, Jack. Princeton Country Club: 50th Anniversary. Princeton, Kentucky: Princeton Country Club, 1981.

Peper, George. Golf Courses of the PGA Tour. New York: Henry Abrams, Inc., 1986.

Peper, George. The 500 World's Greatest Golf Holes. New York: Artisan, 2000.

Peper, George. The Story of Golf. New York: TV Books, Inc., 1999.

Quirin, William. America's Linksland: A Century of Long Island Golf. Chelsea, Michigan: Sleeping Bear Press, 2002.

Ross, Donald J. Golf Has Never Failed Me. Chelsea, Michigan: Sleeping Bear Press, 1997.

Seelig, Pat. Historic Golf Courses of America. Dallas, Texas: Taylor Publishing Company, 1994.

Shackelford, Geoff. Alister Mackenzie's Cypress Point Club. Chelsea, Michigan: Sleeping Bear Press, 2000.

Shackelford, Geoff. The Captain: George C. Thomas Jr. and his Golf Architecture. Chelsea, Michigan: Sleeping Bear Press, 1997.

Shackelford, Geoff. The Golden Age of Golf Design. Chelsea, Michigan: Sleeping Bear Press, 1999.

Shackelford, Geoff. Masters of the Links. Chelsea, Michigan: Sleeping Bear Press, 1997.

Steinbrenner, John. Golf Courses of the U. S. Open. Taylor Publishing, 1996.

Thomas, George C. Golf Architecture in America, Its Strategy and Construction: Los Angeles: Times Mirror Co., 1927 (Facsimile of 1927 edition by Sleeping Bear Press, 1997).

Tillinghast, A.W. (edited and compiled by Robert S. Trebus, Richard C. Wolfe Jr. and Stuart F. Wolfe). The Course Beautiful: A Collection of Original Articles and Photographs on Golf Course Design. New Jersey: TreeWolf Publications, 1995.

Tillinghast, A.W. (edited and compiled by Robert S. Trebus, Richard C. Wolfe Jr. and Stuart F. Wolfe). Reminiscences of the Links: A Treasury of Essays and Vintage Photographs on Scottish and Early American Golf. New Jersey: TreeWolf Publications, 1998.

Tillinghast, A.W. (edited and compiled by Robert S. Trebus, Richard C. Wolfe Jr. and Stuart F. Wolfe). Gleanings from the Wayside: My Recollections as a Golf Architect. New Jersey: TreeWolf Publications, 1995.

Trimble, Francis. One Hundred Years of Champions and Change. Austin, Texas: Austin Country Club, 1999.

Ward-Thomas, Pat, et al. The World Atlas of Golf. London: Mitchell Beazley Publishers Limited, 1976.

Wethered, H.N. and Tom Simpson. The Architectural Side of Golf. Worchestershire: Grant Books, 1995 (Facsimile of 1929 edition).

Wexler, Daniel. The Missing Links: America's Greatest Lost Golf Courses & Holes. Chelsea, Michigan: Sleeping Bear Press, 2000.

Wexler, Daniel. The Lost Links: Forgotten Treasures of Golf's Golden Age. Chelsea, Michigan: Clock Tower Press, 2003.

Endnotes

[1] Pearl Hawthorne, Miss Pearl's Notes, Caldwell County Times (Princeton, Kentucky), 16 November 1978.

[2] Charles Evans, "Perry Duke Maxwell," in The Chronicles of Oklahoma, 31 (Oklahoma City, Oklahoma, Oklahoma Historical Society, 1953), 134.

[3] Evans, 134.

[4] Evans, 134.

[5] Bob Davis, "Photo-biographies – No. 33" in The American Golfer (American Golfer, 1935).

[6] Prairie Dunes: The First Fifty Years 1935 – 1985 (Hutchinson, Kansas, Prairie Dunes Country Club, 1985) , 16.

[7] Extract from land purchased by Perry Maxwell in 1914 provided by Jerry Westheimer, Jr.

[8] James Watson, Early Days (Ardmore, Oklahoma, date unknown), 2.

[9] Mac Bentley, Daily Oklahoman (Tulsa, Oklahoma), 23 May, 1993.

[10] James W. Finegan, 2001 US Open Championship Program, (Far Hills, New Jersey, United States Golf Association, 2001), 114.

[11] Finegan, 116.

[12] Davis.

[13] Mac Bentley, Daily Oklahoman (Tulsa, Oklahoma), 27 April, 1986.

[14] Del Lemon, The Story of Golf in Oklahoma (Norman, Oklahoma, University of Oklahoma Press, 2001), 81.

[15] Tom Doak, Dr. James S. Scott & Raymund M. Haddock, The Life and Work of Dr. Alister MacKenzie, (Chelsea, Michigan, Sleeping Bear Press, 2001), 29.

[16] The Bartlesville Enterprise, (Bartlesville, Oklahoma), 12 January 1926.

[17] The Bartlesville Enterprise

[18] Doak, 129-130.

[19] B. A. Bridgewater, Daily Oklahoman (Tulsa, Oklahoma) 15 September 1945.

[20] PBS.Org, People & Events: Surviving the Dust Bowl: Works Progress Administration, 2003

[21] Cal Lloyd, A Lost Treasure Brought to Light, (Golf Course Management, April 1993), 90.

[22] Lloyd, 96.

[23] PBS.Org, People & Events: Surviving the Dust Bowl: Black Sunday (April 14, 1935), 2003.

[24] PBS.Org, People & Events: Surviving the Dust Bowl: The Drought, 2003.

[25] PBS. Org, The Drought.

[26] Vol I and Vol II, Southern Hills Country Club: A Fifty-Seven Year History, 1935-1992 (Tulsa, Oklahoma, Southern Hills Country Club, 1992), 2.

[27] Whitten, Ron, Golf Digest Article(Golf Digest, August 1994), 73-76

[28] Tillinghast, A.W, Letters to President of the PGA dated January 13th through 18th, 1936 (Courtesy of the USGA).

[29] Tillinghast

[30] Tillinghast

[31] Tillinghast

[32] Emory, Pamela, Prairie Dunes: An American Original (Links Magazine, September 1994) 54-58.

[33] Prairie Dunes, 17

[34] Prairie Dunes, 29

[35] Prairie Dunes, 18.

[36] Gordon, 165

[37] Gordon, 165

[38] Dick McEwen, "Hiker's Paradise," Horizons 13 (Ames, Iowa, 3rd Quarter 1938),9.

[39] Trueblood, Charles, Reynolda's "Dream" Course To Be Finished This Fall (Winston-Salem Journal, July 20, 1939).

[40] Trueblood.

[41] Goddard, David, The Maidstone Links (Maidstone Golf Club, 1997).

[42] Jenkins, Dan, Sports Illustrated's: The Best 18 Golf Holes in America (Time, Inc., New York, 1966), 51.

[43] Peper, George, Golf Courses of the PGA Tour (Henry N. Abrams, New York, 1986), 136.

[44] Roberts, Doug, A History of Lakewood Golf at The Grand Hotel (Lakewood Golf Club, Point Clear, Alabama, 2001), 3.

[45] Trimble, Frances, Austin Country Club: One Hundred Years of Champions and Change (Austin Country Club, Austin, Texas, 1999).

[46] Bentley, Mac, Daily Oklahoman (Tulsa, Oklahoma) April 18, 1995

[47] Evans, 132.

[48] Bentley, Mac, Daily Oklahoman (Tulsa, Oklahoma) August 26, 1994.

[49] Evans, 134-136.

[50] Finegan

[51] Davis

[52] Davis

[53] Davis

[54] Davis

[55] Davis

[56] Davis

[57] Davis

[58] Bulletin of Green Section of the United States Golf Association (USGA, Far Hills, NJ, 1924) 34

[59] Bulleting of Green Section

[60] Bridgewater.

[61] Gordon, John, Great Golf Courses of America (Firefly Books, Buffalo, NY, 1997) 164.

Printed in the United States
By Bookmasters